Understanding Fashion

Elizabeth Rouse

with illustrations by Carol Rouse

BSP PROFESSIONAL BOOKS

OXFORD LONDON EDINBURGH

BOSTON MELBOURNE

D0233468

First published 1989

British Library
Cataloguing in Publication Data

Rouse, Elizabeth
Understanding fashion.
1. Western costume, to 1982
I. Title
391'009

ISBN 0−632−01891−7

BSP Professional Books
A division of Blackwell Scientific
    Publications Ltd
Editorial Offices:
Osney Mead, Oxford OX2 0EL
    (Orders: Tel. 0865 240201)
8 John Street, London WC1N 2ES
23 Ainslie Place, Edinburgh EH3 6AJ
3 Cambridge Center, Suite 208,
    Cambridge, MA 02142, USA
107 Barry Street, Carlton, Victoria
    3053, Australia

Set by Setrite Typesetters Limited

Printed and bound in Great Britain by
MacKays of Chatham PLC, Chatham,
Kent

Contents

Preface

The majority of students of fashion and clothing in the past have approached the academic understanding of clothing and fashion through the perspective of the history of costume. In particular they studied the history of changing styles and the contribution of 'key' designers. Traditionally this perspective focused on form and its aesthetic qualities, and fashion changes tended to be explained in terms of influential individuals or the 'creative genius' of individual designers.

The aim of this book is to provide at an introductory level an additional perspective to this well-established approach. It takes as its main focus clothing and fashion as *social phenomena*. It examines the role clothing plays in social life, and explores changes in the style, production and consumption of clothes and particularly fashionable clothes in their social and historical context.

In the early chapters I have tried to present in simplified form some ideas and theoretical perspectives from the social sciences which can help students develop a critical understanding of the social dimensions of dress. The later chapters deal with specific historical examples: changes in women's styles of dress and the development of markets for fashionable clothes in Britain since the mid-nineteenth century. In the chapters on women I relate dress to the social conditions in which it is worn. Why for example was the crinoline worn in the Victorian era and not in the twenties? Obviously part of the answer lies in the evolution of one style from another but the nature of the style is also related to ideas about women, women's own views of femininity, and general conditions of life at the time. In the final chapters I examine the interrelationship of such factors as demographic change, social change, technical change and changes in retailing in the emergence of new markets for fashion this century.

This book was written for students on BTEC courses in clothing and fashion, though it may be of interest to students concerned with fashion marketing and distribution. It is essentially an introductory text which draws together a range of material which it is hoped will heighten their awareness of the social dimensions of dress and develop their understanding of the implications of social change for the way clothing is produced, bought and worn and thus provide support for their own creative work and for aspects of their business studies such as marketing.

Acknowledgements

I would like to thank Helen Stanley who encouraged me to get this project off the ground, my family for their forbearance while it was being written, and Richard Miles for his help and infinite patience. I would also like to thank the following individuals and organisations for their assistance and for granting permission to reproduce illustrations; Batsford Ltd, BBC Hulton Picture Library, Chatto and Windus, the Hogarth Press, the Suffolk Collection, Ranger's House, English Heritage, Mary Evans Picture Library, Grafton Books, Peter Clarke and *The Guardian*, the Imperial War Museum, Marks and Spencer, *The Observer*, Chris Richards, Selfridges, Miss Selfridge, Smirnoff, Slaymaker Cowley White and Triumph International, and the staff of the London College of Fashion Library.

Elizabeth Rouse
1989

1 Why Do People Wear Clothes?

Why do people wear clothes? Students of primitive societies still argue about whether there are, or ever have been, any truly 'naked savages', or whether the wearing of some form of clothing is part of all human behaviour. What does seem to be true is that all people modify their appearance. The use of body covering is one type of such modification; the arrangement of hair, the altering of the surface and shape of the body itself are others. It is argued that even if it is not worn in everyday situations, clothing is used for ritual purposes or special occasions amongst apparently 'naked' peoples. (1) Is clothing, as a kind of body modification, peculiar to human beings? Other mammals such as chimpanzees delight in decorating themselves with flowers or any other objects which happen to be at hand. A television advertisement for tea shows them apparently enjoying the experience of being dressed up in clothes and wigs. However, I would suggest that the human propensity for body modification and the wearing of clothes is quite different. It is not simply a matter of individual or random experimentation; nor is it a game. Human beings have created definite patterns in their appearance and dress. They learn how to modify their appearance, how to make it acceptable to others. They are able to construct the items they need. They share a particular mode of dress and decoration with other people. Why has this kind of behaviour developed amongst human beings? Why do people wear clothes?

Most people would respond to such a question by pointing out that we need clothes to keep us warm, to protect us from the elements. Some might suggest that we wear them because we would feel indecent without them and others would say that we wear them to make ourselves look attractive. In other words they would explain the wearing of clothes in terms of practical function, morality or aesthetic qualities. Writers on dress have often attempted to explain both the development of clothes in the first place and their importance today in these terms but just

1

how important are such factors and do they really explain why people wear clothes and decorate their bodies?

Protection

Many writers have argued that clothing was born out of necessity. For example, Malinowski, an anthropologist, suggested that clothing was created by people in response to a physical need for shelter and protection. (2) But other animals do not need clothes, so why do we? Like other mammals we are warm-blooded and we possess a number of physiological mechanisms for regulating our body temperature such as sweating and shivering. Some people have developed these organic controls to a high level of efficiency. Eskimos, for example, have a higher metabolic rate. But, it is not known whether this is a result of their high fat diet or a biological adaptation. However, most physical anthropologists argue that the migration of people to regions like the Arctic after the melting of the ice caps was too recent for the slow workings of biology to have brought about such changes. (3) As people evolved as tropical animals, it is suggested that as they migrated to temperate and arctic climates clothes, among other tools, were developed to enable them to survive in these harsher environments. The dress of the Eskimos is an excellent example of this kind of clothing development. The closely-fitting garments, consisting in winter of two layers of skin, effectively trap and hold warmth next to the body. At the other climatic extreme, the long robes of the Arabs give good protection against the intense heat of the sun and shield the wearers from blowing sand.

However, the development of protective clothing by those living in what *we* would consider to be harsh climatic conditions is not inevitable. The Australian aborigines live in temperatures which range between 23°F (−5°C) and 117°F (47°C). They wear only brief loin cloths and sleep in the open air curled around a fire. Another example of a people living in a severe climate with very scant clothing which has often been cited is that of the Yaggans of Tierra del Fuego, at the tip of South America. It is said that Darwin saw snow melting on the skins of these people, and when they were given blankets they tore them into strips which they divided between them and used as decoration.

This disregard for physical comfort is not confined to far off places and times. Some of our own recent styles left much of the body exposed to the elements. Girls braved snow drifts and below freezing temperatures in the cold winters of the late sixties in the briefest of mini-skirts and coats. The wearing of hats in any season is no longer customary for most people in Britain today, although it is well-known that a great deal of body heat is lost from the head. In a lecture entitled 'A Scientist looks at the Functions of Clothing', R.G. Stansfield points out how we have failed to put our advanced technology to best use as far as the practicality and protective value of ordinary clothing are concerned:

'Early this year (1978), two schools ran out of oil for their central heating. The headmistresses did not send notes to the parents saying "the school buildings will be rather cold tomorrow, so make sure your daughters come wearing the right clothes for sitting in classrooms at a temperature of about 8°C". No, they said, "the school will be closed until we get more oil for the boilers".

'So, I thought about the behaviour of the two schools, and how it is really rather odd, that − as the headmistresses knew, quite correctly − most of the girls would not possess clothing which could be closed up to keep them warm enough while sitting in cold classrooms, and then opened up to be cool enough to wear in the periods of high physical activity in the playground or gym. What this shows, I suggest, is that our everyday clothing just does not make real use of 20th century technology − the sort of technology that clothed the astronauts...who landed on the moon in much tougher conditions of heat and cold.

'Modern technology certainly helps, but we shouldn't forget what pre-20th century technology could do...(The Eskimos') clothes were warm enough for a man to sit for hours in the cold wind by a seal-hole in the ice; and when he was lucky and harpooned a seal, he could fling open his fur wraps so as not to get boiling hot in his violent struggle with the seal.

'The challenge to clothing technologists now, as I see it, is to use the new resources of materials and knowledge to produce clothes which will be simple to wear and will preserve freedom of movement and yet which will keep us warm when needed.' (4)

What factors have inhibited the development of such clothes? As Stansfield is well aware, problems of technology are not the only considerations in the design and production of clothes. If they were, we would perhaps all be wearing identical versions of an adapted boiler suit or 'baby-gro'. In recent years we have seen the development of duvet coats and thermal underwear, both highly practical and protective in their intention and style. But despite the claims made about their warmth and their popularity with certain groups of people, many people *choose* not to wear them. There are functions of clothing which override or undermine those of protection and practicality. People seem frequently to wear clothes which are uncomfortable and unsuited to their physical environment. I mentioned earlier the mini-skirt; *this is an example of how being 'in fashion' was more important to many women than being warm!*

We can find many more extreme examples of fashionable clothing which not only fails to protect the body but actually does it harm. In the past the corset, which created the tiny waist so desired by the fashionable Victorian lady, displaced the internal organs and restricted the rib-cage making it difficult for the wearer to breathe properly (Fig. 1.1). The design of present-day shoes is also interesting when examined from this point of view. Shoes, it would seem, ought to provide an example of design reflecting comfort and practicality. However, many shoes worn today are flimsy, let in water, and in the case of high-heeled shoes are extremely uncomfortable for walking any distance. Most fashionable shoes are only made in one width. Moreover, many styles do not take into consideration the actual shape of the foot. They are based instead on a symmetrical shape (Fig. 1.2) which may be thought to be aesthetically more pleasing than that of the natural foot. As a result most people in our society have damaged feet and many suffer the agony of corns, callosities and bunions. Both these examples show that body coverings are not merely practical, or functional objects but also *aesthetic* ones. They are judged by the standards of current fashionable taste. The topic of fashion will be examined more closely in a later chapter; suffice it to say here that clothes have to fit socially accepted standards of what looks good.

However, it is not merely a matter of looking good but also looking 'right', socially correct and proper. In Fig. 1.3 you will see two people dressed quite differently. It is hard to believe that they can be dressed to feel comfortable at the same temperature. The man is wearing a shirt, tie, a woollen long-sleeved jacket and woollen trousers. The woman, by contrast, is lightly-clad in a dress which exposes her arms, shoulders and neck, but does cover her legs. If clothes had the primary function of protecting the body, surely their dress would be more similar, as in the case of Eskimos. Why do they appear so different? Can you imagine how this picture would look if the models exchanged clothes? Obviously each person is appropriately dressed in social terms and they conform to widely accepted ideas of how a man and woman should look —

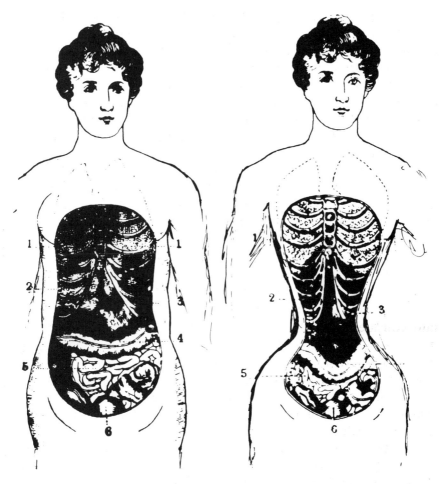

Fig. 1.1 Diagram indicating the detrimental effects of wearing a tight corset.

in this case for, say, for an evening out. In our society we do expect men and women to dress differently and even thermal underwear which is designed to be protective is produced in different styles for men and women. But why is it that it is the woman who is most flimsily dressed? Why do women's vests expose large areas of the chest while men's do not?

Our interpretation of what is socially proper is also a factor in our choice of clothes and which garments we choose to keep on in

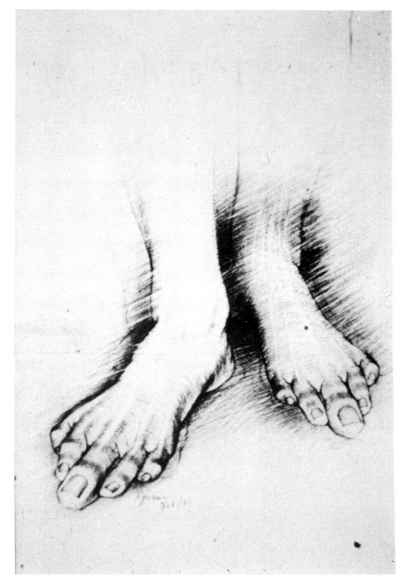

Fig. 1.2 The ideal foot?

changing climatic conditions. In the heat of summer, businessmen will often retain their ties and jackets in order to appear correctly dressed for meetings etc. Manual workers, on the other hand, strip to the waist, but only if they are men! The notion that certain areas

Fig. 1.3 Proper dress?

of the body should be covered or displayed takes us to a consideration of another major explanation of clothes – modesty.

Modesty

It is quite commonly believed that we wear clothes because certain parts of our bodies are shameful and need to be covered. Attitudes of this kind have their origins in the religious mythology of Judaeo-Christian tradition, in particular in the story of Adam and Eve.

> 'And they were both naked, the man and his wife, and they were not ashamed...And when the woman saw the tree was good for food, and that it was pleasant to the eyes, and a tree to be desired to make one wise, she took of the fruit thereof, and did eat, and also gave unto her husband with her; and he did eat. And the eyes of both of them were opened, and they knew that they were naked; and they sewed fig leaves together, and made themselves aprons...Unto Adam also and to his wife did the Lord God make coats of skins and clothed them.' (5)

For a long time this allegory was accepted as literal fact, and it has had a tremendous influence on our attitudes to our bodies and on our feelings about nakedness. Were clothes invented then as a result of feelings of shame and a sense of sinfulness?

The theory of evolution has done much to undermine the general acceptance of the Genesis story, and naturist and nudist groups have attempted to challenge the notion that the naked human body is sinful, or something to be ashamed of. But, there are very few amongst us who would not feel embarrassed if we found ourselves sitting on a bus, or walking down our local high street stark naked. However, we are not experiencing the same kind of shame as Adam and Eve. It is not just a matter of covering certain prohibited areas of the body as the Genesis story implies. Even if we wear our underwear and, therefore, are theoretically decent, we would still be embarrassed. *This is because modesty or shame is relative.* The amount and type of clothing varies according to social context and we feel embarrassed if we are not wearing the appropriate type and number. We are quite happy to appear in minimal clothing on a beach but not in a bus queue. All over the world people have different ideas about what one should be modest about. An Australian Aboriginal woman for example has only the minimal attire of a belt round her waist and necklace whereas a Muslim woman will reveal nothing of her face and figure (Figs. 1.4

and 1.5). These examples undermine the view that covering certain parts of the body is universal in mankind. In Britain, a study of fashionable dress in the last hundred years would show quite dramatic shifts in standards of modesty. In the Victorian period, women concealed their ankles but displayed their shoulders and breasts; in the twenties women exposed more of their legs than ever before; and in the thirties they exposed their backs in evening dress cut to the waist. Today, we are witnessing changes in ideas about decency as nudist beaches become more popular and topless sunbathing for women becomes popular in the Mediterranean, if not in Britain.

It seems then that our sense of embarrassment and modesty comes not from shame of particular parts of the body but the loss of what we are accustomed to wearing or feel is required in a particular situation. A Muslim woman would be embarrassed without her veil, the Victorian lady without her long skirts, and the conventional English holidaymaker without her bikini top. Embarrassment is not necessarily linked to lack of clothes. As Marilyn Horn points out: 'Among the Suya Indians of Brazil, for example, neither men nor women are the least bit embarrassed by their naked bodies, but are humiliated if caught without their lip disks'. (6) A lip disk is the customary form of body decoration among the Suya, an essential part of normal appearance.

People do not have an innate sense of shame; young children are conspicuously lacking in a sense of modesty. As they grow up, they are taught which parts of their bodies should be concealed. They learn this along with many other kinds of knowledge and behaviour necessary for life amongst the group of people in which they live. A child is not embarrassed by a lack of clothing until he has become accustomed to wearing them. Children brought up in groups where very little clothing is worn are not embarrassed by their near-nakedness. *It must be said that modesty or shame was not a causal factor in the initial development of clothes, but is merely a result of the habit of wearing them.*

Attraction

The modesty theory has been attacked from another point of view. Clothing, it has been suggested, does not draw attention away from the body, or reduce an awareness of it as is implied in the term 'modesty'. Rather, the converse is true. Clothing actually

Fig. 1.4 Modest dress — Muslim woman.

Fig. 1.5 Modest dress — Australian Aborigine.

serves to display the body and exhibit it in order to gain admiration. One writer, Rudofsky, compares the wearing of clothes to the sexual displays of birds and animals:

'It seems that man's and animals' clothes serve much the same purpose — sexual selection. Only the roles of the sexes are reversed. In the animal kingdom it is the male who infatuates the female with his gorgeous garb. She falls for his looks rather than his strength and aggressiveness. In human society, on the other hand, the burden is on the woman. Hers is the first move; she has to track and ensnare the male by looking seductive. Being devoid of anything comparable to the extraordinary antennae and giant legs that serve animals for prehending a partner she exerts her powers by way of artificial plumage. To prevent the male from escaping, she has to keep him perpetually excited by changing her shape and colours by every means, fair and foul. In the traditional battle of the sexes, dress and its accessory arts are her offensive weapons.' (7)

James Laver makes a similar point:

'It would seem, in fact, that our clothes are dictated to us by the deepest unconscious desires of the opposite sex. Throughout the greater part of history and prehistory, men have chosen their partners in life by their attractiveness as women. Therefore, women's clothes are intended to make their wearers as attractive, as women, as possible. Women, on the other hand, have, for the greater part of human history, instinctively chosen their husbands for their capacities to maintain and protect a family.

'Women's clothes are governed by what might be called the Seduction Principle – that is, they are sex-conscious clothes. Men's clothes, on the other hand, are governed by the Hierarchical Principle – that is, they are class-conscious clothes.

'In general the purpose of clothes for women has been to make them more sexually attractive and the purpose of men's clothes has been to enhance their social status.' (8)

The implications of Rudofsky's argument is that clothing is necessary for the maintenance of sexual interest and therefore, implicitly, to the future of the human species. Laver contends that the dominant function of women's clothing is that of sexual attraction. For both of them, it is universally true that it is the role of the female to attract, and to be chosen on the criterion of her attractiveness, and that clothes are a key factor in this process. Their views rest on quite dubious assumptions about 'human nature' and 'instincts'. *They play down the role of culture in both shaping sexuality and dress styles, and show a considerable disregard for historical accuracy.* Their ideas may describe some uses of clothing in sexual relationships in our society during specific periods in history but they do not constitute an adequate explanation of all forms of clothing nor do they represent accurately human behaviour in all periods and places. For example, at various times in our own society men have worn decorative clothes. They have worn jewellery, rich fabrics, extravagant trimmings and lace (Fig. 1.6). They have worn make-up, wigs and perfume. Can we assume that the attraction of these objects only operated in one direction and only served to attract men to women, even when they were wearing these objects themselves?

However, this is certainly not to deny that some clothes worn by women are designed to be sexually attractive. To take one example, women's eveningwear is often made of silky or sensuous fabrics; it is designed to reveal the shape of the body, or to reveal certain parts such as the breasts or legs. Many women possess some garments which are intended to attract attention to or show off the body. This is the case because it is the custom in our society at present for people to select their partners on the grounds of finding

Fig. 1.6 Decorative dress for men. Richard Sackville, 3rd Earl of Dorset by William Larkin (The Suffolk Collection, Ranger's House Blackheath, English Heritage).

Fig. 1.7 Enhancing and displaying the body (Triumph International).

them sexually attractive. Along with face, figure and personality, clothing can play a part in such an assessment. The dominance of the idea of romantic love in our society as a basis for marriage has led to the notion that sexual attractiveness is an essential ingredient for a successful match. In particular, it has been seen as a woman's duty to be sexually attractive and this has had implications for the clothes women wear. But this is not part of the human condition: in other societies, and at other periods in our own history, partners were selected on quite different criteria. The dress of women in strict Islamic societies is not a form of sexual display; it is not intended to provoke desire. In fact, it has quite the opposite intention. In some Islamic societies, the sexual partnership of marriage is arranged by relatives and not by the couple concerned, who may not necessarily know each other. Laver's assertion that 'Throughout the greater part of history and prehistory, men have chosen their partners in life by their attractiveness as women' does not hold true for many non-European societies. How people select their sexual partners is not merely a matter of instinct as is implied by Laver, and by Rudofsky's comparison with animals − it is controlled and constructed by a complex of learned cultural attitudes and norms. *Clothing cannot be reduced to a mere trigger for a biological mating instinct.*

Even in our own society, it just does not make sense to explain all the clothing worn by women in these terms. Women do wear clothes which are designed to be *not* sexually attractive; their purpose may be entirely different. One example is that of nun's clothing; other perhaps more commonplace examples these days are the uniforms of the female traffic warden and policewoman. If these uniforms were seen as 'sexy', the authority and respect required by these women to do their jobs effectively would be undermined. They would find it difficult to exert the control necessary in their dealings with the public.

Communication

The clothing of the traffic warden introduces another interesting aspect of dress. The uniform as a type of clothing demonstrates very explicitly a principle which could be very fruitfully applied to all forms of clothing − that of the *expressive* or *communicative* function of dress. The traffic warden's uniform acts as a signal or sign to the observer. It informs him or her that the wearer is doing a particular job, performing a particular role. The observer can use this information; it can influence his or her behaviour. Anyone parked on double yellow lines, on catching sight of the distinctive uniform, will probably take hasty action to avoid getting a parking ticket. In hospitals, uniforms, night clothes, and ordinary clothes are all crucial marks of people's status within the institution. The distinctive appearance of nurses, doctors, ward staff, patients and temporary visitors makes social interaction between all parties more straightforward. *By observing the appearance of an individual, we have one set of information on which to base our dealings with them.*

How far have we got in our attempt to shed light on the reasons people wear clothes?

We have seen that modesty is the *result*, not a cause of wearing clothes. Attempts to explain clothing in terms of attraction also raise many problems. They may offer some insights into attitudes to dress in our own society at certain historical periods but they do not stand up to cross-cultural or historical generalisation.

We have found that the theory which stresses the protective function of clothing can offer only a partial explanation. The protective function of clothing has been compromised by aesthetic considerations and social requirements in many societies including our own. It cannot explain the tremendous variety of styles of clothing, nor why certain clothes are worn by some people and not others, and on certain types of occasion.

How can we explain the diversity in styles of dress? As we have seen clothing can tell us things about each other, it can communicate information. Differences in dress in hospitals communicate differences between people. If an important function of clothes is to communicate information, such diversity would be an essential element. We will consider how and what clothing can communicate in the next chapter.

References

1. Fischer, H. (1978) 'The clothes of the naked Nuer'. In: *Social Aspects of the Human Body*. ed. T. Polhemus. (Penguin).
2. Malinowski, B. (1916) *Science and Culture*.
3. Downs, J.F. and Bliebtreu, H.K. (1969) *Human Variations: An Introduction to Physical Anthropology*. (Glenco) 201.
4. Stansfield, R.G. (1978) 'A scientist looks at the functions of clothing' lecture given at *Science and Clothing Conference*. (April 1978).

5. *Genesis*, **2**, 5 and **3**, 6, 7, 21.
6. Horn, M. (1968) *The Second Skin.* (Boston : Houghton Mifflin Co.) 3−4.
7. Rudofsky, B. (1971) *The Unfashionable Human Body.* (New York: Doubleday and Co.) 12−13.
8. Laver, J. (1969) *Modesty in Dress* (Boston : Houghton Mifflin Co.).

2 Clothing Culture and Communication

One of the distinctive features of human clothing is that groups of people share particular patterns of dress. Clothing is not a random or totally individual affair; it is a social activity. The overall pattern of our dress, be it grass skirts or tailored clothes, is a consequence of the society in which we live − in much the same way as the language we speak, the food we eat and the god or gods we believe in. *The way we decorate our bodies, what we wear and how we wear it is part of our culture, our socially learned way of life.* What is the significance of these patterns of dress?

Human behaviour is not based to any great extent on instinct; we are the least biologically determined of all the species. Unlike animals for whom behaviour is largely, though not entirely, instinctual, the human child is virtually helpless. The human child depends on others for its survival for a comparatively long period while the long process of socialisation takes place. This is the process by which children *learn* the technical skills necessary for the acquisition of food and material objects, and the ways of thinking and acting of the group to which they belong. Individuals come to share the ideas and beliefs of their society and to participate in the social arrangements which order people's lives through the transmission of culture from generation to generation and from individual to individual.

It is the development of these complex and varied cultural patterns which characterise human societies. But the transmission of these learned ways of life is only possible because human beings have a highly developed and specialised ability to communicate. Clearly, language is the most important form of communication but recently some sociologists and anthropologists have argued that it is only one of the forms through which people communicate. They argue that culture is a complex of communicative systems. One such anthropologist is Edmund Leach who in his book *Culture and Communication* sets out to investigate how culture communicates. His ideas are particularly useful in explaining how non-verbal aspects of culture such as clothing and body decoration *communicate*.

Leach argues that three aspects can be distinguished in human behaviour:

(1) biological activities of the body such as breathing and heartbeat;
(2) technical actions which affect the material world outside oneself such as digging a hole or boiling an egg;
(3) expressive actions which say something about the world.

In his definition of expressive actions, Leach includes not only verbal utterances and gestures such as nodding the head and pulling faces but also behaviour such as wearing a uniform or putting on a wedding ring. He contends, however, that these three aspects of behaviour are never completely separable in reality. The act of breathing 'says' that 'I'm alive'. Even the simplest technical actions have both biological and expressive importance. Leach uses the example of making a cup of coffee. This action alters the world out there, water is boiled, etc. It affects the drinker's metabolic processes but it also 'says' something about the drinker. The kind of coffee used, the way it is prepared and served; all can communicate information about the cultural background, lifestyle or even aspirations of the person who makes and drinks it.

This interpretation of behaviour has obvious relevance to our understanding of the wearing of clothes. In the first chapter we encountered problems with attempting to account for clothing purely in terms of its practical function, in other words, the biological and technical aspects of wearing clothes. A garment may be used as a tool to keep one warm but it also *'says'* something about the wearer. In the case of the traffic warden, her clothing communicates her job. The attire of the woman in Fig. 1.3 communicates her sexual identity and a lifestyle. Leach's argument allows us to see that the balance of these aspects of behaviour may vary in any action. In some cases the wearing of clothes may be predominantly 'technical' in the sense of protecting the body but in others it may be predominantly expressive. However, as Leach points out, these aspects of behaviour are not separable and so *the wearing of clothes is inevitably expressive*. The protective robes of the Arab also announce the wearer's Arabness, and are worn as a symbol of Arab identity by businessmen visiting the un-desertlike climate of London or New York. The building worker who wears a hard hat to protect his head communicates the dangerous nature of his work and in addition his compliance with site safety rules.

Wearing a raincoat has both technical and biological aspects but it also says something about the wearer. The Burberry trench-coat and the Peter Storm nylon cagoule say quite different things. What do they communicate to you? We must now turn to the problems of *how* clothes communicate and of *what* they communicate.

How clothes communicate

Many writers have referred to the 'language of clothes' – most recently Alison Lurie in her book of that name. Her book compares clothes with the superficial features of language rather than its structure. For example, she compares articles of clothing to foreign words, and slang words; accessories and trimmings are compared to adjectives and adverbs. Although she asserts that the language of clothes has a grammar, she does not describe it. She simply equates garments with words. This leads her to suggest that rich people who have more clothes have more 'words' and therefore can express more than poorer people with fewer clothes. Would you agree that rich people are more expressive with their clothes? Are more messages communicated because you have a choice of ten silk shirts instead of three cotton? Surely, it is a matter of repeating the same message of wealth just using different garments to express it?

Leach also suggests that non-verbal dimensions of culture such as clothing are organised in a way analogous to language and that one can talk about rules which govern the wearing of clothes in the same way that one can speak of grammatical rules governing speech, However, he sees an important difference in the way we communicate using non-verbal behaviour:

> 'The grammatical rules which govern speech utterances are such that anyone with a fluent command of a language can generate spontaneously entirely new sentences with the confident expectation that he will be understood by his audience. This is *not* the case with most forms of non-verbal communication. Customary conventions can only be understood if they are familiar...a newly invented "symbolic statement" of a non-verbal kind will fail to convey information to others until it has been explained by other means.' (1)

Leach argues that non-verbal communication is more limited and its structures much more simple than spoken language.

It may be useful to examine more closely how communication takes place and in particular how the model of language can help us understand non-verbal communication. People cannot communicate directly with each other by transferring messages brain to brain. We have to express our message in a form that can be perceived by other people. We have to use something to *stand for*, to represent our message. The vehicle we use is called a *sign*. Language has been described as a coded systems of signs. (2) A sign is made up of two parts; the message bearing entity, the physical form which can be perceived and the message itself. Words, letters and sounds are signs in the sense that they can be perceived and are used to stand for, or represent something else. The word 'apple' is a sign; it stands for the fruit we eat (or a computer). If we say 'Please eat this apple' the words represent an object, and action, and a desire to the listener. Signs work in sets to convey meaning and a sign like 'apple' may have different meanings in different sets.

How do signs acquire their meaning? The different words for apple − pomme, mela, ringo show that speakers of different language refer to the same object using different words. The sound chosen seems quite arbitary. In fact it does not matter what something is called as long as the community share the same meaning. Meaning is attached to particular words by social convention. Individuals have to learn those socially agreed meanings. When you learn a language you learn to attach a particular meaning to each sound pattern, you learn what each pattern stands for. In other words you have to learn the *code*.

Non-verbal communication takes place in the same way. Let's take the example of space and distance and see how they convey meaning.

How close you stand to someone carries meaning, it is a sign and like all signs it is conventional and its meaning is learned. The significance of particular distances varies from culture to culture, and this can give rise to misunderstandings. The English and Americans tend to keep a polite distance between speakers whereas, as E.T. Hall suggests, Latin Americans tend to reduce it:

'In Latin America the distance is smaller than in the United States. In fact, people cannot speak comfortably unless they are very close, a closeness which evokes aggressive or erotic intent in the USA. The result is that when they approach we move away, and they think we are distant, cold, reserved and unfriendly. We, in turn, perpetually accuse them of breathing down our necks, or of spluttering all over us.

'Americans who have lived in Latin America for some time use subterfuges: they barricade themselves behind their desks and use furniture to keep the Latin American at what they consider to be a comfortable distance. The result is often that the Latin American may go so far as to climb over the various obstacles until he reaches a distance that he finds comfortable.' (3)

The perceptible aspect of the sign conveys quite a different meaning to members of different cultural groups. However, even within the same cultural sign system, the perceptible aspect of a sign is capable of carrying more than one meaning. This is because the signs do not really convey meaning on their own, as isolated units, but as parts of sets. We say they form a code. The message conveyed by 'closeness' of 'erotic intent' or 'aggressiveness' emerges through the combination of that sign with other signs such as facial expression, gesture, tone of voice and probably verbal utterances.

Signs also acquire meaning by contrast with other signs within the system. Nodding of the head means 'yes' in contrast to shaking the head which means 'no'. In the extract above, 'closeness' and 'distance' are contrasted in both cultural systems to produce meaning, but the resulting messages are quite different for each group. It also illustrates the conventional and customary nature of non-verbal communication which was outlined by Leach. *Unlike language, one cannot make individual or entirely inventive statements and communication can only take place through already established meanings.*

Clothes can act as signs too. They carry messages and convey meaning in the same ways. When you go to a party, or meet an individual or group of people for the first time, you observe the people around you. You observe their faces, their hairstyles, their clothes and on the basis of that observation, you decide their age, their sex, possibly what social background they come from, what kind of job they do, even what kind of person they are. You form an impression of that person from the information conveyed to you by their appearance before you speak to them. We all interpret clothing signs; the process may be so automatic that you may hardly be aware of it.

If you look at Fig. 2.1, you will see how clothing signs work. This advertisement relies on clothing signs to convey its message

Fig. 2.1 The perfect couple? (Smirnoff).

about the kind of people who drink this particular brand of vodka. The key signs are the apron and the brief-case but they have to be put into the context of the other signs. What information do the two key signs convey to you about the two people portrayed in the advert? How is their relationship different for 'the perfect couple'? What does the woman do for a living? What impression do the man's jeans and denim shirt give? What about the woman's style of dress, why is she wearing a skirt? The advertisement links the vodka to an unconventional lifestyle, to role reversal whilst still presenting the man and woman as attractive members of their respective sex; she is not unfeminine, he is not effeminate.

Another good demonstration of the power of clothing signs is the way they can be used to convey a false impression. Like other forms of communication, clothing can be used to mislead the recipient of the message. In our society, signs of female identity include dresses and skirts, make-up, particular hairstyles, high-heel shoes and certain types of jewellery. These objects are used to great effect by female impersonators to convey the message of femininity. They use clothes and cosmetic techniques to simulate the natural indicators of femininity such as breast development and lack of facial hair, as well as the culturally defined signs listed above. It is interesting to note that the impersonators use clothing signs, in addition to other techniques, to conjure up quite different types of women − of different ages, nationalities and classes. A few of the most famous would be Dame Edna Everidge, Hinge and Brackett, Danny La Rue and Les Dawson's impersonation of working class wives. All rely for their characterisation on clothing and cosmetic signs.

Signs have meaning when they are worn together; on its own each sign does not really have a meaning. The signs combine to signify a sexual role. The trilby hat has carried various meanings in different sets of signs − it is part of the costume of middle-aged men, mods, bookies and on occasions part of the dress of 'fashionable' women. The kilt is worn in English society by women and girls. It has been worn as part of a school uniform for girls, a 'classic' for women, and in the sixties the mini version was a sign of being 'in fashion'. In Scotland and amongst members of the English Royal family, kilts have traditionally been worn by men.

A garment itself acts as a sign but in addition, the fabric, the stylistic features of the garment, the colour, the way the garment is worn, all these aspects can act as signs and communicate meaning. Traditionally the pattern of the fabric from which a kilt was made acted as a sign of clan membership, and tartans are still associated with particular surnames. The side that garments such as shirts, trousers, coats and jackets are fastened signifies a masculine or feminine garment. Women's and girls' clothing have the fastening flap on the right, whereas for men it is on the left. Despite the unisex revolution of the seventies this distinction continues even if it is largely unnoticed by many. The colours pink and blue are often interpreted when used for baby clothes as signs of the sex of

Fig. 2.2 Male and female skirts.

the child. It is not entirely reliable as an indicator as little girls are often dressed in pale blue, but pink is hardly ever worn by boys. The way a garment is worn can act as sign; the top button of man's shirt if left undone means 'casual', 'relaxed', 'informal' whereas the opposite meaning is implied if it is fastened and worn with a tie. Nearly all these examples show how opposing signs are used to define meaning. Left and right, pink and blue are used to convey masculine and feminine, open and closed to convey formal and informal.

Like other signs, clothing signs are coded and the meaning has to be learned. Figure 2.3 shows a Melanesian woman. As mere

Fig. 2.3 Melanesian woman. What does her appearance mean?

onlookers we do not understand the significance of her appearance. The shaven head, the painted face and grass skirt convey to those familiar with the code that this woman is a widow. In our own dress code, the sign of recent bereavement is the wearing of black, or at least dark, sober colours, and widows often wear black and a sometimes black hat with a veil. We cannot interpret the clothing of other societies, we cannot understand their significance, if we have not learned the code. In Japan, for example, colour is an important signifier of age in both traditional and western clothes. Older women wear dark or muted colours and small patterns; only young women wear brightly coloured clothes. There are strict codes of dress for the wearing of traditional clothes. The type of fabric, the colours, the type of design or pattern on the fabric, the length of the sleeves, the way the sash is tied, all act as signs and carry social meanings. In Fig. 2.4 the light coloured and highly decorated kimono with long sleeves are worn by young women and girls to indicate their youth and unmarried status. In the centre of the picture is a woman wearing a dark kimono with a border print and short sleeves; this costume denotes her married status.

We also have to learn the dress codes of our own society and particular social groups may have clothing signs you may not understand. For example, young Rastafarians wear hats and sometimes other clothes and badges emblazoned with the colours red, green and gold. Do you understand their significance? You probably know that two stripes on the sleeve of an army uniform 'means' corporal, and three stripes means sergeant but would you know the signs used to distinguish a captain, a major or a general? *Do you know the code?*

What clothes communicate

It is obvious that the kind of information that is communicated by clothing is of a restricted and specialised kind. Clothing signs could not be used to express a desire for a door to be opened or to argue the case for euthanasia. We would use another mode of communication, one better suited to our purpose such as words or gesture, even if those words were 'worn' displayed on a tee-shirt or badge. Our bodies and clothes constitute our physical presence in the world, and particularly the social world in which we live. They are the means by which our place and our participation in that social world are signified. Clothing signs express an individual's social identity. It is one of the basic conditions of social life that individuals know with whom they are dealing, they have to be able to recognise each other's social identity. They need to know the role or roles each person is playing, the groups they belong to, their status within those groups and even their status within society as a whole. There are innumerable ways that this kind of information

Fig. 2.4 Guests at a wedding, Oato (photo. Chris Richards).

is conveyed to an onlooker but clothing can be an important vehicle for social communication in many situations. An everyday example is the use of clothing signs in the retail trade. In large and crowded shops, it is essential for the smooth running of business for the customer to be able to identify the assistants and cashiers. In most shops, the staff wear uniforms, or distinctively coloured clothes or badges to differentiate themselves from the public and to announce their role. In the absence of such signs customers are forced to look for other clues such as their not wearing outdoor clothes or carrying bags. We have already discussed the importance of uniforms in institutions such as hospitals as communicators of roles and status.

Most uniforms are compulsory, their form is rigidly laid down and individuals have to wear them in the prescribed form. But there are many patterns of dress in our society which are not compulsory in the way that military or police uniforms are, but are just associated with a particular role, status, or group. Men who work in offices and business usually wear a suit, shirt and tie, and frequently carry a brief-case. The clothes communicate to an on-looker the kind of work a man does, they are signs of his occupational role. The men who wear this kind of informal uniform are not coerced; they wear it voluntarily. They are, however, conforming to certain social expectations of dress. When an individual adopts a style of dress associated with a particular role, status or group, he or she *not only signifies a particular identity but a willing participation in that role or willing adherence to that group and acceptance of a particular status*. It is a sign of an individual's involvement and commitment. The tramp whose clothing is scavenged from any available source communicates his lack of participation in conventional groups and roles; he communicates his social marginality. Clothing signs are very important as signs of social participation, and the degree of an individual's active and willing participation.

Although in any society there are basic ideas about what constitutes appropriate and respectable attire for its various members, this does not mean that everyone who is a businessman or a member of the upper class will wear identical dress. Individuals will interpret those ideas in a slightly different manner; there will be individual variations. Rules of appearance are often unstated but there will always be limits to the range of individual variation. The rules cannot be bent too far before the individual is criticised, or even excluded from the group. A bank manager may be permitted a flamboyant tie but if his dress strays too far from what is expected by wearing shorts and tee-shirts in summer, his clothing signs will give a confusing message to his colleagues and customers. He will be accused of 'not looking like a bank manager' and people will begin to doubt his fitness for the role. People expect a bank manager to look soberly dressed, reliable and trustworthy − not flash! Similarly, if a member of a punk group started to wear her hair in a neat bun and to wear twinsets and pearls, she would be regarded as having changed. She would no longer be regarded as a punk and would probably be excluded from the group.

Clothing and other forms of modification of the body such as hair styles, make-up, scarification or tattooing can communicate quite precise information about an individual's social identity. Because societies in different parts of the world are organised in different ways, quite different sorts of groups and roles have developed. The major social divisions in any society tend to be given visual representation in styles of clothes and appearance. For example, in a caste society like India, each caste has distinctive markings. In a society like the Nuba which is organised in terms of clans and age grades, each clan has a distinctive colour of clay used in body decoration and each age grade has particular hairstyles and forms of body painting associated with it. In our own society not all aspects of our social identity are communicated by clothing signs. Let us examine some of the most obvious.

Groups

Perhaps the largest group to which we belong is a national group. The dominance of fashion in the industrial and westernised world has led to a growing uniformity in the dress styles of the western and westernised nations, but it is still possible to recognise members of national groups by their style of dress. In societies which have maintained their traditional form of dress − such as areas in the East and Africa − costume clearly announces national identity. The kimono or the sari are both easily recognisable signs of the national identity of their wearers. We also easily recognise the Nigerian's white embroidered robes as African, even if we are not sure of the exact country of origin because of our ignorance of dress codes. But do the clothes of the American, French or German tourists communicate their national identity to you? If you have travelled abroad, have you been able to spot the other British people by their clothes and general manner? If you live in an area which is popular with foreign tourists, or if you have travelled abroad yourself, the codes of foreign clothing signs become more familiar and recognisable, as do differences within those groups. The clothes of different nationalities and societies do not only signify 'difference', they also express the values and way of life shared by the national group. The style of dress adopted by the Chinese in the aftermath of the Communist Revolution was modelled on the fighting clothes of the revolutionary army. There had been no difference between ranks, all soldiers wearing the high-collared tunic and soft-peaked cap in green. After the victory in 1949, men and women wore identical suits in green or blue, and wore their hair short. The style of dress expressed the self-conscious attempt to create an egalitarian society; it was a socio-political statement. As the political system has become less rigid, allowing some private production of goods, so there is more personal variety in dress. *Clothing signs therefore do not only delineate the boundaries of social groups, they express what kinds of group they are.*

In our own society, we do not have a uniform style of national dress in the way the Chinese did in the 1950s. Divisions of class, race, religion, age, and sex all produce differences in dress styles. In Britain a hundred years ago, it was very easy to distinguish the *social classes* by their styles of dress. The classes led quite different life styles and the differences in wealth produced widely divergent standards of living. Dress was a clear indicator of both wealth and class. Since then, a number of factors have intervened to complicate both the class system and the styles of dress associated with the classes. These factors include an increase in the affluence of the lower classes, a rise in their standard of living, an increase of social mobility, changing patterns of work, the development of a 'generation gap', and in the field of clothing, the development of mass-produced fashion. The distinctions between the classes have become less clear cut and the lifestyles within the classes more varied. But class remains a major social division within our society. Class groups are cultural groups whose members share common values and tastes and, as such, class identity is an important part of the social identity of an individual which is expressed by clothing. The working class man may have changed his boiler suit and hobnail boots for jeans, a bomber jacket and trainers, the middle class housewife may have exchanged her tweed skirt and twinset and pearls for dungarees or a Laura Ashley dress, but both are class styles of dress. So is the suit, trench coat and executive briefcase of the middle class business executive, and the short skirt, acrylic sweater and white high-heeled shoes of the working class girl. They express the taste and values of the group, and are just one means of signifying one's identification with those standards.

Most of us belong to a *family group* and to a *local community*. The nature of our society has lessened the importance of such groups and we do not signify our membership of them in our dress. In some primitive and peasant societies, large extended family groups are often an important focus of social and cultural identity; it is an economic, political or religious unit. On important occasions, members of such family groups will distinguish themselves from other groups by clothing signs or bodily decoration. The Nuba of the Sudan are organised into clans (each clan traces its descent from a common ancestor) and the members of each clan decorate themselves with a particular colour of clay. The Scottish clans each wore a distinctive tartan. In our society family groups are small and their activities are limited. Few are economic units and many of their previous functions have been taken over by outside institutions. If asked to identify oneself socially, one is much more likely to do so in terms of occupation than in terms of a family group. Similarly local communities have little sense of a corporate identity in the way that peasant communities were self-sufficient economic and social units. As a consequence our dress does not signify that one is a member of the Jones family rather than the Browns, or that one lives in Billericay rather than Harlow.

Britain is often described now as a *multicultural or multi-ethnic society*. This is because the population includes numerous groups of people who came themselves, or are descended from, people who came from different parts of the world. Many have come from former British colonies in Africa, Australia, India and Pakistan, Canada, Hong Kong, Cyprus and the West Indies but others have come from Europe, like the Italians, and others have come for political reasons like the Poles, Jews and Vietnamese. Many of these people have retained something of their old way of life, their culture. It may be their religion, their food, their marriage patterns or their traditional occupations. Some remain quite separate and distinct communities retaining as much as possible of their traditional ways of life, while others forge new but still culturally distinct identities. Dress is an important indicator of allegiance to a particular group and of the degree of allegiance to its values. Many Asian

Fig. 2.5 Women in Southall, London (BBC Hulton Picture Library).

women retain the sari as a form of dress despite its impracticality in British winters because of its social significance within their culture and as an expression of loyalty to that way of life. Their daughters' Western clothes signify their position 'between two cultures', caught between the values of their family and of the society which surrounds them in education and in work. As well as conforming to traditional values, experience of racial discrimination and rejection has led to the overt expression of separate cultural identity. Clothing signs are obviously one means of asserting ethnic pride. 'Why shouldn't I wear a turban? I'm a Sikh and proud of it, so why should I pretend that I'm not? Perhaps it will make it more difficult for me to get a job, but it won't make much difference. Everyone can see that I'm an Indian whether I wear a turban or not.' (4) Some second-generation West Indians who feel neither Jamaican, for example, nor fully English have forged a new black identity which is focused on particular forms of black music such as reggae or soul, and which involves particular types of behaviour and forms of dress, and hairstyles.

Black youth are not the only ones to form style groups. Throughout the population, adolescents are involved in *peer groups*. From schoolchildren to adults in their twenties, peer groups serve as sources of social identification and this identification is expressed through a style of dress. Amongst groups of adolescent school children hairstyles, bags, clothes, ways of knotting a tie can all signify membership of an 'in-group'. In clothes and shoe shops all over the country, parents and children stand arguing about purchases. The parent, not understanding that the particular shade, the type of pleat in a skirt or, more often these days, the particular brand name can guarantee membership of the style group, argues about school rules, quality or cost, all irrelevant to the would-be member. A recent vogue amongst London schoolchildren was for garments bearing brand names or logos such as Fred Perry or Benetton sports shirts, Pringle sweaters, Kicker shoes or Nike trainers and Burberry accessories such as hats and scarves. This style obviously is a form of conspicuous consumption and perhaps it expresses the current preoccupations and aspirations of these young people at a time of high youth unemployment. But it is only one of the styles produced by the young in recent times. Since the 1950s the identification of those of similar age and backgrounds has become an increasingly important and visible feature of our society. In the post-war period a large variety of youth cultures have emerged, each with their own sets of values, patterns of behaviour, tastes in music and distinctive styles of appearance.

Membership of *religious groups and organisations* is sometimes signified in styles of dress and appearance. Members of religious orders and the clergy signify their position if only by the wearing of the dog collar, although their participation in religious rituals is usually signified by a special form of dress. But ordinary lay members of the major Protestant and Catholic churches do not signify their religious affiliation through clothing signs. It is the more marginal religious groups or those who wish to maintain a separate and exclusive existence whose members are clearly distinguished by their appearance. New converts to sects such as the Hari Krishna sect are required to give up their former life and this dramatic change is symbolised in their appearance. The men almost entirely shave their heads, leaving only a small area at the crown, and both men and women wear long saffron robes in the style of Asian Buddhists. Their appearance clearly signifies their separate and distinct identity. In the case of the very orthodox Hasidic Jews of New York and London, their dress not only marks them out from the rest of the population and from other Jews, it also signifies the degree of their religious commitment and observance. A study by Simon Poll of the Hasidic community in New York, revealed six different levels of religious commitment, each with a form of dress appropriate to it, from the near secular Yid who wears only the standard long outmoded double-breasted suit which buttons from right to left to the Rebbe who has a full beard, side locks, kapote (a long black jacket) sable hat, bekescher (a Hasidic, coat of silky material), and schick and zocken (slippers and white knee socks). Comparable distinctions in dress can be seen in the Hasidic community in North London (Fig. 2.6). Such clothing signs are reminders to wearer and observer alike of an individual's religious

Fig. 2.6 Hasidic Jews, Stamford Hill, London (photo. Mike Abrahams, *The Observer*).

affiliation. As one Hasidic Jew remarked, 'With my appearance I cannot attend a theatre or movie or any other places where a religious Jew is not supposed to go. Thus my beard and my side-locks and my Hasidic clothing serve as a guard and shield from sin and obscenity'. (5) This must be true also for the vicar, priest or nun British society; they must behave in an appropriate manner.

As we saw above, the Sikh's turban in the context of British society is a sign both of his religion but also his participation in a cultural tradition. The Rastafarian's dreadlocks and tam serve as signs of religious affiliation but also of a distinctively 'black' identity within British society based on the concern of Rastafarianism with the roots of black people in Africa.

Membership of *political groups* is only expressed in certain situations. Obviously there are times when people actively conceal their political affiliations; for example, during underground or resistance activities, members of such groups will carefully control clothing signs which would reveal their identity or lead to their detection. In other situations, however, when people feel it is necessary or wish to show loyalty to a particular group or cause, or when it is necessary for political boundaries and divisions to be clearly visible, clothing signs can be used. During the French Revolution, the rough trousers of the poor, the *sans culottes*, became the sign of commitment to the Revolution. In Africa, supporters of SWANU (South West African National Union) used their party colours of blue, red, green and yellow in their clothing as a simple visual symbol of their support. In Northern Ireland, where political and religious affiliation divide the country in bitter conflict, clothing signs take on an important role in expressing loyalties. The Protestant Orange Order march in public parades wearing the insignia of the Order and the IRA march in their para-military uniforms. The fact that these uniforms are outlawed is indicative of their significance. In mainland Britain, we do not have particular styles of dress which signify membership of each party, but of course during the thirties the British fascists wore distinctive black shirts. There was an attempt during the 1983 election campaign by *The Guardian* newspaper to define the image of a typical candidate for each party in terms of their dress and appearance (Fig. 2.7). It relied heavily on class stereotypes and their assumed voting patterns. On the whole, the British do not display their allegiance to any political party explicitly, only a very few dedicated party workers wear rosettes on election day. But people are prepared to express their sympathies for political issues such as nuclear disarmament or animal rights by wearing badges or tee-shirts bearing symbols or slogans. These are worn particularly during demonstrations, sometimes to indicate membership of a pressure group such as CND and sometimes merely to express a political opinion.

We could continue almost indefinitely to discuss the great multitude of different kinds of groups that people belong to − from educational establishments, places of employment, interest groups such as freemasons, voluntary groups such as charity workers, to sports and recreational groups, and from highly formal groups such as the army to informal and transient groups such as friendship. However, its only purpose would be to repeat the argument, *that members of any group are expected to look like members by their fellows and by outsiders except in very special circumstances. In some cases the group imposes or generates a style of dress which signifies membership; in others the group is formed by selecting people whose appearance already suggests they are 'one of us', 'our kind of people'.*

Role and status

Within a society and within social groups, individuals occupy a certain *status*, position or rank, and they play certain *roles*. Some roles are very brief and are played only for a few hours, such as a guest at a wedding; others extend over a number of years, such as occupational or family roles; and a few are permanent, such as our sexual role. Not all, but many of the roles we play and the status we occupy are signified by our dress and adornment. Leach suggests that clothing acts as a marker of the various roles we play:

> 'Taken out of context, items of clothing have no "meaning"; they can be stacked away in a drawer like the individual letters which a typographer uses to make up his typeface but, when put together in sets form a uniform; they form distinctive markers of specified social roles in specified social contexts. Male and female, infant, child and adult, master and servant, bride and widow, soldier, policeman, High Court judge, are all immediately recognisable by the clothing they wear.' (6)

Obviously some roles such as those of sex and age have a biological basis but the content of those roles, the behaviour and attributes expected of those playing them, is socially defined and varies from culture to culture. In the case of our sexual roles, neither our

CONSERVATIVE

LABOUR

HER county-lady tweed suit: affluence, traditional, wholesome values, probity, motherliness. Jaunty hat and aggressively feminine spectacles: acknowledgment of femininity and secondary role to lord and master, identification with the natural order of things, rejection of feminism. Crimped hair: belief in order, tidiness next to godliness, meals on time. Sturdy handbag after HM The Queen Mother: competence, preparedness, willingness to be encumbered since someone else will open the door. Gloves: breeding, a knowledge of correct behaviour. Sturdy walking shoes: 'I am taking this election seriously.' Extravagant bow: 'I do not, however, wish to be thought aggressive or unfeminine.'

HIS Savile Row pin-stripe old-fashioned cut suit, old-school tie, starched collar, highly polished shoes: upper class assurance, the right background, born to rule, know what's what, it's in the blood. Military tache: 'I know where my duty lies.'

HER clashing patterns, bright too-short skirt and bright even-shorter coat: passion, commitment, lack of funds to spend on herself, lack of time to educate taste, vague feeling that if you want to be listened to, you've got to make them look at you. High-heeled sandals: 'I've got good legs − my old man always said so − and you need all the height you can get in this game.' Wrinkled stockings: 'What! Where? Who's got time to worry?' Messy hair, scrubbed face: 'Life is too interesting to bother.' Scatty but lovable, involved and concerned, approachable. Shopping bag: so much to do and think about and sort out.

HIS anorak, jeans and sneakers: working class uniform, class identification. Earring: support for Gay Lib. Saggy patterned garish sweater: knitted as an act of love by mate/clonè, its scruffiness is not so much ignored as unnoticed. Handbag: they are fashionable for men, John Lennon glasses: they were fashionable for men last time he thought to visit an optician. Long hair and beard: anti-establishment.

Fig. 2.7 Political stereotypes (illustration Peter Clarke, *The Guardian*).

LIBERAL

SOCIAL DEMOCRAT

HER pale pink track suit, pale grey legwarmers and pink/grey striped woolly hat: highly developed fashion sense translated into practical if posy outfit; fashionable in all things including ideas. The Social Democrats are all too middle-aged and middle-class, couldn't vote Tory, Mummy does, Labour is going a bit far. The Liberals are frightfully nice and so young and committed. Huge bag: contains term paper, exercise class tights and leotard, Jane Fonda tape, High Fibre snack, leaflets.

HIS polytechnic lecturer's tweed jacket: reliability, anti-establishment, academic respectability. Creased cords, button-down-shirt, thin tie; nostalgia for the sixties, student revolt, an end to the academic gerontocracy, Lucky Jim. Smelly pipe: poverty, nervousness, academic standing. Desert boots: romantic affection for old clothes, long-held ideas; new ones make him nervous. Long hair shaggy moustache and Van Dyck beard: peer-group uniform, anti-establishment but slightly vain, self-conscious, image-conscious.

HER droopy, flounced Laura Ashley purple print skirt, Peruvian cardigan, frilled T-shirt, gypsy earrings, ethnic goatskin bag: eclecticism, romantic attachment to Third World and the idealised rustic life. Pretty T-bar shoes and coloured stockings: imagination, flair, interest in decoration, sensuous/sensual appreciation of life. Short-cropped but well-cut hair: seriousness, purposefulness, good at organisation.

HIS Marks and Spencer suit, shirt and shoes: middle-management or creative occupation; conformity for ambition's sake. Hideous flashy tie: non-conformity for vanity's sake, affectation, self-consciousness, resentment of necessity to conform. Expensive, youthful haircut: passionate desire to be called a "whizz kid"; fear that it is almost too late; desperation, opportunism.

behaviour nor our appearance can be attributed to any great extent to biological difference; we have to learn how to be a man or woman in our society and how to look like one. Anthropologists have shown that the behaviour, tasks and essential characteristics associated with male and female roles differ quite dramatically from one society to another. In some societies, it is considered a natural task for a woman to carry heavy loads whereas in others it is considered a task for a man. Spending time adorning oneself is considered a feminine activity in one society and masculine in another. Most of what constitutes 'maleness' and 'femaleness' varies from one society to another and from one historical period to another, because the differences are socially created; they are learned. *Clothing and adornment act as important signifiers of those learned roles, but their meaning depends on their social context.* In many societies it is the men who paint their faces, grow their hair and spend long hours adorning themselves, whereas in our society these activities would be seen as signs of femininity.

In our society, *sexual roles* are an extremely important part of a person's social identity. They provide an ever present background to social behaviour, and the base from which other roles are played. Clothing and adornment which act as signs of sexual roles act as important cues for our behaviour which is quite different towards men and women. People feel very uncomfortable if they cannot establish the sexual identity of an individual from his or her appearance. In our society the sexes are usually clearly distinguished by their styles of clothes, hair, shoes, jewellery, and the use of make-up and perfume. People feel outraged when the signs of one sexual role are adopted by members of the other sex. When young men in the sixties began to grow their hair, older people seemed to be shocked and said they were unable to tell the sexes apart. When women first wore trousers, they were ridiculed and condemned as unnatural and unattractive. Of course, trousers are now worn by both sexes but there are different types and styles available to each sex. Despite the unisex fashions of the sixties and a vogue for cross-dressing by pop stars such as Boy George and Annie Lennox in the early eighties, the distinctions between the sexes remain. Garments such as skirts, brassieres and high-heel shoes remain signs of femininity; men continue to wear trousers, heavy shoes and shirts, have shorter hair and on the whole do not wear make-up.

Clothing signs can be used to communicate the individual's interpretation of or attitudes to their sexual role. As in the past, those interested in the emancipation of women borrowed a masculine style of dress and during the late seventies feminists were seen in dungarees or boiler suits, with short hair cuts and flat shoes or boots. Others continued to wear high-heels, dresses, skirts, make-up, nail varnish and to have carefully coiffed long hair, as an expression of their interpretation of a woman's role.

At one time it was popularly believed that homosexuals wore effeminate clothes and lesbians wore masculines ones, but there is no evidence that the majority of gay people want to dress in the clothes of the opposite sex. In the past, of course, many homosexuals had to keep their sexual identity secret for fear of the legal and social consequences of discovery, and so the majority dressed like everyone else. In the era of gay liberation, gay people were less afraid to indicate their homosexuality and to 'come out', and certain styles of appearance became associated with gays. Alison Lurie describes one such style in America, which is also found in Britain:

'Many gay men, in fact, have now adopted the "macho" look, and to the casual observer seem more masculine than most heterosexuals. They wear work clothes (especially when not at work): plaid shirts, jeans, athletic shirts, coveralls and heavy work shoes; they also favour Western gear, particularly cowboy hats and boots. To complete the image, they often grow large bushy mustaches and exercise for hours in the gym to develop their muscles.' (7)

This was, of course, the style of only *some* gay men. But clothing signs have been used as a means of communicating between homosexuals for a long time. Alison Lurie also refers to an article, 'Signifiers of Male Response' by Hal Fischer, in which he argues that urban homosexuals in America have evolved a system of clothing signs which can inform possible sexual partners of their sexual preference. He suggests that those who wish to play an active or masculine role wear a bunch of keys, an earring, or a bandanna in their back left pocket and those who prefer to play a passive or feminine role wear one or more of the indicators on the right. This form of communication has obvious advantages in gay bars and pick-up situations where people do not know each other.

Like sexual roles, *age roles* have some biological basis. The process of ageing is continuous and inevitable but the way an individual's life history is divided into various stages, and the role and status associated with each of those stages is culturally determined. In some societies people are considered to be adults from their early teens; in others, not until they are in their thirties. In

Fig. 2.8 The social progress of the Tohikirin Indians of South America through the age stages from infancy to old age is marked by distinctive styles of body painting and ornamentation.

our society, adult rights and obligations are taken on by most people from their late teens or early twenties. The status or value attached to different ages also varies; in some societies it is the very old who have highest status, in others it is the middle-aged and in some the young. In most societies, clothing and modifications of appearance serve to show in visible terms the individual's progress through the various social stages from infancy, through puberty and adulthood to old age. Some societies are organised in terms of age sets. In such societies membership of age sets or grades determines economic, political and ritual activity. The men of the Nuba of south-eastern Sudan are organised into three age grades and different economic, sporting and political activities are assigned to each grade. The youngest grade, involving youths from eight to seventeen years old, are mainly involved in cattle-herding chores, bride service, decorating themselves and wrestling. The second grade, young men from seventeen to thirty-one years old, devote much time to decorating themselves with body paintings, and to fighting and dancing. It is in the third grade of men over thirty-one in which they 'settle down', retire from sports and become involved in leadership and decision-making. The third grade do not decorate themselves except for ritual occasions and, unlike the two younger grades, wear loose clothes. Each grade and subgrade in the younger age sets has its own style of decoration and prescribed hair style. The women do not have age grades. Their body decoration tends to act as visible signs of their progress through the reproductive cycle and to mark their status as bearers of children. At the age of ten, a girl will begin a series of body scarification; first a set of scars is made at the beginning of breast development, another at the onset of menstruation, and a final set when her first child is weaned. This final scarring is regarded as very beautiful, and this is when a woman is most sought after by lovers. A young married woman signifies her status by wearing a white or coloured skirt, but after the menopause women wear dark blue skirts.

In our society, there are no formal age grades, or rules laid down that particular styles or colours should be worn at particular ages or stages in our development. In the past, the conventions were stricter. In the Victorian period, girls wore skirts which were made longer as they approached maturity. At eighteen they wore long skirts and put their long hair up as signs of their entry into adult society. Boys wore skirts, then short knee breeches and after puberty went into long trousers. Bush and London, writing about America, suggest:

> 'it was possible, until the beginning of the Second World War, to distinguish most American boys younger than six or seven from those between the ages of seven and puberty. Those in their pre-school years generally wore shorts while those in grammar school wore knickers. It was further possible to distinguish the prepubescent boy from the adolescent on a similar basis, namely the former's wearing of knickers and the latter's wearing of long trousers. The extent to which the

receipt of one's first pair of long pants was associated with pubertal ceremonies, the anxious and pleasurable anticipation attending the wearing of these pants, and the perception of this event as an affirmation of impending manhood, indicates the degree to which *differences in trousers were used as a means of differentiating one stage from another*, this change having something of the import of a rite of passage.' (8)

This custom of wearing long trousers after puberty continued in Britain until the sixties but now many children wear long trousers from a very early age. For girls, puberty is still marked by the wearing of the 'first bra'. This remains an important sign of growing up and becoming a woman, as does the wearing of make-up, high-heeled shoes and more adult styles of clothing. Perhaps it is because of the earlier onset of puberty or because of changing ideas about the role of child and adolescent that the signs are not as clear-cut as in the past and the boundaries are not so rigidly defined between the stages.

Nevertheless, informal age grades continue to exist in our society, even if the divisions are becoming rather blurred. Children, young adults, the middle-aged and the old do dress in different styles which signify their social age. This is recognised by the makers of clothes who provide different styles for each age group. Although there is pressure in our society on women to prevent and mask physical signs of ageing such as wrinkles and grey hair, there is also considerable disapproval of both men and women who dress in ways which signify an age which is very different from their actual or apparent age. If a person looks physically young then more youthful styles of dress are tolerated but generally 'mutton dressed as lamb' is pitied or laughed at.

Unlike the Nuba who signify 'motherhood' by scarring of the body, kinship and family roles are not marked in our society. There is no visible indication of a person's status as a parent. It may be possible to distinguish a mother and housewife by her dress but the style of appearance is associated with her occupational role rather than her status as mother. We do, however, mark marital status by the wearing of rings. In many societies unmarried and married women are distinguished by their appearance. In traditional Japan, the length of the kimono sleeves and the fabric used acted as signs of marital status. Similarly in Europe:

'In many European folk-cultures, women's dress was especially differentiated to signalise marriage. Even in villages where the dress of the unmarried girl and the married woman were almost uniform, there would be a subtle variation − a tell-tale change in the colour of the Haube, the flowered pattern of the apron, or some other detail, as, for instance, hair down for the unmarried girl and hair up and under the Haube for the married − that would define the difference.' (9)

Indicators of a man's marital status is less common.

Many of the roles a person plays are impermanent; children become adults, single women become wives and later perhaps widows. *As we have seen, the change from one status to another is often marked by changes in dress; the individual's movement across social boundaries is visibly expressed.* On the occasion of a particularly important change in status, a ritual or ceremony may be performed to mark the change and the participants nearly always 'dress up', putting on special clothes. The individual, whose status is changed wears special clothes so the boundary he or she is crossing can be seen to exist. A good example from British culture is a wedding. Despite the decline in Christian belief and church-going, many people still choose to mark their marriage by a church ceremony and even those who marry in a registry office observe many of the same conventions. All the guests and the families involved 'dress up', many people buy new clothes, wear hats and of course, carnations. Their appearance signifies their participation in the event but, in particular, attention is focused on the bride and her appearance. The bride usually wears a long white dress which is very distinctive in the context of the others participating in the ritual but also within the context of normal dress. The white dress is a symbol of purity and virginity, and draws attention to the transitional role of the bride as she is about to cross the social boundary from single woman and virgin to a married woman and non-virgin. The marriage ceremony seems to focus on the woman's change of status − the couple are pronounced man and wife, not husband and wife, and the dress of the groom is not that different from that of other participants such as the best man. When the ceremony is over, both the church rite and the ritual meal which follows, the bride changes out of her special dress into new but more ordinary clothes and embarks on her life as wife. When a woman 'leaves' her married status and becomes a widow, her change of status is marked by the wearing of black. In some cases the widow continues to wear black for the rest of her life, as in Greece; in England it may only be for the funeral.

Another very important aspect of our social identity is our

occupation — what we do, our job or more broadly how we spend our time — perhaps as students, international playboys or house- wives. It is one of the first questions we are asked: 'What do you do?' In the past, the wealthy indicated their leisure by styles of dress and the professions and the working class trades and occu- pations had distinct costumes. We have already seen that clothing signs are used to indicate occupational roles in hospitals, and in the uniforms of traffic wardens. But many jobs have a required costume from High Court judges and barristers to the services, and from archbishop to school dinner lady. In some occupations the clothes not only signify the occupational role but are also protective and necessary to the job being done. Work clothes may also indicate the company or institution you work for rather than the actual job. However, there is usually a distinction made in the dress of each grade in the organisational hierarchy. Even if there are no uniforms or prescribed forms of dress, most types of work have a style of dress associated with them that performers of that role are expected to wear. We have already discussed the style associated with the job of bank manager. We would not expect him to look that different from, say, a chartered accountant whose work is of a similar type and requires similar qualities. However, we would expect a coal-miner, a car mechanic or a butcher to look quite different.

Occupations have a *status*, a relative level of prestige attached to them. This status is one factor in establishing the overall standing of the individual in society. Often, though not always, the relative status of an occupation is linked to the income received for the job. In our society, those who possess wealth, either earned or inherited, are accorded high status. The rich are admired and envied. Veblen, an American sociologist, suggested there is no better means of indicating or implying wealth than through the use of clothes: '*Expenditure on dress has this advantage over most other methods, that our apparel is always in evidence and affords an indication of our pecuniary standing to all observers at first glance*'. (10) Veblen termed such displays of signs of wealth 'conspicuous consumption'. In the past the luxurious and exravagant nature of fashionable clothes, the fine fabrics and excellency of the cut were signs of wealth. In recent years the labels and logos of manufacturers and designers have become one of the most common means of conveying the purchasing power of the wearer, as they act as signs of the price paid for each garment. There are numerous examples —

the distinctive lining to Burberry raincoats, Daks' distinctive check fabric, the designer labels on jeans from Pierre Cardin to Fiorucci, and the whole gamut of sportswear logos, Pringle knitwear, Lacoste, Ellesse, Fila, Nike. Originally prestige labels such as Gucci or Hermes were worn by the rich. In London, young upper class women, labelled 'Sloane Rangers' by the journalist Peter York, wore a fairly distinctive style of dress which proclaimed their wealth and social class; with the velvet jacket and pleated skirts, they wore Gucci shoes and handbags with the discreet logo and Hermes headscarf. Increasingly, 'exclusive', labels have been worn by those wishing to 'borrow' some of their high status and prestige. *They are now worn by those who wish to give the impression of wealth.* Some individuals are prepared to spend a large proportion of their income on expensive clothes even if it means hardship or deprivation. Others cheat by buying a Harrods carrier bag, thus implying they shop there when in reality they shop at Tesco's or Marks and Spencer. William Davis, in a newspaper article in 1983, argued that the over-popularity of prestige goods, bearing distinctive labels was resulting in a change in their meaning. (11) As Lacoste sweaters, Ralph Lauren sports shirts and Gucci crocodile skin shoes appeared on the football terraces of London they lost their image of exclusivity and their association with most socially prestigious groups in society. Perhaps these particular signs of wealth will be replaced by others but as long as there are differences in wealth and in the prestige accorded to the different levels, people will continued using clothing as signs of their relative position and of their aspirations.

Another source of prestige is the political power associated with *leadership*. In institutions like the army and the church, the superior status and power of high-ranking officers and church dignitaries is communicated through distinctive and often sumptuous forms of dress. In some societies, the political leaders have a special form of dress − insignia of office such as a crown or special head-dress or particularly extravagant and luxurious clothes to communicate their high status. In our democratic and parliamentary system of government, elected leaders do not generally wear any mark of their office. In local government, many mayors still wear the traditional chain of office when carrying out official duties. The insignia of political roles which are worn tend to be traditional, even archaic, expressions of former roles. These include the robes of the Lords, and of course Her Majesty the Queen's crown and sceptre. The real leaders, the real decision-makers, i.e. the Prime Minister and the Government of the day, do not wear any badge of their status even on official occasions.

Clothing signs can act as markers for long-term roles and establish status, but they are also used to express *the performance of very brief roles*. As we saw in the example of the wedding, special clothes are worn as signs of participation in an event which lasts only a very short time. Women buy expensive wedding dresses which are worn only once for a few hours for their role of bride. Special clothes are worn to indicate participation in rituals of this kind but also on many social occasions such as parties when we express our role as guest. The social divisions of the year and day are also signified through clothing. Although this is probably less true than in the past, we change our clothes according to *the time of day* and *the activity in which we are engaged*. We change our clothes according to whether we are staying at home to clean up, going out for an evening, going to play badminton, or just going to bed. Even if you choose your clothes for cleaning and sport on practical or functional grounds, such actions still have a communicative aspect, as Leach pointed out, *they communicate to others what activity you are engaged in*. If someone is still wearing her nightie at midday, the observer assumes that person has just got up or is still making the transition between waking up and getting on with the activities of the day — it says something to the observer. It also communicates how the individual is feeling and we will now turn our attention to the relationship of the individual and his or her clothes.

References

1. Leach, E. (1976) *Culture and Communication*. (Cambridge University Press) 11.
2. Saussure, de, F. (1916) *Cours de Linguistique Generale*. (Paris).
3. Hall, E.T. (1959) *The Silent Language*. (New York: Doubleday).
4. Watson, J. ed. (1977) *Between Two Cultures*. (Blackwell) 147.
5. Poll, S. (1965) 'The Hasidic community'. In: *Dress Adornment and the Social Order*, eds. M.E. Roach and J.B. Eicher. (New York: John Wiley and Sons) 146.
6. Leach, E. (1976) *Culture and Communication*. (Cambridge University Press) 53.
7. Lurie, A. (1981) *The Language of Clothes*. (New York: Random House) 259.
8. Bush, G. and London, P. 'On the disappearance of knickers.' In: *Dress Adornment and the Social Order*, eds. M.E. Roach and J.B. Eicher. (New York: John Wiley and Sons) 69.

 9. Dorson, R. ed. *Folklore and Folklife*. (University of Chicago) 305.
10. Veblen, T. (1931) *The Theory of the Leisure Class*. (New York: Random House Modern Library) 170.
11. Davis, W. 'The Logo's a No Go' *Daily Mail* 14 November 1983.

3 The Individual and Dress

What is the relationship between the individual and the way he or she dresses? So far we have examined the ways in which clothing and the various forms of body modification act as forms of *social communication*, transmitting information about the social identity and activities of the wearer. They tell us about the individual in relation to the community to which he belongs. As we have seen, clothing and other forms of adornment are used to emphasise *social similarities*, to communicate a *common identity*. There are many examples of dress being used to suppress individual differences and create the illusion of total conformity.

However, in our society, the idea of totally uniform or rigidly controlled styles of dress is abhorrent. In fact, it is sometimes used as a form of punishment, when it is seen as a sign of the loss of individual freedom. In many Western cultures, there is a highly developed sense of *individualism* and individual freedom, and the idea of individuality in dress is part of that same ideology. It is, of course, true that every individual is unique in terms of character or personality and many people seem to believe that our choice of clothing reveals our individual character.

Human beings are born with a strong visual sign of their unique personal identity that makes the use of clothing to differentiate between particular individuals redundant. With the exception of identical twins, everyone has a unique face which distinguishes him or her from other people. So, does clothing act as a means of *personal* communication in the sense of expressing the individual's unique personality? Does everyone have a unique style of dress, a distinctive look?

There certainly is a close identification between the individual and his or her particular clothes. From the day we are born we spend most our time wearing some form of clothing. In fact, some people in our society are only without clothes for the briefest periods whilst they change or bathe. Clothes are a kind of second skin, an extension of our bodies. But are they an extension of *ourselves*? When we lend someone a garment or an outfit, is that friend borrowing our identity or character for the evening? For some people the identification with their clothes is so close that they will not lend them at all, and others will only lend them to close friends or members of their family. Lovers sometimes exchange garments as a mark of physical closeness, or as a token of their continual presence even when apart. The closer items are worn to the skin, the more reluctantly they may be lent out. You might quite readily offer to lend your coat to a comparative stranger for a few minutes but what about the shirt off your back or an item of underwear?

We also identify with the clothes we wear to the extent that criticism of them is often experienced as criticism of ourselves, and praise as praise of ourselves. After all, our clothes are hung on *our* bodies and do reflect *our* taste and judgement to some extent. You might argue, of course, that you would look quite different if you had more money or more time to spend on your appearance. Also, the importance we attach to the remarks of others depends very much on *who* those others are. Whose criticism or praise would you take to heart most, that of your grandmother, your father, your friends, or your boyfriend? Why are some people's opinions more important to you than others? Does your clothing reflect *your* personal taste, or a taste shared with others?

Notwithstanding these problems, there is a widely held belief that clothing is a form of self-expression. How does this expression take place and what aspects of self are communicated? There are two rather contradictory and conflicting views. For some people, clothing is an expression of personality, an almost inevitable and unconscious revelation of one's 'true self'. Others see it as a means of 'putting across an image', something which can be manipulated to improve the impression we give of ourselves to others. John T. Molloy, author of *Dress for Success*, capitalises on both views. In his book, he advises the reader on how he can manipulate his appearance either to imply he has the qualities desired in a particular situation, or to mask undesirable ones: in other words, how to give a particular impression of himself which may well be false. Molloy promises 'I can help you look successful, fatherly, honest, sexy...'. (1) He regards clothing as a tool which can be used to get jobs, get promotion, be successful with women and even make an individual more likable! He directs his advice to lawyers seeking to influence juries and politicians seeking election. Can a charismatic leader be created by a change of suit and tie, as he claims? (2) However, Molloy's theories rely on the majority of the population reading clothing and general appearance as *reliable* indicators of personal qualities and attributes, otherwise they would see through the ploys he suggests in his book. Where does the truth lie?

Let us examine in some detail these two approaches to the expression of self in dress.

The expression of personality — 'the true self'

The notion of a personality or individual identity is not quite as simple as it might appear at first sight. We must decide what we mean by *personality* and then how it could be communicated by our appearance and clothing?

In everyday speech, when we talk of someone's personality we usually mean his or her individual character. We think that we can learn about that character by getting to know the person, watching him or her and generally forming an impression of how he or she is likely to react and behave. We tend to describe people's personalities in terms of characteristic traits — shy, kind, aggressive, generous. We sometimes talk about people having 'lots of personality' when we mean they are lively or socially adept and having 'no personality' when they are shy or withdrawn. But, of course, everyone has an individual character. Sometimes we may borrow terms from psychology like 'extravert' and 'introvert'. However, even psychologists are by no means in agreement about what personality is, and those who wish to explore and explain individual differences have developed a number of approaches to this issue. We are going to look at *some* of those approaches and assess the extent to which they help us understand the relationship between individual personality and dress.

One of the earliest theories of personality attempted to classify individuals into personality types on the basis of their appearance, and in particular in relation to body build. A short plump person, an *endomorph*, was said to be sociable, relaxed and even-tempered. Other personality types were associated with thinness or muscular build. (3) This theory is now discredited, and subsequent research has shown that there is little correlation between specific personality characteristics and body build. Nevertheless, body size and physical type may well influence personality development in more subtle ways and we will return to this issue when we discuss self-image and self-esteem later in this chapter.

Other personality typing theories have been based on purely psychological characteristics. Carl Jung divided all personalities into *introverts* and *extraverts*. An introvert is characterised as shy and often choosing to work alone, whereas the extravert is sociable and chooses to work with people. We may all feel that we know a 'typical' extravert or introvert but it is also likely that most of our friends fall somewhere in between the two extremes. This is the problem with type theories: most typologies involve a continuum of differences rather than discrete types. A dichotomy must over-simplify the range of personality and the range of behaviour each individual is capable of.

Even if we accept that there are typical extraverts, is their clothing and appearance also 'extravert'? If so, what does this mean? Many people would, in the first instance, associate bright, flamboyant or eye-catching clothes with an extravert personality. But I would suggest that one could equally find a very sociable, outgoing person dressed in rather subdued, even dull clothes. Does this mean they are not 'extravert' or that dull clothes are 'extravert'? Similarly, are all those who wear eye-catching colours, etc., auto-matically extravert? I think not. Sometimes bright or dull colours are fashionable and people wear them for that reason without it being an indication of their personality type.

Instead of classifying people into types, the proponents of *trait theory* assume that *a personality is made up of an accumulation of traits*. The individual's personality traits are measured or rated on a scale, or point on a continuum between polar opposites such as tidy-careless, calm-anxious. Here is an example of such a continuum produced by Hans Eysenk in which traits are shown in relation to the two dimensions of introversion-extraversion and stability-instability.

Critics of trait theory argue that despite decades of work devising questionnaires and tests, the trait theorists have had little success in predicting behaviour. This may be because many of the traits they examine do not reflect fundamental attributes of a person but may in fact be *highly dependent on the situation*. Someone may be an aggressive competitor in sport but very passive and gentle in other spheres. Trait theory also tends to focus on particular isolated traits; it does not help us know which are most important or how the traits relate to each other to form a personality. If we take Eysenk's example in relation to dress, just how many of those

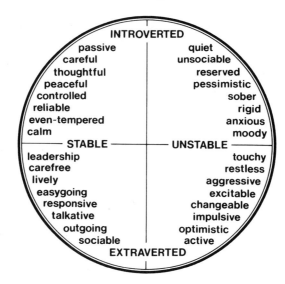

Fig. 3 After Eysenk and Eysenk.

traits could be deduced from clothing? What would be the significance of that deduction for an understanding of the individual's personality?

We could perhaps argue that traits such as carefulness, sobriety, rigidity, responsiveness to change could be observed but these traits may only be related to clothing behaviour, and even then only in certain situations. Does a careful or fastidious approach to dress always accompany, for example, a careful approach to financial matters or study? A study of students in America in 1974 showed that although the investigators assumed that personal neatness was one component of 'conscientiousness', their results showed otherwise. (4) For most students the neatness of their room, for example, was not related to other measures of conscientiousness such as completing assignments on time or arriving promptly for classes.

Behaviour depends on situation to a large extent: you may be honest with your friends but not in your attitudes to charges for parking or library fines. People may appear soberly dressed if their work requires it but dress flamboyantly during their free time. A smart executive may have been positively scruffy during his student days. At best, it seems that we can deduce, from the way people dress, how they behave in relation to the selection of clothes and ways of dressing! Only if we have knowledge of other aspects of their behaviour could we say that they are sober, honest or whatever. But even then there is no evidence to support the view that we could *predict* that individual's future behaviour. Increasingly, psychologists have acknowledged the importance of situation in determining behaviour.

A radically different approach to personality is that of *psychoanalysis* which is based on the work of Freud. Freud's theory of the personality focuses on the unconscious and the development of sexuality. According to Freud the personality is composed of three major systems − the *id*, the *ego* and the *superego*. The id incorporates innate biological needs and drives especially the libido (sexual energy defined very widely). It operates according to the 'pleasure principle', that is, it seeks immediate gratification of pleasure-seeking impulses. The ego relates to external reality. It develops to restrain the impulses of the id and direct them towards socially acceptable forms of expression. The ego acts according to the 'reality principle'. The superego develops from the ego and represents internalised morality, standards of behaviour and cultural values. The ego has to manage the tensions which inevitably arise between the id, superego and outside world. This frequently requires the use of defence mechanisms such as denial and displacement to repress instinctual drives.

Aggressive impulses which are socially unacceptable in many contexts may be 'displaced' on to a more acceptable activity such as sport. An impulse may be 'repressed' by pushing it out of awareness into the unconscious. It may be 'denied' by the person disguising even from himself the real motives for his behaviour. 'Reaction formation' takes place when the anxiety-provoking impulses are so successfully suppressed that the individual behaves in a way that is directly opposite to that impulse. For example, a strong sexual impulse may be reversed and appear as extreme puritanism.

Freud's work on the unconscious led to his discovery of infantile sexuality. He argued that the libido is focused on different parts of the body as the individual develops. He outlined three stages − the oral, the anal and the genital − through which an individual must pass before mature sexuality is achieved. The individual's progression through these stages has profound consequences for his or her psychosexual development.

The ideas of Freud have interested many of those wishing to understand the motivations behind clothing behaviour, most notably the psychologist J.C. Flugel, author of *The Psychology of Clothes*, but also more popular writers such as Laver. Using psychoanalytic theory, Flugel attempts to explain the differences in individual attitudes to clothing and appearance, and in the pleasure taken in clothes.

Like Freud, Flugel argues that behaviour is motivated by pleasure-seeking impulses of the id and experiences in childhood in relation to these impulses shape personality. The two impulses with which Flugel is particularly concerned are those derived from the naked body and from exhibiting it — auto-eroticism and narcissism. Flugel suggests that small children initially show very little interest in clothes but these two impulses can be 'displaced' on to clothes and 'when thus displaced, become *the main source* of the development of interest in dress in the individual...'. (5)

Auto-erotic pleasures, skin and muscle eroticism, can be displaced on to clothing. Displacement of the pleasures of the wind and sun on the skin may be found in the sensations created by the feel of fabrics on the skin. The free play of the muscles, Flugel suggests, is best appreciated when naked, although compensation may lie in the pleasurable pressure afforded by tight garments. (This view has been used to explain the wearing of tight corsets and belts, particularly by women.)

Narcissism is the tendency to admire one's own body and to display it to others. Clothing is used to augment this display, but an interest in clothes can become distinct from interest in the body itself and can actually be substituted for it.

Flugel devised a typology based on the extent and nature of an individual's displacement of narcissism and auto-eroticism. The following are examples of his types. The 'rebellious type' is someone who demonstrates very little displacement on to clothing, who in fact prefers to be naked, resents the restrictions of clothing, and is not inhibited by social expectations about dress. 'It would seem highly probable...that individuals of this type constitute the main body of supporters of the 'nude-culture' movement..' (6) The 'prudish type', on the other hand, has conquered exhibitionistic impulses to such an extent that exposure of the body is regarded as disgusting and any extravagance of dress is disapproved of. This is an example of 'reaction formation'. The 'sublimated type' simply displaces instinctive pleasures on to clothes: 'It is this type which is most fully capable of the satisfaction that sartorial display can give; and, where there is aesthetic capacity also present, it is to this type that we may look for the most satisfactory development of clothes'. (7) Because of the relatively strong narcissistic tendencies in this type, Flugel suggests it may lead to an excessive interest in clothes display.

I am sure we all know some people who do not seem to care how they look, some who think it is almost immoral to worry about fashion, and others who are obsessed with their clothes and devote hours to appearance. So, Flugel does raise some important questions about why it is that individuals do vary so greatly in their attitudes to clothes, the pleasure they get from them, the interest they take in them and the amount of energy they devote to the way they look. But, as Flugel admits, his typology is provisional and requires further study. Do the types he outlines actually represent the ways pleasure-seeking impulses are manifested and controlled in the individual personality?

Freud has been criticised for the universal and ahistorical nature of his theory of personality for his emphasis on instincts and his neglect of social experience in shaping the personality. These criticisms could equally apply to Flugel. When discussing the 'rebellious' type Flugel himself mentions the popularity of nudism and naturism in Germany in the 1920s. The existence of large groups of naturists in Germany and Scandinavia raises questions about the universality of the type and highlights the importance of understanding the development of the individual within specific historical and cultural conditions.

For Flugel, the motivation for clothing behaviour is *unconscious* and must be inferred from that behaviour. Let us now contrast this with a quite different approach to human behaviour, one which suggests that the individual is *consciously* and continuously manipulating his action and his appearance to give a particular impression.

Putting across an image

Some American sociologists have taken the view that the individual does not have a fixed or continuous self, a given identity which moves from one situation to another. (8) They challenge the commonsense notion of a fixed personality which could be expressed through or deduced from dress. Instead, they argue that the self is continuously created and re-created in each social situation.

Social interaction is seen from the perspective of a dramatic performance; the participants, like actors, take on roles and play parts in the drama of social life. For example, in a classroom, participants arrive with expectations of the behaviour and responses of those involved — in this case teacher and students. Their expectations define the situation, and if their expectations correspond the interaction is likely to run smoothly. A role is a typified response to typical expectations. Like in a script, the role of teacher is already written; the teacher must look and act like a teacher in order to fulfil the expectations of the student and evoke the expected responses from them. If they have not met before, the students will observe closely the appearance, manner and actions of the teacher in order to get some sense of his or her expectations of them. Will the teacher be strict, easy-going, humorous or boring? Of course, there is considerable variety in the way any role is played but there is sufficient similarity for students to recognise who is a teacher.

Individuals play a multiplicity of roles in society which demand quite different behaviours and attitudes. 'The person's biography... appears to us an uninterrupted sequence of stage performances, played to different audiences, sometimes involving drastic changes of costume, always demanding the actor *be* what he is playing.' (9) The playing of roles then is not quite as cynical or detached as the analogy with drama might suggest. A social role is not just a script of required actions and simulated emotions, it involves the participant in an identity. The teacher or student is not just acting out a role; even if they feel a little uncomfortable in the role at first, they eventually begin to *feel like* a student or a teacher, and to adopt the attitudes and feelings associated with that identity.

This identity is not just 'given', it requires social recognition, it has to be confirmed and supported by the responses of others. If students refuse to accept the authority of the teacher and do not treat him like a teacher, he may begin to doubt his identity, or he may try to find another teaching situation where the responses do meet his expectations. Looking 'the part', like a teacher, like a student, like a woman, like a reasonable person, is part of establishing that identity with others.

In his book, *The Presentation of Self in Everyday Life*, Goffman shows how the individual tries to control the impression he or she gives to others. Every social encounter is a performance which has to be 'stage-managed'; clothes, houses and job situations are all 'props' to be used in the performance. Goffman argues that individuals seek to present themselves in the most favourable light for their purpose. But, in the process of each individual projecting an image of himself or herself and forming impressions of others. She is trying to reach *beyond the social façade* in order to evaluate her trustworthiness and the reliability of the image she is putting across.

Is clothing used as a kind of 'prop' by the individual? Do people select their clothing in order to present what they consider to be an appropriate and acceptable impression of themselves, given what they judge to be the requirements of the situation?

Everyone has faced the dilemma of 'what to wear', at some time. Perhaps we are most conscious of our need to look 'right' and the problems of stage managing our costume (Is it clean? Can we afford a new one? Is it too tight? Can I wear brown shoes with a blue suit?) on occasions like meeting people for the first time or going for an interview. In both situations we are going to make an impression on people and clothing is an important element in that impression. People are going to make assumptions about us from our appearance as well as from what we say and our manner, but we often have to guess at what their expectations and criteria for judgement are.

Most of the time we have some idea of their expectations; we have built up some knowledge through experience. For example, most people acknowledge that there is an expectation that, at interviews, the interviewee will 'dress up' for the occasion, that his or her dress represents a special effort and is not how they would necessarily appear everyday. However, the interviewee has to balance this with the expectation to look the 'part' of the job he or she is applying for. Most people realise that you should not dress in overalls if you are applying for a job in management, and that a potential fashion designer or a legal secretary would dress quite differently for their interviews. Of course, people do make mistakes in their attempt to create the right image; they misjudge the situation or the meaning conveyed by their appearance. Some students arrive at college for the first time dressed up in their smartest clothes, obviously wishing to make a good impression but perhaps also having an over-glamourised notion of student life. They soon realise that they look 'too smart', 'too keen' and opt for the more casual style worn by other students.

We cannot guarantee that the impression we are trying to convey will be understood in the way we intend. As we have seen in Chapter 2, the meaning of clothing signs is socially established and different groups attach quite different meanings to the same garments. It is also clear, from the wide variety of styles which people choose and like, that people's tastes also vary. An outfit which for one person is bright and cheerful can be seen by others as gaudy and vulgar; what is subtle and tasteful to some can be rather drab and dull to others; what is fashionable to one person is just 'a mess' to others. Our choice of clothes is influenced by the opinions of those around us. As children our tastes were shaped by our family but as we get older peer groups, friends, work environments or the standards set in magazines and the media may affect our taste. Our choice is influenced by what we think others like, or expect, in a situation but we cannot guarantee that we share an identical clothes language.

People use clothing to create *different impressions* of themselves in *different situations*. This is particularly true of people who play a variety of roles. For example, a career woman may wear smart tailored suits and shirt blouses for work, a seductive evening dress when she goes out in the evening, and sporty clothes at weekend around the house. On one level these clothes express her participation in certain kinds of activity but her choice also expresses how she wishes to be seen and treated. Her clothes 'give off' an impression of the kind of person she is. Her work clothes suggest efficiency and a serious approach to her career; they express her desire to be treated as a colleague. Her evening dress, on the other hand, may stress her identity as a woman and one who wishes to be seen as attractive and treated as such. *Her selection of clothes are an important indication of which aspects of herself − which roles − the woman is emphasising at any time.*

Not everyone modifies his or her appearance according to the social situation. A skinhead tends to look the same wherever he goes or whatever he does. He expresses his identity as a 'skin' above all else and his loyalty to the group values of toughness and aggression. His refusal to adapt to others' expectations may provoke antagonistic feelings or even hostility in others. Similarly there are women who adopt an extreme and stereotypically feminine style − lots of make-up, long or fussy hairstyles, lots of jewellery, high-heeled shoes, flimsy or sexy dresses − and maintain this style whatever they are doing be it working at the office, climbing up a mountainside, going dancing or going to the launderette. Their style announces that their identity as a very feminine woman is paramount.

However, *clothing is not used just to create an image or impression for others; it also helps establish a sense of identity for the wearer.* Putting on certain types of clothes can make you feel different.

Berger suggests that 'One feels more ardent by kissing, more humble by kneeling, more angry by shaking one's fist. That is, the kiss not only expresses ardour, it also manufacturers it'. (10) In the same way, if you put on a long-flowing, elegant evening gown and you begin to move around in it, it can make you feel elegant and sophisticated. If you put on tennis shoes, pick up a racquet, begin to bounce around and practise strokes, you begin to feel like a tennis player. Of course, clothing cannot completely transform people's sense of themselves. Someone with a strongly developed sense of masculine identity is not going to feel elegant in an evening dress — he would probably feel ridiculous. Even a woman may feel awkward and clumsy if she identifies herself as not 'the type' for such garments.

Nevertheless, clothing seems to be an important element in the way social identities are established for others and for oneself. In his article, 'Changes in person perception as a function of dress', Hamid suggests:

'Early in a child's life he learns to identify behavioural intentions from facial expressions and gestures of his parents. He also learns that there are quite marked differences among people according to the clothes they wear. Such distinctions enable the child to identify men, women, policemen, firemen, soldiers, nurses, etc., with speed and reliability. Dress therefore provides efficient cues for the classification of others. Thus, just as emotions can be attributed to certain facial expressions, so too actions and activities can be attributed to persons in different modes of dress.' (11)

In other words, clothing is recognised as a tangible sign of identity. During the process of socialisation, children become familiar with those signs and the appearance of others has meaning for them.

Clothing is used by children in play to help establish a sense of role. Many of the games played by children involve trying out adult roles — mummies and daddies, doctors and nurses, playing at shopping, keeping house, etc. Dressing up is an important part of such play. G. Stone, who did research amongst American men and women, found that 65 per cent recollected dressing up in adult clothes and most of them had dressed in the clothes of the same sex. (12) In particular, children's play seems to be concerned with learning sex roles — how to be a man or woman in society. Initially children model themselves on parental behaviour but soon begin to include other models of masculinity and femininity. Props such as clothes, guns, handbags, dolls and cars seem essential to the acting out of the roles and to the process of identifying with them. It seems that these dramatic props aid the performer throughout life. 'It is likely, indeed, that the psychology of clothing has too often been conceived in terms of simple narcissitic delight in one's appearance; clothing is largely a means of making real the role that is to be played in life.' (13) Note the contrast here with the views of writers like Flugel.

Children also learn very early in life that their own appearance and clothes evoke certain responses from others. Little girls soon learn what kind of clothes evoke comments like 'don't you look a pretty little girl, then!' They also become aware of the fact that approval is given to people and children with particular types of appearance and is witheld from those who lack the necessary attributes or clothes. Children are very sensitive to the social significance of clothing and the effects their appearance has on their social interactions. They show a willingness, even determination, to acquire certain items of clothing in order to produce a desired impression on others.

The reactions of other people affect the way the individual feels about himself or herself. Writing at the turn of the century, Cooley saw the opinions and judgements of others as crucial to the development of an individual's sense of identity, their self-image:

> 'As we see our face, figure, and dress in the glass, and are interested in them because they are ours, and pleased or otherwise with them according as they do or do not answer what we should like them to be: so in imagination we perceive in another's mind some thought of our appearance, manners, aims, deeds, character, friends, and so on, and are variously affected by it.
>
> 'A self idea of this sort seems to have three principal elements: the imagination of our appearance to the other person; the imagination of his judgement of that appearance, and some sort of self-feeling such as pride or mortification. The comparison with a looking-glass hardly suggests the element, the imagined judgement, which is essential. The thing that moves us to pride or shame is not the mere mechanical reflection of ourselves but an *imputed sentiment* − the imagined effect of this reflection upon another's mind.' (14).

Cooley draws attention to the way the individual formulates a *self-image* by *imagining* how he or she appears to others. The imagined judgements of others contribute to the individual's sense of *self-esteem*. However, we also check our imagined self against 'reality'.

This helps to explain our concern with the way we look, our fascination with images of ourselves. It is not necessarily vanity which makes us look back when we catch sight of ourselves in a mirror or shop window, or makes us want to see photographs, videos or films of ourselves, but *the desire to know how others see us*.

When we are trying to decide what to wear, we conjure up a mental image of how we think we are going to look. When we are buying clothes we try to visualise how we will look in them and our hopes are fulfilled or crushed in the changing rooms where with the aid of mirrors we try to see ourselves from every angle. We want to know what 'image' other people will see, what impression we will make. Some people take along friends, members of the family, boyfriend or girlfriend so they can have their opinions straight away. As Cooley suggests, we are far from indifferent to what we see in a mirror, we do feel pleased or disappointed, and sometimes we are shocked. 'Do I really look like that?' Our assessment of the likely reaction of others leads to the formation of a poor or good self-image, and the reactions of others will help sustain or undermine our own assessment.

It is perhaps pertinent here to mention the role of physical appearance in the formation of a self-image. Clothing, after all, is only one aspect of appearance. Our physical self has a substantial influence on our self-image and on the ways we can use clothing to give particular impression of ourselves. In the discussion of personality, Sheldon's attempt to develop a typology of personality linked to physical types was mentioned. This could be seen as an elaboration of the stereotypes which exist in everyday parlance: thin lips are associated with meanness, fat people are often thought to be placid and good-natured, etc. Sheldon's theory has largely been rejected but physical types do evoke certain reactions just because the stereotypes exist. The individual's self-image may be shaped by the expectations implicit in the stereotype and by the responses and reactions of others.

A tall, well-built woman is likely to be perceived by others as capable and able to look after herself, not a 'damsel in distress' type. A very petite woman on the other hand, might have difficulty convincing others that she does not need someone to take care of her. Physical types have not only been associated with personality types but also social roles. In the past, men were *supposed* to be big and strong and women were *supposed* to be dainty and weak. Although, these days, ideas have changed about the roles of men and women and what they should look like, we still do compare ourselves and other people to the ideal physical types associated with particular roles in our society. Our physical type and body size may affect the degree to which we can identify with certain roles, and in turn this may affect our self-esteem.

There is considerable variety in what different people might feel is the ideal body type but people use clothing to help them create as far as is possible the illusion of conforming to one of them. People use clothing to mask undesirable physical attributes or to draw attention to their 'good points'. Women wear clothes which conceal fat waistlines or fat legs; they wear padded bras to increase their bosom and corsets to hold in their stomachs. Men wear jackets with padded shoulders to make them look stronger and built-up shoes to make them look taller.

However your body type may prevent you from identifying with certain ideal types and it may not always be possible to use clothing to achieve a desired image. For example, it seems that it is very difficult for a very plump woman to think of herself as fashionable or to be seen as fashionable by others. The image of a very tall, slim woman has dominated the world of fashion for some years now. Most fashionable clothes are designed to show off slim bodies and to look good on tall people. They are always modelled by tall, slim, young people on the catwalk and in magazines. Some designers even say that they would prefer people over size 12 not to wear their clothes and most of the clothes featured in magazines are only available in sizes 10, 12, and 14. But even if the individual decides to resist such images and fight the stereotype, she is likely to run into practical difficulties in obtaining suitable clothes unless she is prepared to make them herself. (15) Finally, will she persuade others to see her as *fashionable*?

Not everyone is concerned with their appearance to the same degree. Some people are willing to accept a poor self-image as far as appearance goes and focus their attention on more 'important' aspects of self. However, for many people, appearance and therefore clothing is an important element in their self-esteem. Few aspects of self provoke so much direct comment or produce so much readily expressed admiration. People are much more likely to comment on a new item of clothing or hairstyle than on a person's character or abilities. The comments are very likely to be positive rather than critical. Just think how many times people have remarked upon your appearance recently in comparison to your personality.

They are more likely to say 'I like your dress' than 'I think you are a wonderful person', or 'You are really intelligent' or whatever. Obviously such remarks help build up and maintain social relationships and it is easier and more socially acceptable to comment on clothes rather than some other aspects of a person. Nevertheless, such comments do bring pleasure and sometimes increase self-esteem.

Being admired is not just a matter of simple pride or vanity. Most of us learned in our childhood that looks do matter. In 'The importance of being beautiful', Bull summarises the findings of various pieces of research which show that people who look attractive do gain social benefits. It is suggested, for example, that attractive looking people may receive lighter prison sentences than plainer individuals in certain categories of crime. Clothing is an important factor in the assessment of attractiveness. Various studies have shown that the same individual, when dressed in different outfits, is assessed quite differently and meets with quite different responses. Not many people would be surprised by the results of some research carried out by Athanasiou: 'A female experimenter stood in a lay-by near her car, which had its bonnet raised. The experimenter was dressed in either an attractive, sexy way, or unattractively. During the three days of observation far more offers of help. . .were received if the experimenter was attractively dressed.' (16)

During the process of socialisation we learn the correct way of dressing for various social situations and the inability to 'dress the part' can cause the individual to feel socially uncomfortable or ill at ease, even depressed and frustrated. Loss of our clothing props may have important consequences for our sense of identity. Goffman has shown how in total institutions such as prisons and mental hospitals inmates may be systematically stripped of their 'identity kits' – the means by which the individual controls how he or she appears to others – clothes, cosmetics, combs, washing equipment, shaving sets, etc. The individual lacks the means to maintain his former image and as a result experiences a 'defacement' of self. (17)

In contrast, some mental hospitals in the United States have experimented with 'fashion therapy'. It is suggested that clothing and cosmetics can be used to restore feelings of self-esteem and therefore promote social confidence and aid recovery.

'For some patients in the group, effects of the fashion project were dramatic and immediate. One woman in her early thirties had persistently

refused to enter any socialising activities and had even been unwilling
to use her privilege of going out in the grounds. She finally admitted
that she was ashamed of her appearance and said that she never went
to parties or dances because she "looked so terrible". After being
fitted with proper foundation garments, she looked in a mirror and said
"My, I look so different". At the fashion show she went on stage in her
new dress looking confident and happy.' (18)

The benefits of new and pleasant clothes in terms of boosting
morale and self-image are not confined to patients in hospitals.
Most of us feel better if we think we are looking good. Clothing
has an important role to play in maintaining a positive self-image
and high self-esteem.

Clothing, then, is not simply something which individuals can
manipulate at will in their relationships with others, a dramatic
prop to be used to good effect. Clothing and physical appearance
'act upon' the individual. They contribute to establishing and maintaining identification with social roles, to the formation of a self-
image and to a sense of self-esteem.

References

1. Molloy, J.T. (1975) *Dress for Success*. (New York: Peter H. Wyden).
2. *ibid*. See Chapter 12 'How to dress up your case and win judges and juries' 6
   'A few years ago a Midwestern politician running for minor office called me
   in as a consultant when the political pros told him he had no chance of
   achieving even that lowly position because he lacked charisma. I changed his
   dress and his image. He is today Governor of his state.'
3. Sheldon, W.H. (1954) *Atlas of Man: A Guide to Somatyping the Adult Male
   of All Ages*. (New York: Harper and Row).
4. Bem, D.J. and Allen, A. (1974) 'On predicting some of the people some of
   the time. The search for cross-situational consistencies in behaviour.' In:
   Psychological Review.
5. Flugel, J.C. (1930) *The Psychology of Clothes*. (Hogarth Press and the
   Institute of Psychology) 85.
6. *ibid* 93.
7. *ibid* 100.
8. This perspective has largely been developed in the United States, building on
   the work of Herbert Mead and Charles Cooley.
9. Berger, P. (1971) *Invitation to Sociology*. (Penguin) 121.
10. *ibid* 113.
11. Hamid, P. (1969) 'Changes in person perception as function of dress'. In:
    Perceptual and Motor Skills, **29**, 91–4.
12. Stone, G. (1965) 'Appearance and self'. In: *Dress Adornment and the Social
    Order*, eds. M.E. Roach and J.B. Eicher. (New York: John Wiley and Sons)
    216.
13. Murphy, G. (1968) 'Personality: A biosocial approach to origins and structure'.
    In: *The Second Skin*, ed. M. Horn. (Boston: Houghton Mifflin Co.) 123.

14. Cooley, C.H. (1902) *Human Nature and the Social Order.* (New York: Charles Scribner's and Sons) 152.
15. Some retailers such as Marks and Spencer do market fashionable styles in size 16, and in two or three lengths but the majority of shops selling fashionable clothes for the young only stock up to size 14 and only one standard length. As 47% of the population of women are size 16 or over, some of them must be young and many of them may wish to be fashionable if they could obtain the clothes.
16. Bull R. 'The importance of being beautiful.' *New Society.* (14 November 1974).
17. Goffman, E. (1971) *Asylums.* (Penguin) 28.
18. Muller, T.K., Carpenter, L.G. and Buckey, R.B. (1965) 'Therapy of fashion'. In: *Dress Adornment and the Social Order*, eds. M.E. Roach and J.B. Eicher. (New York: John Wiley and Sons) 267.

4   Fashion

So far in our discussion of clothing and appearance we have left aside the issue of *fashion*. We have not confronted the problem of what fashion is, or examined the extent to which people wear a certain style of clothing, shoes, jewellery or a particular hairstyle because it is in fashion. Yet fashion is an important influence on what we wear and what we think. It is part of the social world we inhabit; we constantly meet with references to it; we are surrounded by shops which sell it; and we judge clothes by its standards.

Fashion is *news*. International and British fashion shows, the styles young people wear, street fashion, the clothes of famous people are all given coverage on television, radio and in the press. Articles about fashion are featured regularly in most national and local newspapers, as well as constituting a major subject area of most magazines for women. Despite its high profile in the media, fashion is not generally regarded as a topic serious enough to appear on the 'real news' pages. Fashion is a luxury, a trivial and frivolous bit of fun. Perhaps this accounts for the way fashion is treated as a woman's topic − even men's fashions appear on the 'Women's Page' of newspapers like *The Guardian*, and of course in women's magazines. It is assumed that women are interested in fashion in a way that most men are not. Women, in particular, are bombarded by images of fashionable clothes, fashionable shapes and colours, fashionable bodies, fashionable faces and fashionable people. Are women more interested in fashion, or more susceptible to its influence?

Fashion is also *big business*. The fashion industry is enormous: a network of designers, manufacturers, wholesalers and retailers who make fashionable clothes available, and a network of public relations officers, journalists and advertising agencies who promote them. The fashion industry is not simply concerned with production of adequate or pleasant clothing, it is concerned with the production of 'new' styles, with style innovation. Unlike the producers of commodities like cars who claim improved mileage or greater speeds in a new model, the producers of fashion do not claim that a new style is necessarily better — they do not claim that the garment will last longer or keep you warmer — it is just different. Fashion seems to be about change for change's sake, and the illusion of novelty. Each year designers and companies launch their *new* collections, and each year each designer and each company hopes that their styles will become fashionable. However, only some will be successful and, what is more, some of the styles which do become fashionable will not have their origins in the fashion industry at all.

Fashion, then, is more than a commodity, the product of a particular industry, it is an attribute with which some styles are endowed. For a particular style of clothing to become a fashion it actually has to be worn by some people and recognised and acknowledged to be a fashion. It is not enough for a manufacturer to produce blue socks and for people to wear them. After all, plenty of people wear blue socks, but they are not a fashion. 'Blue socks' have to be recognised as *the latest style*. How does a style become a fashion?

When we talk about the fashions of a particular era like the twenties or the sixties we mean in the first instance the characteristic styles of those periods, the styles which were different from those that had gone before and those that followed. They are not necessarily the styles that the *majority* of people wear. For example, in the Edwardian period the majority of women did not wear the 'merry widow' hat. Many women could not afford such extravagant headgear but it was fashionable. By fashionable we also mean the most admired styles, the styles with the special significance of representing the current ideal.

Those who wear fashionable clothes share in that special significance. In the past a 'man of fashion' and members of 'fashionable society' referred to those of high social standing and substantial fortune who could afford to indulge themselves in both a luxurious lifestyle and extravagant clothing. Nowadays it is not just the rich or upper class who are fashion conscious; it is not confined to those who feel themselves to be socially or financially superior to the mass of society. Despite the accessibility of fashion and its supposed triviality, are not fashionable people still regarded as a kind of élite in our society, in some way superior to the unfashionable?

Fashion is sometimes seen as a way of *differentiating* the wearer from the majority. It makes the individual stand out from the crowd, to seem somehow more individual, more creative, more daring, more up to date. But, of course, the act of being fashionable does require *conformity* − but to a new standard rather that an old. It involves being the same as some other people. One cannot be 'fashionable' all by oneself.

Whether we like it or not, fashion plays a part in our judgement of clothes, those worn by others and those we buy for ourselves. Even those who do not follow fashion themselves are aware of and can identify major stylistic changes. Anybody who watched TV or read a newspaper in the early eighties could not help but know about the gender benders of that time, or the fashion for wide padded shoulders for women.

Fashion is a standard by which we judge people and obviously the greater our knowledge of fashion trends the more subtle our judgements. We do categorise clothes and the people who wear them as more or less fashionable, more or less up to date, too way out or very *passé* and so on.

Fashion also influences what we like. Some people feel that their choice of clothes reflects their personal likes and dislikes but it is very difficult to separate out a notion of personal taste which escapes the influence of fashion. Everyone has probably thrown away clothes in good condition or stuffed them to the back of the wardrobe because they are out of fashion. We liked them once but now...In the early seventies people really liked flared trousers, hot pants and platform-soled shoes; they thought they looked good. Now those styles look ugly and totally unwearable and some people may deny *they* ever wore such things.

Our tastes do change with fashion and nothing demonstrates this more clearly than looking at old photographs of ourselves. We are amazed that we thought that particular dress or coat looked good and we wonder how on earth we had the nerve to walk round in them. Similarly, you may have said 'I'll never wear that!' when a new style appeared, only to find yourself several weeks later not only wearing it but liking it.

The influence of fashion goes beyond individual taste and our perceptions of how we looked in the past; it moulds our concept of what is beautiful. Fashion has an impact on face, hair and body shape as well as clothing styles. In fashion plates, the models look as 'old-fashioned' as the clothes. Edwardian beauties like Lily Langtry do not correspond to modern ideas of feminine attractiveness; they are too heavy for modern tastes. Ideas of what is beautiful seem to be inseparably linked to what is considered fashionable.

The film *Some Like It Hot*, released in 1959, provides a good illustration of this. Set during Prohibition in America, the film stars Tony Curtis and Jack Lemmon as two musicians trying to escape from a group of mobsters who are pursuing them. They escape by dressing up as women and joining an 'all-girl' band. Their appearance in 'drag' follows fairly accurately the styles of the twenties — their hair is bobbed, their silhouette is straight and slim and they wear cloche hats. Jack Lemmon in his role as 'Daphne' is complimented on her flat chest. But the band's *beautiful* and *sexy* singer Sugar, played by Marilyn Monroe is a typical fifties' beauty. Her appearance bears no resemblance to the styles of the twenties. Her hair is blonde and cut in a style popular in the fifties. Her silhouette certainly is not 'boyish'; it is curvaceous and plump. Her costumes draw attention to her figure and particularly her breasts, waist and hips — the antithesis of twenties style. It was in order that she appear beautiful and sexy to the audience of the day that Marilyn Monroe was chosen for the part, and her clothes are in the style of contemporary fashions rather than those of three decades earlier.

The word fashion is mainly used to refer to clothing and styles of appearance. But of course there are 'fashions' in other aspects of intellectual and social life. There are fashions in interior decoration, architecture, dancing and cookery but also in fields like medicine and theoretical subjects like philosophy or sociology, when one particular view holds sway for a while only to be replaced by another, or where one area of research becomes very popular but is eventually superseded by another. The expectation of change which characterises our approach to clothing styles pervades many aspects of our social and intellectual life.

To take our understanding of fashion further let us consider the following issues:

(1) In what social contexts does fashion exist?
(2) How can the system of changing styles of dress be explained?
(3) What status do fashionable clothes bestow on those who wear them?
(4) How are fashions spread or promoted in our society?

THE WHEN AND WHERE OF FASHION

We have established that fashion is to do with innovation, the illusion of novelty. It is characterised by change, change in the past but also an expectation of change in the future. Fashion is part of our social world. But the system of changing styles of dress is not universal, it is not found everywhere. Not everyone in our society wears fashionable clothes and many of the styles of dress we described in Chapter 2 were not 'fashionable'. For example, the dress of traffic wardens and Hasidic Jews, the wearing of skirts by women and trousers by men are the styles of dress associated with particular groups or roles.

Many people in the world wear a 'traditional' form of dress like the sari or kaftan, the basic form of which appear to have changed very little over many years. Some people decorate their bodies or mould them in permanent ways — for example, by shaping the skull or scarring the skin. By their very nature, it would be impossible for such forms of decoration to be incorporated into contemporary fashion which changes so rapidly.

These styles are not 'unfashionable'; they are not failed attempts to be fashionable. One would not call a woman in a sari or a traffic warden's uniform 'unfashionable' in the way one might define a woman wearing tight shiny 'disco' pants these days as unfashionable or *passé*. It seems that there are two systems of dress and that fashion cuts across other more stable forms of dress in our society.

What differentiates *fashion* from *non-fashion*?

Flugel distinguished between what he called 'fixed' and 'modish' forms of dress and he suggests that:

> 'The differences between the two types becomes most clearly apparent in the opposite relations which they have to space and time. "Fixed" costume changes slowly in time, and its whole value depends, to some extent, upon its permanence; but it varies greatly in space, a special kind of dress tending to be associated with each locality and with each separate social body (and indeed with every well defined grade within each body). "Modish" costume, on the other hand, changes very rapidly in time, this rapidity of change belonging to its very essence; but it varies comparatively little in space, tending to spread rapidly over all parts of the world which are subject to the same cultural influences and between which there exists adequate means of communication.' (1)

He goes on to say:

> 'It is this latter type of costume which predominates in the western world today, and which indeed (with certain important exceptions) has

predominated there for several centuries; *a fact that must be regarded as one of the most characteristic features of modern European civilisation*, since in other civilisations, both of the past and of the present, fashion seems to have played a very much more modest role than with ourselves. Outside the sphere of western influence, dress changes much more slowly, is more closely connected with racial and local circumstances, or with social or occupational standing — it exhibits, that is to a much greater degree, all the distinguishing features of the "fixed" type.' (2)

Flugel suggests that fashion is linked to a particular type of social organisation, a particular type of society and culture — that of the West, the European-American lifestyle. Before the spread of Western influence, was fashion peculiar to European culture?

In non-Western societies there seems to have been a tendency for dress styles and forms of adornment to remain fairly stable, to change very slowly. If this is the case, why is it so? What kind of society developed in Europe which stimulated the development of fashion? Why do some people in Western societies *not* wear fashion?

Are there societies without fashion?

Let's look at some societies where it seems that a recognised system of style change did not exist and briefly examine the major characteristics of such societies and their forms of clothing and adornment.

Fashion does not seem to occur in so-called 'primitive' or simple societies, societies like the Australian Aborigines, the bands of Indians like the Kayapó who live in the equatorial forests of Brazil, the people living in the New Guinea Highlands or the Kalahari Bushmen. The way of life of many such peoples has been destroyed by contact with the West, by colonial settlers. The traditional way of life of those groups which remain has become increasingly difficult to maintain in the face of outside influences.

However, these societies are traditionally characterised by their egalitarian structure, organisation in terms of kinship, simple division of labour, simple technology and a subsistence economy. Although their life is materially very simple, such people have highly developed knowledge of their environment, and highly developed skills in relation to survival, and their religious and social life is often extremely complex.

Such societies live by hunting and gathering, and perhaps simple agriculture, but natural resources are not owned by individuals. All members of these societies have access to land, grazing or hunting rights. In many such societies, there is a tendency only to 'work' as much as is necessary for survival. Where surpluses or excesses exist, they tend to be shared out, redistributed or given in exchange. Individuals do not accumulate great wealth; prestige and status are frequently gained by generosity.

A particular example of exchange is found amongst a group in New Guinea:

> 'Hagen is a competitive society. Within it there are no hereditary offices of chiefship nor any rigid hierarchical relations. It is small political groups and their self-made leaders (called big men) who are continually competing for temporary advantage over each other. The main arena for this competition is an elaborate ceremonial exchange system (the moka), in which groups try to outdo each other by the size of their gift of shell valuables and pigs.' (3)

Special forms of decoration are worn at these exchanges and a great deal of time and energy is devoted to preparing one's appearance for such rituals. Individuals and groups try to outdo each other in the splendour of their appearance. However, 'Decorations do not mark out lasting relations of superiority and inferiority, but are assertions that one's own group has succeeded in the current bout of exchanges'. (4)

The raw materials for ordinary dress and ritual decorations are largely gathered from the immediate environment although some items are obtained through trade. 'The Hageners use shells, feathers and plumes, grasses, leaves, dyes and grease to decorate themselves. In other societies, the skins of animals or bark cloth may be used. Techniques of tattooing, scarring, piercing and shaping the body are also widely used. These forms of adornment are as important as clothes in the individual's notion of being properly 'dressed' and are regarded signs of the individual's humanity.

Body decoration and clothing are used to signify the social divisions of the society — clan membership, age grade or marital status or to reflect social values about, for example, social solidarity, fertility or health. The choice of immutable forms of decoration is in strong contrast to fashion; it implies a confidence that social and aesthetic values will remain the same. It is inconceivable that there should be a 'fashion' for head-shaping like that practised in the past by the Kwakiutl Indians of Vancouver Island, because the style could not be changed within the individual's lifetime.

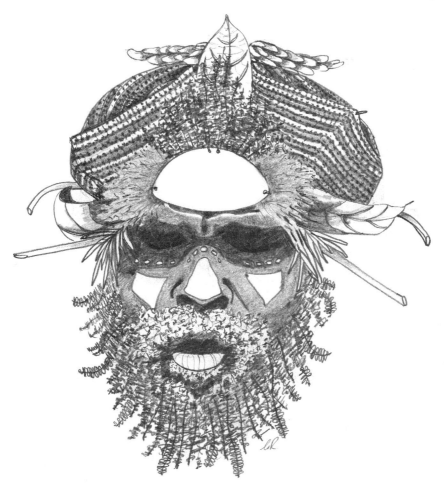

Fig. 4.1 Man from New Guniea Highlands in ceremonial decorations.

These societies are based on tradition, cultural stability and an *apparently* unchanging way of life, and the appearance of the members of such societies reflect these values. Like the societies themselves before contact with the West, their appearance *seems* to have remained unchanged for hundreds of years.

Primitive societies are very small-scale homogeneous groups, sharing a common culture, and often living in isolation. But what of the larger scale civilisations based on settled agriculture and trade like those of South and Central America, Egypt, the Middle East, India and China, and of course feudal Europe.

Fig. 4.2 Padaung woman from Burma wearing neck rings. Such permanent forms
of body decoration could never be part of fashion. In Padaung society the neck
rings symbolise the status of the wearer and her submission to her husband.

Did they have changing forms of dress? If one looks at the
history of dress in societies like India, China or Japan, it is apparent
that changes have taken place, sometimes as the result of invasion
and domination by a foreign power but one is also struck by the
continuity of dress styles over prolonged periods. There has been
no system of fashion change, regularly changing the shape and
style of clothes, as developed in Western Europe.

In the past, the development of settled agriculture was associated
with hierarchical social organisation, such as feudal systems and
caste systems. The agricultural surplus produced by one section of
the population was used to support classes not involved in agricultural labour. In such societies status was usually hereditary, with
little chance of social mobility. The social hierarchy was legitimised
by and enshrined in religious belief, such as the Hindu caste

Fig. 4.3 Bedouin boy in an apparently timeless costume (BBC Hulton Picture Library).

system, or notions of divine kingship. The dominant source of prestige and wealth was ownership or control of land, and this was usually confined to an hereditary elite within the society.

In contrast to 'primitive' societies, crafts and arts were well developed, as were written language and trade, and there was a much more complex division of labour. It was in these societies that spinning and weaving technology became highly developed. India, for example, developed the technique of spinning and weaving cotton into fine muslins. The Chinese developed methods of spinning and weaving silk. In societies where production is a laborious and long drawn out process, there is the tendency to use fabric with care and a reluctance to cut the fabric. The Egyptians, the Greeks and the Romans all used rectangles of cloth to make their clothes with very little cutting. The Indian sari and Japanese kimono also follow this kind of attitude to fabric. Another interesting feature of these two garments is the emphasis on the fabric design rather than changing the features of the garment itself.

In such societies, differences in role and rank were clearly expressed in dress. Differences in wealth and position associated with control of land produced sharp divisions within society and these were reflected in dress. The landholding classes and possibly the priesthood were the most likely to have fine clothes. Social differences were expressed by the number of clothes worn, the kind and quality of fabric or skin used, the dyes used in the fabric, the amount of decoration and the amount of jewellery, etc., worn.

Differences in dress, however, were not only the result of differences in wealth; people were expected to know their place and to not dress above their station, even if they had the money to do so. There are many examples of statutes laying down the appropriate dress for particular ranks. In Imperial China, different forms of dress were specified for each rank of the gentry.

In the seventeenth century in Japan, the Tokugawa shogunate established a feudal type of system to ensure political stability and limit social mobility. Society was divided into four main classes – the samurai, the peasants, the artisans and the merchants. Everyone was expected to behave and dress according to their station. Deviations, including the wearing of dress unsuited to one's station, were punished. However, the political system which required the leaders of the warrior class to spend alternate years at the capital and to leave their families behind there when they returned to their lands crippled them financially and many fell into debt to the merchants. Although in theory the merchants had the lowest status in the social hierarchy they were able to acquire considerable wealth. The wives of merchants were able to dress in some splendour. The Tokugawa period is characterised by swings between extravagant display and the imposition of harsh sumptuary laws by which the shogunate sought to control the dress of the merchant class. They responded by inventing new decorative and dyeing techniques in order to circumvent these laws. Dress remained fairly stable in form until the mid-nineteenth century when contact with the West brought wide ranging changes to Japanese society.

Rigid social hierarchies seem to have effectively inhibited changing patterns of dress. In the event of challenges to the political status quo, the elite use sumptuary laws to control the dress of those seeking to rise above their allotted station, and to emphasise their political dominance.

How did fashion develop in Europe?

It has been suggested that fashion developed in Europe with the breakdown of feudalism and the advent of fitted clothes. Until the fourteenth century, dress styles changed but they changed slowly. They remained relatively stable between the eleventh and fourteenth centuries. But from the fourteenth century, styles began to change more quickly, the rich began to throw clothes away because they were 'out of style' and by the sixteenth century it was thought to be a sign of inferiority to wear clothes not 'in fashion'. The system of changing styles of dress seems to have coincided with the rise of mercantile capitalism and town life.

Under the feudal system, dress had been closely linked to one's rank and position in society. Social position was largely hereditary, and there was little opportunity for social mobility. During the late Middle Ages, society was changing. The power of the aristocracy was being undermined and its authority challenged. A number of factors contributed to these changes — the Crusades which took place from the eleventh to the thirteenth century, the Black Death, which it is estimated killed one-third of England's population, and the growth of trade. Trade was growing not only within Europe, but also with the Middle East. This was combined with, and contributed to, the growth of towns and to the growing class of town dwellers who made their living from crafts and commerce — the bourgeoisie. The merchant class and particular individuals within it were able to amass substantial wealth. New ideas, new goods and new sources of wealth all challenged the *status quo.*

Von Boehn, describing the situation at the beginning of the fourteenth century, explains the emerging system of fashion in this way:

'The chief change was the apparent loss of a standard of what so far had passed for propriety. In the arrogance of its newly acquired wealth the rising middle class recognised no bounds; it must and would enjoy life. It did not desire to emulate the knights but to outshine them. This aim naturally manifested itself most obviously in dress, for dress is the agency which any new consciousness of the world and one's particular milieu is most speedily proclaimed. Not only did new modes arise, but they changed with far greater frequency than before; fashion, in the sense of incessant fluctuation, perpetual striving after improvement, now came on the scene.' (5)

There were many attempts to hold back the flow of fashion by the use of sumptuary laws. In 1327, Edward III enacted a law to control 'the outrageous and excessive apparel of divers people against their estate and degree'. (6) In the sixteenth century many laws were passed. Elizabeth I expressly forbade anyone to copy her dress. But these laws were impossible to enforce; as wealth came into the hands of more people they used it to express their social ambitions, which of course posed a threat to established power.

Town life offered a new arena for social interaction, and must have contributed to the use of changing styles of dress as a form of prestige:

'The medieval castle gave little opportunity for individual display; its society was too isolated and its life too primitive. Moreover, town life was more gregarious and more socially mobile. A person's pedigree was not as important as before and his position at a given time carried greater weight. Outward display was therefore a method by which he could give overt expression of his wealth'. (7)

The development of fashion seems to have occurred in societies which were changing, where that change is valued by some groups within the society, and social mobility is possible. Fashion is not possible in totally egalitarian society nor in a rigid hierarchy. 'There must be differences of social position, but it must seem possible and desirable to bridge these differences'. (8) It is essential that at least two groups in a society have sufficient means to indulge in the wastefulness of fashion.

The development of Western Europe in terms of urbanisation and then industrialisation obviously provided an ideal setting for fashion. Town life, and then the development of large industrial cities, increased the reliance of dress cues in social interaction as social relations became more anonymous and society became more heterogeneous. Fashion served as indicator of status and orientation.

Industrialisation not only increased the sources of available wealth and contributed to a growing complexity in the stratification of society, it also led to the mass production first of cloth and then clothes which enabled more rapid production of clothes and made fashion more widely available. Industrialisation also led to accept-ance or, at least, awareness of change. Technological and social change are an acknowledged part of life in an industrial society.

Why not everyone wears fashion

In his book *Fashion and Anti-Fashion*, Polhemus argued that within our own society different people will have different attitudes to change, and this will be manifested in their approach to dress. To demonstrate his point he uses the example of two dresses in the public eye in 1953 — the Queen's coronation gown and Dior's 'tulip line':

'The Queen's coronation gown is traditional, "fixed" and anti-fashion; it was designed to function as a symbol of continuity, the continuity of the monarchy and the British Empire. Dior's gown also created a stir in 1953 but then Dior had been creating a sensation since 1947...each year he had created a new New Look...Likewise in 1954 Dior changed the "tulip line" into the "H-line", and in 1955 replaced the "H-line" with the "A-line". In this way he captured the essence of fashionable attire; its function as a symbol of *change, progress and movement through time...Anti-fashion adornment, on the other hand, is concerned with time in the form of continuity and the maintenance of the status quo'*. (9)

Polhemus argues that the two systems are based upon alternative concepts of time:

'If traditional, anti-fashion adornment is a model of time as continuity (the maintenance of the *status quo*) and fashion is a model of time as change, then it is appropriate that Queen Elizabeth II should not have chosen a fashionable gown for her coronation. It is rational that she should have worn a gown which proclaims a message of continuity over hundreds of years, a message of timelessness and changelessness. In short, her social, economic and political situation suggests that she should prefer things to change as little as possible, and she expresses this attitude in her dress and adornment especially at her coronation. On the other hand, a social climber who is, or would like to be, on the way up will use the latest fashions to reinforce and project an image of time as change and progress. His or her fashionable attire constitutes an advertisement for socio-temporal mobility and will remain so as long as he or she stands to benefit from social change rather than the social *status quo*.' (10)

Polhemus emphasises once again the association of fashion with an ideology of social change, and a situation in which change is both possible and desirable. In some societies the dominant ideology is antipathetic to social change and notions of 'progress', but in our own society different groups and individuals have more or less interest in change, or more or less interest in preserving the *status quo*.

WHY DOES FASHION CHANGE?

We have examined the kind of context in which fashion is likely to exist, and in which people are going to endeavour to be fashionable. Let's look now at some of the explanations which have been put forward to account for the changing pattern of styles of dress.

One commonly held view is that fashion is the result of a conspiracy on the part of makers of clothes to make us spend more money. That is, designers, clothing manufacturers and businessmen impose new fashions in order to stimulate the market and increase their trade. It is sometimes said that designers have conspired together to produce a dramatic change in fashion which will involve those wishing to remain in fashion throwing away most of their wardrobe. For example, the New Look launched after the war made clothes from the preceding years look very dated. But did the designers of the day conspire to achieve such an effect?

There are many examples of dressmakers and couturiers attempting to manipulate the public by paying society figures or models to wear their designs at particular society occasions or events where they would be noticed and even photographed. The intention here was to give their designs the appearance of having been accepted by leading members of society. It has been suggested that Dior used this technique to launch the New Look in the United States. These days it is perhaps more likely to be pop stars who give a designer's clothes publicity and create the impression they are established as 'fashion'.

This kind of explanation does seem attractive especially when you are having to discard perfectly good clothes just because they are out of fashion. Sometimes it *feels* as if there is a conspiracy to prevent you from buying what you want. If, for example, you particularly like black crew neck sweaters and buy them regularly, you may go to the shops to find only pastel coloured sweaters because they are in fashion and no-one is stocking black this year.

How often have you searched in vain for something you wanted, and then bought what was available in desperation?

However, a sustained conspiracy would be extremely unlikely given the structure of the fashion industry and, even if it did exist, would it really explain fashion change? First of all, designers and manufacturers are in competition; they do not all produce a 'new look' at any one time. They are always seeking to be the first, ahead of their competitors. When Dior's New Look took hold, many manufacturers lost money as they were left with dated and undesirable stock. A change of fashion can ruin designers and manufacturers just as it can bring profits. Secondly, although the 'New Look' was accepted, many of the design ideas put forward are not. Designers and manufacturers may try to influence or even manipulate the public, but the public can, and often does, refuse to accept their suggested style changes. Lastly, frequent fashion changes have characterised clothes for women for many years, so why has not the same technique been used in marketing clothes for men? (In recent years more 'fashion' has been creeping into mens-wear, so perhaps the rewards of selling high fashion are beginning to outweigh the risks, or has there been a fundamental change in men's attitudes to clothes and fashion?)

It is frequently suggested that individuals change the course of fashion. Sometimes it is designers like Dior or individuals like the Princess of Wales. Princess Diana, according to some newspaper reports, was personally responsible for the popularity of ball gowns, and the wearing of hats (although hats are not much in evidence for daily wear). Like her predecessor Princess Alexandra, Princess Diana has been dubbed a leader of fashion. But we must ask ourselves to what extent they really led fashion. Neither of them revolutionised fashion, they did not introduce something totally new or reverse trends already in existence. Princess Diana may have made the brushed back bob and frilly collars more popular but she did not create the look. Since her marriage she has been advised by 'fashion experts' and the more she conforms to such advice the more frequently she is hailed as a trendsetter. She leads only to the extent she is representative of certain trends within fashion – in fact, a traditional, rather safe image. She is not associated with the daring innovative designers but those who produce more 'classical' styles.

As for designers, can they change the face of fashion, alone? In the case of Dior's New Look, he was not alone, or the first, to propose such a style. Attempts had been made to introduce similar styles before the Second World War but the war had intervened. Chanel, for example, had broken with her general style to show a wasp-waisted full-skirted suit, and Molyneux was showing full dirndl skirts in 1939. Designers are a kind of community: they talk to each other; they look at each other's work; they inhabit the same 'fashion world' and cannot help but be influenced by each other. (We will return to the issue of why designers sometimes arrive at similar styles if they are working in competition and in secrecy.)

Also, in the same way that the industry as a whole cannot impose fashion change, no individual designer can *impose* a radical change in style. The public has to be ready to accept such a change and therefore fashion change is always a matter of tailoring stylistic innovation to the limits of acceptability for the customer. A designer is successful when he or she is able to anticipate the direction in which taste is moving.

Another commonly held view of fashion change is that it is produced by boredom. At one level this seems to be true; we do buy new clothes because we have grown tired of the ones we have got. Can we really explain fashion in such terms? Nystrom thinks we can:

> 'The specific motive...for fashion interest and fashion changes, in addition to the physical reasons for change such as occur at the end of each season, are the boredom or fatigue with the current fashion, curiosity, desire to be different, self-assertion, rebellion against convention, companionship and imitation. There may be other factors in *human nature* promoting fashion interest, but these are sufficiently effective and inclusive upon which to build a practical theory of fashion.' (11)

If fashion change is produced by human nature, why is it not universal? As we have seen, changing styles of dress are not found everywhere. Indeed, some forms of adornment are permanent and cannot be changed even if the individual should become bored with them. Throughout the world, people are content to wear the costume handed down by their predecessors relatively unchanged.

Is not our own sense of boredom created by the existence of fashion in our society, the fact that we are surrounded by images of changing styles and are encouraged to adopt them? Human beings are no doubt inquisitive and curious creatures but there is no evidence that these characteristics are always manifested in relation to styles of dress. There is also a contradiction in the notion that fashion changes represent a desire to assert the self, and to rebel against imitation. If these motives were really at work, surely there would be an infinite variety of individual styles which change at the whim of the individual. What actually happens is a fairly ordered change by quite large numbers of people from one style to another. Although some may lead and others follow, a large degree of imitation and conformity is involved.

Hollander in her book *Seeing through Clothes* suggests that changes in fashion are motivated by the visual 'need' for a new image. She argues that 'the way clothes look depends not on how they are designed and made but on how they are perceived...perception of clothing is achieved...through a filter of artistic convention' and 'Changes in style of clothing are consequently inextricable from changes in the medium of art in which the human figure usually appears. (12) It is the visual need for change rather than practical considerations, or social influences which is crucial in Hollander's view: 'only certain [shapes, lines and textures] will do at a given moment; these are the ones the eye seems to require'. (13) If dress changes in relation to changes in styles of art, how do we explain the changes in styles of art? Who experiences this visual need?

Another theory of fashion which rests on a supposed need for novelty is the shifting erogenous zone theory. Laver popularised this theory drawn from psychoanalysis, he quotes Bergler:

> 'Stripped of its essentials, fashion is no more than a series of permutations of seven given themes, each theme being part of the human (female) body: the breasts (neckline), waist (abdomen), hips, buttocks, legs, arms and length (or circumference) of the body itself. Organs "appear" and "disappear" as the theme of fashion changes, and one by one and then another part of the body is emphasised by succeeding styles. The breasts and legs are "opposite" in fashion; if in one season, the neckline plunges and breasts consequently become the centre of attraction, one can be sure that in subsequent seasons breasts will be covered and the spotlight will be on legs, and so on, in endless variations.' (14)

This view does seem to describe what happens as a result of fashion changes — different parts of the female body are emphasised by the changes in style. But for Laver it becomes an explanation of the system of fashion itself. He believes that the word fashion should be applied only to women and he argues that there are no male 'fashions'. Having distinguished between male and female dress in terms of the Hierarchical and Seduction Principles, he suggests that 'Fashion is a function of the Seduction Principle with its need of perpetual novelty and change'.

Laver argues that because women lack a 'natural' focus of eroticism which is equivalent of the male phallus

> '...in imagination the whole female body is desirable. In practice this is not so, as anyone who has visited a nudist camp can testify; complete nudity is anti-erotic as soon as the shock of novelty has worn off...If complete nudity were common we should probably become seasonal in our impulses like animals. Our characteristic *permanent* eroticism is kept alive by clothes.
>
> 'But clothes can only keep it alive by continually altering the emphasis, drawing attention to all aspects of the female body in turn by exposure, semi-concealment or by other devices well known to every dress designer. This altering of emphasis is the "Shifting Erogenous Zone" and is the whole basis of Fashion.' (15)

In view of cross-cultural and historical evidence, Laver's explanation of fashion as a necessary stimulus to sexual desire seems absurd. People living in societies in which changing styles of dress are not found are not 'seasonal' in their sexual behaviour. It is not true that the focus of eroticism must constantly be shifting in order to maintain sexual interest. For example, in Imperial China, the bound foot was the focus of erotic interest for hundreds of years. But one would also like to ask whether men's costume has not drawn attention to different parts of the male anatomy as focus of erotic interest. Why was it that menswear in the fifties tended to emphasise the shoulders and pectoral muscles, whereas in the sixties tight trousers drew attention to the genitals and in comparison with the fifties, the shoulders and chest were narrow and underdeveloped?

Despite considerable reservations about Laver's explanation of fashion in terms of sexuality, the 'Shifting Erogenous Zone Theory' does have value. It draws attention to the way in which the focus is moved from one part of the body to another as fashion changes.

In the thirties, two anthropologists, Richardson and Kroeber attempted to analyse statistically how styles of women's dress changed over three centuries. (16) Using fashion plates and portraits of fashionable women they measured six dimensions of women's formal dress — including the depth of decolletage, skirt-length and the diameter of skirt. They identified two types of fashion change. First, the annual changes of a trivial nature which served to distinguish this year's clothes from last year's or five years before; and, second, longer cycles of change, more stable and slower moving forms which each year's changing style takes for granted and builds upon. They found that styles of women's dress moved with regularity between the maxima and minima of the dimensions they measured. For example, skirt widths were at a minimum in 1811, and then again in 1926; and at their fullest in about 1749 and then again in 1860. So between 1749 and 1811 there had been a swing from full to narrow skirts, followed by a swing back to full, followed by a further swing back to narrow.

Agnes Young adopted a similar investigation and studied the skirt shapes in the period from 1760 to 1935. (17) She identified three major types − full, tubular, and skirts with back-fullness and she found these appeared in regular cycles of roughly thirty-five years (Fig. 4.4).

Richardson and Kroeber, and Young, regard fashion as an 'independent' system with its *own logic of change*. There is a pattern of change established within the system and for them the ability of individuals to mould styles is slight. What causes the change from one style to another, or the movement towards the opposite extreme? For Richardson and Kroeber, social and political change are the cause of a disruption in the style pattern. For example, they argue that changes in style pattern coincide with eras such as those of the French Revolution and the Napoleonic Wars, and of the First World War and the post-war period.

They do not argue that particular events or social conditions will produce a particular style:

'The explanation propounded is not that revolution, war, and socio-cultural unsettlement in themselves produce scant skirts and thick and high or low waists, but that they disrupt the established dress style and tend to its overthrow or inversion...By contrast, in "normal" periods dress is relatively stable in basic proportions and features; its variations tend to be slight and transient − fluctuations in mode rather than changes of style.' (18)

They are therefore ruling out the kind of suggestion ever popular with commentators on fashion that short skirts are necessarily to be found in times of economic growth and long skirts in times of

Shape	Period	No. of Years
Bell	1725–1759	34
Back-fullness	1760–1795	36
Tubular	1796–1829	34
Bell	1830–1867	38
Back-fullness	1868–1899	32
Tubular	1900–1937	38

Fig. 4.4 Recurring cycles of fashion (after Young).

depression. In 1982, Suzy Menkes presented this argument again:

'The idea that the stock market rises and falls with the hemline can be charted quite precisely this century. Up above the knee went the skirts of the "roaring" 1920s, ankle deep in the depression, up with the war effort, down with the New Look, thigh high in the expansionist 1960s and down to maxi levels in the oil war of the 1970s.' (19)

She uses this idea not only to comment on British fashions but to relate the fashion predictions for countries like Japan, Germany, the USA and France to their economic prospects. Such generalisations have a peculiar charm for fashion journalists wanting to write a witty article but there can be no real correlation between economic growth and skirt length before this century and Menkes' international survey is not thorough enough. For example, Japan has imported fashion looks from the West, despite quite different rates of economic growth. No causal link has yet been established between movement in share prices and the length of skirts.

But what of Richardson and Kroeber's views? There are obvious and immediate problems. They examined only fashion plates and not what people actually wore, and they dealt only with formal attire. Both their's and Young's research ended in the thirties and fashion has changed dramatically since then. Even if we were to choose a similar category for contemporary study, such as evening-wear, there is no identifiable single style – there are short dresses, long dresses, even trousers for women. Fashion cycles seem to change more rapidly in the twentieth century. Society and the fashion industry have changed and we cannot assume that the forces which produced the cycles they describe are still influential today.

Young pointed to what she thought was the basic style patterns in skirt shape but since then length has become another significant variable in skirt shape, and back-fullness seems to have disappeared. What produces the inclusion of such a new variable or dimension within the system? How can this be explained in terms of their ideas? Finally, does the analysis of one element help us understand style change as it relates to the total effect of a costume?

Despite such problems, their work does raise some interesting questions about the process of innovation and change. If we take the example of skirt-length, there does seem to have been a system of swings between short and long skirts during this century, changing direction at roughly ten year intervals. The logic of innovation does seem to demand that after movement in one direction such as larger and larger collars in order to produce a sense of innovation and change, a change to no collars, or small collars or stand-up collars is necessary. Similarly, after periods of bright or synthetic colours, there may be a move to introduce subtle colours or dark colours. Whether any pattern in such changes could be discovered is another matter and any study of the numerous variables apparent in the wide range of fashionable styles today would be a mammoth task. However, our attention is drawn to the need to understand changing styles of dress as an evolution, one style growing out of another.

Finally, let's look at another explanation of fashion, one which accounts for fashion change in terms of social competition, the desire to imitate the elite in society. This is status theory, or what is sometimes called the 'trickle-down' theory of fashion. Georg Simmel suggested that:

> 'Social forms, apparel, aesthetic judgement, the whole style human expression, are constantly transformed by fashion in such a way, however, that fashion − i.e. the latest fashion − in all things affects only the upper classes. Just as soon as the lower classes begin to copy their styles, thereby crossing the line of demarcation the upper classes have drawn and destroying the uniformity of their coherence, the upper classes turn away from this style and adopt a new one, which in turn differentiates them from the masses; and thus the game goes merrily on. Naturally the lower classes look and strive towards the upper, and they encounter least resistance in those fields which are subject to the whims of fashion; for it is here that mere external imitation is most readily applied. The same process is at work as between the different sets within the upper classes, although it is not always as visible here as it is, for example, between mistress and maid.' (20) (First published in 1907.)

Simmel argues that fashion spreads vertically down the social hierarchy, that the upper socio-economic groups adopt fashion first as symbols of distinction and exclusiveness, and that the lower classes each and in turn try to emulate the upper class leaders. However, at a certain level of adoption the style becomes vulgarised and has to be discarded by the upper classes. They take up new style and so the process repeats itself.

Simmel's theory that styles spread down the social hierarchy may have described the situation in previous centuries and even at the time of writing. But is it true today? Are the rich or the socially prestigious the first to adopt a new fashion, are they the wearers of the most up-to-date styles? These days, people from all classes can wear fashionable styles at roughly the same time. Changes within society and within the fashion industry have actually undermined the system which Simmel outlined. Let's look at the main criticisms that can be made in the light of contemporary experience.

First, fashion change does not occur because the lower classes have copied the style of dress of the rich or socially prestigious. It is no longer the rich who decide when a new style will come into being. The fashion industry introduces *new* styles each season as a marketing strategy, regardless of whether the previous style has worked its way through the social hierarchy. What is more, the styles are no longer chosen by the wealthy or the upper class. The styles created by designers and manufacturers go through an intensive process of selection within the industry and in co-operation with the retailing industry. It is this process which determines what styles will be available to the public as 'fashion' in any season rather than what the upper classes have been wearing. We will look more closely at the process of how a style becomes a fashion below.

Secondly, some styles which have become fashionable were first worn by low status, low prestige groups. The most obvious example would be punk which could not by any stretch of the imagination be deemed a style associated with wealth or the upper classes. This style created by disillusioned and disaffected youth influenced the world of high fashion.

Thirdly, Simmel's theory depends on a time lag between the adoption of a particular style by the upper class and by the lower classes. This is clearly no longer the case. At one time couture houses kept their new styles secret so that personal customers could buy and wear the styles before they were released for copying by ready-to-wear manufacturers and shops. Until after the war, the publication of sketches and photographs of the collections was prohibited for a certain period so there was a suitable delay before the style could be copied. However, since the sixties, ready-to-wear has taken over as the sphere in which style innovations are launched and a structure has developed which leads to the rapid dissemination of styles. The ready-to-wear collections are attended by other designers, manufacturers and buyers, and of course the press. The press, and the trade press in particular, plays an important role in providing information on the latest trends to the rest of the industry.

In one sense a hierarchy remains *within* the fashion industry as 'top' designers provide the lead. Other designers and manufacturers look to them for ideas which are used as inspiration for their own designs, or which are in some cases illegally copied. The timing of the ready-to-wear collections well in advance of the season in which the clothes are to be worn, not only allows time for the clothes to be manufactured to meet orders, but also time for the styles to be 'copied' by other companies. A new style is usually available at a variety of price levels within the same season. The rapidity of style dissemination within the industry combined with the constraints of ready-to-wear production work against any possible vertical flow of fashion in society.

However, although a hierarchical structure does tend to persist within the industry, not all ideas are generated at the top, by prestige designers. Styles such as workwear, sportswear and ethnic styles were already being worn by various groups within society before designers and manufacturers presented them as 'fashion'. In recent years, 'street styles', and the suppliers of avante garde youth fashions have become an important source of inspiration for the fashion industry as a whole. This is a reversal of the 'trickle-down' theory in which styles created by and associated with lower class youth are seen as the latest style and have been copied by designers and manufacturers *for the rich*.

Another development which undermines the system, as defined by Simmel, is the growth of the mass media during the twentieth century. Not only is there no time lag within the trade, there is no time lag between the style being presented in Paris or London and reports in the press or on television. Pictures of styles can be flashed across the world within hours of being on the catwalk. People of all classes who want to know about fashion have access to information about it. Magazines and newspapers provide information mainly for the mass market about what the latest trends are, what to wear and how to wear it.

It is true of course that styles are not available or adopted throughout the market at the same time. There is a time lag between a style being available at high fashion shops and at stores like Marks and Spencer or British Home Stores. Some styles never spread to the more middle of the road shops. This takes us on to an interesting point about the way fashion spreads these days. In the past it was probably true to say that it was those with wealth who tended to adopt a style first, and styles like the crinoline, for example, spread down the social hierarchy. These days, however, amongst the wealthy there are those who wear the latest fashions but also those who wear classic styles; and amongst those who adopt a style first are those who are far from wealthy.

It seems apparent, and this view has been supported by some research, that members of each socio-economic grouping do not behave uniformly and that some members from each group may be amongst the first to adopt a particular style. (21) There is some evidence that styles now spread *across* socio-economic groupings — that is, they spread horizontally rather than vertically. Those adopting a style in its early days are also likely to be the first to abandon it and move on to the next style. Within any socio-economic stratum, there are those who may be termed fashion leaders, those who adopt a fashion early, those who adopt it when it is well-established and those who adopt it when it has become rather dull or who miss it altogether. Such people may have quite different ideas about what is 'fashionable'; for example, fashion leaders are unlikely to regard what is in the high street chain stores as high fashion whereas it may represent the look that others are trying to achieve. Despite such differences, many people do endeavour to be fashionable. Why? Why is 'being in fashion' so important to some people?

BEING FASHIONABLE

People who are fashionable, especially those who are highly fashionable, have a special status in our society. They are admired, envied and criticised for the way they look and what their style of appearance represents. This special status and the admiration they may excite is not the same as the status enjoyed by those who are 'chic', or 'stylish' dressers, people who are admired for their good taste or their ability to put clothes together. People can dress fashionably without dressing well or looking good. Being fashionable is clearly separate from having 'good taste' although an individual may have both good taste and be fashionable. But chic or stylish dressers may wear 'classic' styles which are the opposite of fashion. They last, they stand the test of time in contrast to transient fashions.

Classics are associated with quality and durability, with simple elegance and good taste. They are 'above' gimmicky fashions, and thus represent a good investment. In the first edition of *Working Woman* Jean Muir recommended a classic black skirt, a well-cut pair of black trousers and a black coat as the basis of a versatile and elegant wardrobe which would stand the test of time and be 'value for money'.

As we have seen, being in fashion has been associated by some writers, such as Simmel and Veblen, with wealth and the desire to indicate or imply high social status. For Veblen it was linked with the ability to buy extravagant and luxurious clothing, clothing which implied a life of ease. Fashion was also regarded as an expression of wealth because of the waste involved in changing styles of dress. When one looks at the people who wore fashion and at the styles of dress which were fashionable in the nineteenth century and at the beginning of the twentieth century this does seem to be the case. However, the types of clothes which are fashionable these days are not necessarily luxurious, expensive, or unsuitable for working in. So, to what extent do these ideas have any validity today?

There is still an element of conspicuous consumption and waste implicit in the buying of fashionable clothes at any price level. The willingness to transform your appearance in accord with changing fashions demands regular expenditure on a whole range of items from eyeshadows and lipsticks to coats and shoes which will be used for a relatively short time and then discarded before they are used up or worn out. Within the horizontal groupings across which we have suggested fashion now spreads, wearing fashionable clothes implies a degree of wealth — unallocated money which is available to spend on clothes. Even though we are aware that people may scrape and save to buy clothes and neglect other aspects of necessary expenditure, such as food, there is still an air of 'having money to spare' about people who are constantly buying new fashionable clothes.

Being fashionable also seems to indicate a willingness to devote time and attention to one's appearance, and therefore that individual has 'time to spare' — leisure time when they are not engaged in work, housework or study. After all, maintaining a fashionable appearance does require quite a lot of effort, time spent in shopping for the essential elements of the look, tracking down the right items, and energy to find out exactly what the look is. No doubt the richer you are the less energy it takes to achieve a fashionable appearance. Of course, it is not only the fashionable who take a great deal of care over their appearance. Classic dressers, for example, may also devote much time and energy to their appearance, but their choice of clothes, accessories, etc., tend to follow an established pattern or formula and they do not have to worry whether it is in fashion.

Although 'being in fashion' may imply a certain degree of wealth or leisure, the desire to emulate the upper class or the desire to show off wealth would not be regarded as a dominant motive for being in fashion these days. Why do people want to be fashionable? Blumer suggests that:

'Fashion dies not because it has been discarded by the elite group but because it gives way to a new model more consonant with developing taste. The fashion mechanism appears not in response to a need for class differentiation and class emulation but in response to a wish to *be in fashion, to be abreast of what has good standing, to express new tastes which are emerging in a changing world.*' (22)

He also stresses fashion's links with the notion of modernity – 'Fashion is always modern; it always seeks to keep abreast of the times'. (23)

The notion of being 'up-to-date', linking oneself with the *new* seems to me to be a key element in the concept of being in fashion. By adopting the newest trends in dress styles, you show you are *in touch* with the what is newest in society. What is new may be a revival of a previous style like the dandy or Beatnik looks, but it is still the 'latest', the 'newest' at the present time. You show you have a feel for or a knowledge of the direction in which styles and tastes are moving. To be fashionable is to be 'where it's at' and to be 'in the know'.

Not to be fashionable is to be 'out-of-date', 'out of touch', 'left behind' in the movement towards the future, and these terms, like 'being out of fashion' have definite derogatory overtones.

Rosalind Coward suggests that being fashionable, for women, relates particularly to sexual ideals: 'to be fashionable now is...to express a readiness to keep up with prevailing sexual ideals'. (24) She uses as an example the recent fashion for wearing the bizarre and the extraordinary.

'*19* magazine offered itself with the image of a model dressed rather like the scarecrow, Worzel Gummidge, with the caption: "Some girls wouldn't dare". The essence of fashionableness currently is to dare to wear the extraordinary, to look as if you don't care and still remain attractive. The tendency to clutter the body is all part of this. Layers and layers of padding, leather, three belts; what they emphasise is that the wearer's body is good enough for her not to worry.

'What might have been a parody or rejection of fashion reveals itself to be well within the tradition of clothes geared towards prevailing standard ideals of female sexual behaviour. Here is the legacy of the sixties, the signification of the modern girl who dares everything and because of that attracts her man.' (25)

The fashion industry creates new and daring images, or it follows those created by subgroups. The effect of this constant generation of new styles is to render

'...previous styles ugly or repellent. They have come to signify a *passé* form of behaviour, an outmoded personal behaviour, as a defunct style. To see someone dressed in the style of the sixties is to be confronted with someone who has not kept up with the times, who is, in short a sexual conservative.' (26)

Being fashionable involves more than just a readiness to keep up with prevailing ideas about sexuality; it is more inclusive than that, but certainly to be out of fashion is to be someone who has not kept up with the times, to be a cultural conservative.

There is also a core of *elitism* which runs through fashion, and a system of prestige which attaches itself to varying degrees to those who dress fashionably.

Not only is there a hierarchy of the fashionable and unfashionable, there is a hierarchy within the group who identify themselves as fashionable. Some people will say with scorn 'Oh, I was wearing that kind of thing last year'. They gain a sense of superiority from being among the first to adopt a style, or at least being ahead of the current wearers of the style under discussion. They look down on the less adventurous and enjoy a sense of being ahead of the majority. The elitism is based on what they feel is their ability to know which way trends are going to develop, on their sensitivity to the movement of popular taste.

Recently, with the flow of style innovation coming from the 'street' to the fashion industry, some young people claim to have been among the creators of a particular look or style. They were not just among the first to wear it, it was *their idea*. Amongst the avant garde, and those who regard themselves as fashion aficionados, there is a distain for those whose fashion is the product of the fashion machine – looks assembled by manufacturers and retailers and not put together creatively by the individual.

Creativity is sometimes seen as part of being fashionable. But the notion of creativity has to be handled quite carefully in relation to fashion. Although individuals and groups may innovate aesthetically and technically to create new styles of clothes, the process of *fashion* is the marking out of particular styles which are given a special status and which are emulated.

Of course, these days the nature of fashion has changed. There is no longer a *line* handed down from Paris like in the fifties when Dior introduced A-lines, H-lines, and so on. Fashion ideas are generated by a variety of groups within society. Many commentators now talk about 'looks' rather than particular styles or lines. Recent 'looks' have included the sporty look, ethnic look, androgynous look and poor look. But the individual chooses between the types of fashion, the various looks, and the extent to which he or she is deemed fashionable will depend on that choice and the degree to which he or she adopts that look.

Let's now look at how a style or look becomes *fashionable*, how it becomes recognised as the *latest look*.

STYLES BECOME FASHIONS

In our criticisms of the status or 'trickle-down' theory, we argued that fashionable styles are no longer those chosen by the rich or social elite, but are those styles which are recognised as the newest, typifying the direction in which styles are moving. The dressmaker does not deal directly with her customer; instead, a whole network of public relations officers, journalists and buyers intervene in the process of a style reaching the public. So in this section we are going to look at how certain styles or looks become fashionable today, how they become recognised as the latest look. This will involve examining the way certain styles are selected within the fashion industry and by retailers to be the styles available for the public in any season, and the way the press represents a selection of styles and looks as the fashion, and marks them out or labels them as such.

Selection

The goods available in the shops are the result of an intensive process of selection within the fashion business and by retailers. Out of the many styles created, only some will actually reach the shops, and only some of them will become fashionable.

Perhaps one of the most interesting aspects of fashion is its uniformity; that each year, the products of so many designers and manufacturers working in competition should be so similar. Today, in the mid-eighties it has become commonplace to point out the variety of styles and looks available, and fashion journalists themselves comment on the difficulty of isolating dominant themes but there is still a consistency about fashions. In 1985 black was to be seen everywhere as one of *the* colours along with pinks, electric blues, and jade green, shoulders were big and padded, and knitted garments and the retro mood were influencing all types of fashion. How can we explain this uniformity in the goods available for the public to buy?

Herbert Blumer, writing about the Paris couture designers of the late sixties, argues that their methods of working and sources of inspiration produced common themes:

'There are three lines of preoccupation from which they derived their ideas. One was to pore over old plates of former fashions and depictions of costumes of far-off peoples. A second was to brood and reflect over current styles. The third, and most important, was to develop intimate familiarity with the most recent expressions of modernity as these were to be seen in such areas as the fine arts, recent literature, political debates and happenings, and discourse in the modern world. The dress designers were engaged in translating themes from these areas and media into dress designs. The dress designers were attuned to an impressive degree to modern developments and were seeking to capture and express in dress design the spirit of such developments. I think this explains why the dress designers, again a competitive and secretive group working apart from each other in a large number of different fashion houses, create independently of each other such similar designs. They pick up ideas of the past, but always through the filter of the present; they are guided and constrained by the immediate styles in dress, particularly the direction of such styles over the recent span of a few years; but, above all, they are seeking to catch the proximate future as it is revealed in modern developments.' (27)

In a discussion of developments relevant to fashion design today one would have to add such phenomena as street styles and popular music to Blumer's list. But we would also have to add that there are tremendous differences in the way many designers work within the industry; some are concerned with producing innovatory styles, but others are really only modifying the ideas of others to meet the demands of a particular section of the market or to avoid infringement of copyright.

The majority of designers – for example, those in mass-production – are working under greater constraints than the designers described by Blumer. They work within the frameworks already established by the 'big name' designers, and reported in the press. We described this as the trickle-down effect within the industry and the press has played a very important role in spreading particular styles. Designers avidly read the fashion press, reports in newspapers and magazines like *Vogue* and the trade press such as *Womenswear Daily*. Designers also consult the forecasts – the fabric and fashion predictions now available. Publications like *Design Intelligence – A Service of Advance Trend Information* provide guidance on colours, fabrics and key 'fashion concepts', and 'hundreds' of designs from which to build a composite collection'. They also can consult the fashion videos like those produced by *Draper's Record* – the selective recording of the collections in Paris, Milan, London and New York. The identification of key fabrics, colours and styles provides the starting point for many collections and many designers are therefore trying to produce styles which correspond to already identified trends.

The ideas that are produced by a designer undergo a ruthless process of selection by the designer himself or within the company. The aim is to identify those styles most likely to be most successful, that is those which correspond most closely to the anticipated fashion, as well as work within the constraints of manufacturing capabilities and costing limits. Only a small proportion of any designer's ideas will be made up as samples and included in the designer's or company's collection and shown to customers.

Most clothes these days are not sold direct to the public, but through retail outlets such as shops and mail-order catalogues. Buyers and selectors are the people who are responsible for deciding which styles are going to be sold in the shops, and therefore have a key role in determining what styles can become fashion. Of course, they cannot decide what the public will buy, but they do set the limits within which, on the whole, the public has to make their choice. They act as a filter through which styles have to pass if they are to become fashion.

Buyers select from the styles offered by designers and companies those which they *feel* will sell in their particular retail outlet. Some buyers even influence the styles themselves by asking for changes to the original design, changes in fabric, colour or trimmings. How do buyers know what to buy, what will sell and what will become fashionable?

Buyers obviously build up a knowledge of their customers, their section of the market, and they make their judgements about what to buy in the light of that knowledge. They also have to watch closely what is happening in the fashion world. They do this in a variety of ways: attending fashion shows, exhibitions and fairs; discussions with PRs representing designers, manufacturers and shops, with fashion consultants, with journalists, with designers and manufacturers themselves, and with other buyers; by reading newspapers and magazines concerned with fashion; and by observing the lines sold by their competitors. In this way buyers get a feeling for what they consider to be right next season. Like designers they have to try and anticipate the way in which taste is moving.

Although buyers are a powerful force in the shaping of fashion, they are certainly not invincible. They do make mistakes, and of course, they can never force the customer to buy. However, great assistance to the retailer in his efforts to persuade the customer to buy his goods can be rendered by the media, if a magazine presents the goods for sale, or styles which are similar to the goods for sale as *fashionable*. Influential and large retailers employ the services of PRs to make sure their shops and goods are promoted on fashion pages of newspapers and magazines.

Let's look at the role of the media in defining or marking out what is fashionable; first in relation to the industry itself, and secondly in relation to the public.

Marking out

How is fashion marked out within the industry?

Journalists writing about fashion are also part of the selection process but they also mark out certain styles or stylistic features as having special significance. They select in the sense that they 'pick out' the work of certain designers, clothes from certain manufacturers or shops from the whole array styles and products displayed at fashion shows, exhibitions, from PRs, and in the shops. They do not, they could not, record or describe everything and so they draw attention to a selection of the styles available. In the process they mark out those styles, those features, those clothes as this season's look, *the fashion*.

For a long time fashion journalists have looked to Paris or Milan, to big name designers, for guidance on the looks for coming seasons, although they now include 'young designers' for future developments. They attempt to identify 'themes' in terms of colours, silhouettes, etc., and most attention is given to the designers whose work corresponds to the themes which the journalists have identified.

An article entitled 'Mannish in Milan' by Sally Brampton illustrates this approach. She defines the main theme: 'The influence is emphatically masculine: generously cut double-breasted jackets rubbed broad shoulders with capacious trench coats; baggy flannel trousers and men's shirts were compulsory; everything from the top of the model's closely cropped head to the flat soles of her leather lace-up brogues was once intended for the male'. (28) She then goes on to show how designers like Armani, Versace and Montana exemplified this theme.

A similar process takes places in the articles written for trade journals. Magazines like *Draper's Record* include articles which describe the general trends as represented by various designers, say in Milan, but then they may explore in more detail how these trends are represented in particular types of garments, what the implications of the trends are for fabrics, and the likely reaction of customers.

At fashion shows and exhibitions, press releases and publicity material also point both journalists and buyers towards 'themes'; identifiable trends which other manufacturers can borrow, buyers can interpret for their stores and journalists can pass on to the public. The exhibition brochure not only provides a guide to the exhibitors but also introduces what have been indentified by the compilers as the main trends within the exhibition. When buyers go round the exhibition, the way they perceive the exhibited clothes must be affected by this; they will see them as representing the identified trends or as styles which are different from the identified trends. Not all buyers will be seeking to follow those trends; they may be looking for a different image, or feel that those trends are not suitable for their particular market, but it is likely their perceptions of the styles are changed by this process of 'marking out'.

The trade press can be roughly divided into those aimed at manufacturers, such as *Manufacturing Clothier*, and those aimed at the retailer, such as *Draper's Record*. As well as dealing in general trends, magazines like *Manufacturing Clothier* give guidance to manufacturers on trends in fabrics, their availability and suppliers, and of course they include reports from fabric fairs. There are also specialist fabric journals which include reports of trends in fabrics and associated styles. Such reports direct fabric buyers for companies towards the fabrics available in a way which also points to certain styles or trends. As well as marking out for its readers what are considered to be coming trends, *Draper's Record* also provides statistical information about the way goods are actually selling in the shops to help buyers assess current trends in consumer demand.

The media plays an important role in both identifying trends and defining certain styles as fashion, and in disseminating that information within the manufacturing and retailing industries. It is this common influence which contributes to the uniformity of style available to the public in the shops.

How is fashion marked out for the public?

As we have seen, what the public can buy is largely decided by buyers. Most women get to know about new fashions by looking in the shops, looking at what other women are wearing and, of course, by reading newspapers and magazines. Shops obviously use their windows to display examples of their current stock, and often, by the style of mannequin and other objects used in the display, try to create a mood or a specific look. Members of the public may identify the goods as fashionable because they have seen similar goods in many shops, because the shop itself has the reputation of being fashionable, or because they have seen similar styles pictured in the press. Women observing a new style of garment may see it as a new fashion, if it is worn on the street by someone with a recognisably fashionable image. However, the extent of this influence is very difficult to assess. On the other hand, it is certain that the press has a particular role to play in spreading ideas about what is fashionable.

Most newspapers and periodicals which have a substantial female readership give some space to fashion. It is interesting that the spread of fashion in society, the movement away from fashion led by the elite and restricted to the well-off has been associated not only with the rising affluence of the lower classes and the growth of mass-manufactured fashion, but also with the growth of the media, and in particular the growth of the women's press.

The way magazines have covered fashion has also changed. Early magazines for women such as the *Lady's Monthly Museum* of 1798, merely recorded what society women were wearing. They did not predict styles. In 1860 the *Englishwoman's Domestic Magazine*, a magazine for the middle classes, arranged for the publication of fashion engravings from Paris. As well as merely giving information about Parisian styles, these engravings also promoted these styles in Britain. *Vogue* was launched in Britain in 1916 and gave very detailed accounts of current fashions supported by black and white engravings of designers' models. *Vogue* was to become an arbiter of taste for the better off, an indispensable guide for the fashion-conscious woman – 'Buy nothing until you buy *Vogue*'.

After the war, as the market for fashion expanded so did the number and range of women's magazines. In the twenties and thirties, magazines catering for the lower-middle and working classes were launched such as *Good Housekeeping, Woman's Own* and *Woman*. These magazines, which could not compete with 'glossy' magazines like *Vogue* in fashion coverage, aimed to help women achieve the best results within their limited budgets.

As the market for fashion and other consumer goods became more differentiated, the range of women's magazines became more diversified. Since the magazines aimed at the young in the sixties, such as *Honey* and *Petticoat*, there have been magazines for the single independent woman, like *Cosmopolitan*; for the older career woman, like *Options*; magazines for slimmers; magazines for the fitness fanatic; all of which have been added to the traditional family-type magazines. All have features of clothing and fashion and promote certain looks.

How are those looks promoted?

Magazines very quickly moved from merely recording what was being worn to forecasting the styles which would become popular – what would be this year's look. Although many women's magazines still feature 'personalities' and their dress style, this is not usually their main fashion feature. In general, informative sketches which draw attention to the significant stylistic features have been replaced by colour promotions and features now often extending over a number of pages.

In 1960, magazines started to supply lists of stockists of the featured garments. Lists of garments and their stockists have replaced the description of styles and their main features in some magazines, and fashion features are more like promotions for certain retailers' goods. There is far less advice on how to create a particular look oneself, and more emphasis on where one should go to buy it. It is obviously a great help to the retailer if he can get his stock featured in a popular magazine.

However, there is always a fashion 'story'. Fashion editors generally decide three months or so in advance on the 'stories' they are going to feature. These decisions must be based on fashion predictions, trends in fashion shows and exhibitions, what they think is happening in a sphere of youth style, but also on seasonal themes such as swimwear or party dresses. It is these fashion stories which mark out for the public particular styles or looks which are represented as what is going to be fashion, or what is fashion already. In fact, no-one might ever wear such a garment or style.

These fashion 'stories' have the effect of marking styles out for the public and directing them towards certain looks. For example:

'VERVE TRICOT'
'This winter there are five looks to choose from, and knitwear is the key. We break them down into the plain, the plaid, the pulled, the polished and the pearled. Knit-pick the one that suits you best.' (*Harpers and Queen*, November 1983.)

With accompanying pictures this text directs the reader to the conclusion that to be in fashion she will have to adopt one of the illustrated looks and, in particular, that knitwear has a special degree of fashionability. Anything else just won't do!'
Elle tells its readers:

'DOTTY ABOUT STRIPES'
'Fashion is getting dottier by the month. The spring collections are dancing with polka dots and pinstripes. Here is a selection from the winter collections on sale now. Spot the future and streak ahead.' (*Elle*, February 1986.)

Even if one does not like dots or stripes when one sees these fabrics after reading this article, one will perceive them as 'fashionable', as having been identified as part of the latest look. One's perception is changed. One cannot now look at new striped garments without recognising them as the styles promoted as fashion.

One might even be persuaded to go out and buy such a garment in order to 'streak ahead' and, to help you, *Elle* provides a full list of the stockists of the featured clothes. *There is a neat fit between what is defined and promoted as fashion and what is in the shops.*

Of course, not all fashions as defined in the press actually become fashion. A style may become defined as fashion in different ways, such as gradually spreading from a particular style group, or being worn by figures in the public eye, like pop stars, but there can be no doubt that the media (here we have concentrated on the press for women, but one should include TV and video) plays a very important role in disseminating particular style ideas and in defining them for the public as the fashion.

It seems that for a style to become a fashion, to be transformed from just a style to one of *the* fashionable looks, we need three ingredients: the style itself, a marker in the form of a magazine article or perhaps a shop window, and of course the consumers who accept that definition.

During the punk era, magazines like *ID* tried to move away from the idea that fashion trickled down from the top designers and show the ways innovation was pushing up from the street. Instead of themes and trends, they celebrated diversity and multiplicity to individual style rather than fashion. Instead of 'glamour' shots, *ID* featured 'snapshots' of ordinary people who had created a distinctive look, who were seen as creative dressers. But street styles themselves became the focus of general media attention, and became swallowed up in the business of fashion labelling and dissemination.

Now, *ID* is a glossy magazine and has fashion editorials which define particular 'looks'. They do feature the clothes of young designers and retailers, but also carry advertising for well-established companies such as Wrangler and retail chains such as Benetton. They are now part of the system.

References

1. Flugel, J.F. (1930) *The Psychology of Clothes*. (Hogarth) 129.
2. *ibid* 130.
3. Strathern, A. and M. (1971) *Self Decoration in Mt Hagen*. (Duckworth) 3.

4. *ibid.*
5. Von Boehn, *Modes and Manners in the Nineteenth Century*. **1**, 215.
6. Freudenberger, H. (1973) 'Fashion, sumptary laws and business'. In: *Fashion Marketing*, eds. G. Willis and D. Midgley. (Allen and Unwin) 137.
7. *ibid* 139.
8. Flugel, J.F. (1930) *The Psychology of Clothes*. (Hogarth) 140.
9. Polhemus, T. and Proctor, L. *Fashion and Anti-Fashion*. (Thames and Hudson) 12.
10. *ibid* 13.
11. Nystrom, P. (1928) *The Economics of Fashion*. (New York: Ronald Press) 81.
12. Hollander, A. (1975) *Seeing Through Clothes*. (New York: Viking) 311, xii.
13. *ibid* 312.
14. Bergler, E. (1969) Fashion and the unconscious. In *Modesty in Dress*, J. Laver (Heineman) 37.
15. Laver, J. (1969) *Modesty in Dress*. (Heineman) 37.
16. Richardson, J. & Kroeber, A.L. (1973) 'Three centuries of women's dress fashions: a quantative analysis' In: *Fashion Marketing*, eds. G. Willis and D. Midgley. (Allen and Unwin) 47–106.
17. Brook Young, A. (1973) 'Recurring cycles of fashion'. In: *Fashion Marketing*, eds. G. Willis and D. Midgley. (Allen and Unwin) 107–124.
18. Richardson, J. & Kroeber, A.L. (1973) 'Three centuries of women's dress fashions: a quantative analysis'. In: *Fashion Marketing*, eds. G. Willis and D. Midgley. (Allen and Unwin) 105.
19. Menkes, S. *The Times* (15 June 1982).
20. Simmel, G. (1973) 'Fashion'. In: *Fashion Marketing*, eds. G. Willis and D. Midgley. (Allen and Unwin) 175–6.
21. King, C.W. (1973) 'A rebuttal to the "trickle-down" theory'. In: *Fashion Marketing*, eds. G. Willis and D. Midgley. (Allen and Unwin) 215–27.
22. Blumer, H. (1973) 'Fashion: From class differentiation to collective selection'. In: *Fashion Marketing*, eds. G. Willis and D. Midgley. (Allen and Unwin) 333.
23. *ibid* 334.
24. Coward, R. (1984) *Female Desire*. (Paladin) 34.
25. *ibid* 35.
26. *ibid* 36.
27. Blumer, H. (1973) 'Fashion: From class differentiation to collective selection'. In: *Fashion Marketing*, eds. G. Willis and D. Midgley. (Allen and Unwin) 331.
28. Brampton, S. *The Observer* (18 March 1984).

5 Victorian Women: Their Dress and Social Position

WHY DO MEN AND WOMEN DRESS DIFFERENTLY?

In our society, like in most others, it is taken for granted that the sexes dress differently. Have you ever wondered why this should be the case? Why do men wear trousers, and women wear skirts and high-heels? And why women started wearing trousers? Of course there is nothing intrinsically *male* about trousers or *female* about skirts. Women from the Middle East and the Indian sub-continent have traditionally worn trousers and in other parts of the world men have worn 'skirts' like the sarong, kaftan and kilt. However, in our society skirt means female and most men would be embarrassed if they were forced to wear a skirt in public. Such differences in dress visibly express the wearer's gender; his or her socially defined sexual role.

Although for a long time it was unthinkable for any respectable woman to wear trousers they have now become an acceptable and popular form of dress for women. Even today trousers are considered inappropriate for women barristers and judges, some secretaries and schoolgirls are discouraged from wearing them, and uniforms for nurses, air hostesses, and policewomen are still based on skirts despite some of the more practical advantages of trousers. Neither the Queen, not Mrs Thatcher as Prime Minister have ever been seen in trousers when carrying out official duties. Skirts remain the only proper dress for some women. How can we explain changes like the wearing of trousers by women? Men's dress has remained fairly stable, they have been wearing trousers and suits for a long time. But women's appearance has changed quite dramatically, they have worn crinolines, bustles, short skirts, long skirts, trousers and hot pants. Why has women's appearance changed so much?

It could be argued that the changing patterns of women's dress, the changes in style and the particular looks of periods like the twenties and thirties are the achievements of particularly creative designers who satisfy the demand for new fashions. But designers are part of society and their designs are created within specific social and cultural contexts, their success depends to some degree on their ability to meet the needs and requirements of their clientèle. Courrèges believed a good designer must react to the social environment in which he or she lives: 'A good designer must be a sociologist, he must look at the lives people lead, the way their houses are built, what are their needs and preoccupations'. (1) Speaking in 1979, Courrèges was criticising attempts to introduce a 'forties' look and basing his predictions on what he saw as people's current way of life and needs he accurately forecast the tremendous popularity of sportswear-inspired clothing in the eighties.

Styles of dress do not simply reflect the social position of women or the preoccupations of society. They are themselves part of that social environment process by which people's ideas and aesthetics are formed. As we have seen in Chapter 3, clothes are instrumental in the process of socialisation into sexual roles, they help shape an individual's idea of how women should look, what kind of people they are and how they should behave. When a woman steps into high-heeled shoes, she becomes less stable, less able to move about freely: the restriction of movement and induced fraility are apparent to the wearer and those around her, and those attributes are interpreted as *her* attributes. Styles of dress are part of the process by which attitudes to and images of, both men and women are created and reproduced.

In this and the following chapter we are going to examine changes in women's appearance and dress. Our approach is different from a history of costume which would show in detail *how* styles changed for women – when the bustle first appeared or when Dior introduced his H-line. We will examine the differences between the dress of men and women, and assess the extent to which women's appearance related to their social position, to the kind of life they led and to the ideas held about women. We are certainly not suggesting that changes in styles of women's dress can be understood *only* in terms of changes in gender relations, far from it. Women's appearance, like that of men, is affected by many diverse influences including developments in the visual arts and technology, and by the logic of fashion change itself. By exploring the relation between dress and how the role of women is defined and experienced, we can add an important dimension to our understanding of change.

HAVE MEN AND WOMEN ALWAYS DRESSED VERY DIFFERENTLY?

During the Middle Ages, men and women wore comparatively similar clothes, simple, long, loose-fitting tunics. The neckline and length of the tunic were different but the shape was universal. Fabrics and costly dyes served to differentiate the costume of the social classes. However, with the advent of fitted clothes and the rapid evolution of tailoring techniques from the 1340s onwards, the dress of the sexes began to diverge in construction. By the Tudor period, quite distinct forms of dress had emerged, which clearly expressed the different roles of the sexes. The costume for men consisted of a padded doublet which emphasised or gave the illusion of broad shoulders, and of tightly-fitted hose which emphasised slim hips and legs. Women's costume, on the other hand, had become restrictive and cumbersome. A tight bodice encased the chest and unwieldy hoops held out the large, long skirts. The dynamic and active image implicit in the male silhouette was in sharp contrast to the solid and passive look of women's clothes. *Throughout the subsequent centuries, men's dress continued to allow a freedom of movement denied to women by the many constraining fashions such as stays, farthingales, paniers, crinolines and bustles.*

There did, however, remain close parallels between the *fashionable dress* of men and women, that is, the dress of the affluent classes in society until the end of the eighteenth century. Like women, men of these classes wore ruffs, slashed clothes, furs, jewellery, wigs, lace, silks and delicate fabrics. These fashionable features acted as signs of wealth and status for men and women alike, and served to differentiate them from other classes in society. There were as many, if not more, differences between the dress of the rich and the poor as there were between the sexes. However, it is towards the end of the nineteenth century that another crucial difference began to emerge in the dress of the sexes: a new sobriety began to appear in men's dress. Men adopted a drab and austere image never exhibited before by the upper classes. Despite the revival of flamboyant styles such as the satin shirts and velvet trousers of the sixties, and more recently the styles of cults like the New Romantics and the so-called gender-benders, men in general have continued to dress in simpler and plainer styles, heavier fabrics, more sober colours, and wear a more limited range of garments than women. From this time, women came to be regarded as the decorative sex, prey to the whims and vagaries of fashion in ways that men were not. The nineteenth century was a watershed — the extreme point of difference in the styles of fashionable dress and in the roles men and women played in society. So, it is here we begin.

PATRIARCHS AND LITTLE WOMEN

During the late eighteenth century, the increasing mood of Romanticism and the influence of Rousseau, the French philosopher, had made the idea of a return to the simple life popular. This was reflected in dress by the adoption by the upper classes of a more informal and countrified look. This tendency was given further impetus by the French Revolution. After the fall of Louis XVI and his court, elaborate dress in France was associated with the *ancien régime* and it became dangerous to be seen wearing it. In England too, aristocratic and ostentatious dress became unpopular. Beau Brummell, often thought of as a dandy, was a leading figure in the trend away from aristocratic dress. He set the fashion for well-cut clothes of plain cloth, immaculate linen and top hats. The embroidered coats and tricorne hats of the aristocracy, decorated with feathers and gold, were no more, and wealthy men, regardless of birth, began to share the same style of dress. At the turn of the century, fashionable dress for both men and women had become simpler, influenced by the neo-classical style.

But if there had been a political revolution in France, in Britain there had been a technological and economic revolution. The Industrial Revolution brought far-reaching social changes which included new patterns of work and new lifestyles for many people, new roles for men and women, and of course new changes in dress. By the 1830s there was a clear division between men and women's dress. The Industrial Revolution brought manufacture and commerce to the fore as sources of wealth. Entrepreneurs swelled the ranks of the middle classes which became not only more numerous but wealthier. The men of these classes were deeply involved in the expanding world of industry and commerce; they spent much of their time at the factory, in the office or counting-house, rather than in the drawing-room or riding after the hounds. This rising class, with its emphasis on work and respectability reinforced the trend towards both sobriety of dress and manners. As businessmen, they required clothes which allowed them freedom of movement and which expressed attributes desirable in the world of business — namely discipline, reliability and honesty. In other words, their clothes should express an air of restraint, not flamboyance. However, some of these men had become increasingly rich and most were proud of their achievements.

How could they show off this wealth?

In the past the aristocracy had shown their high social status not only through their possessions, which had included expensive clothing, but also through their lifestyle. For the most part, they led an

Fig. 5.1 The sober patriarch.

honourably futile existence — an endless round of social engage-
ments interspersed with artistic pursuits like embroidery, sketching
or singing on the part of women, or field sports and gaming tables
on the part of men. As we have seen, ostentatious dress would
have been incompatible with the image of a businessman, and
obviously a life of leisure was not possible for those whose fortunes
depended on their involvement in industry and commerce. So it
seems that *the burden for displaying the wealth and thus the importance of these middle class men fell upon their female dependents.* It
was their dress and idleness which acted as *status symbols* for the
men; the increasing extravagance and elaborateness of their dress
and their leisured existence seems to have acted as a compensation
for the increasing severity of men's dress and the growing number
of gentlemen who were carrying out some form of occupation.

Little women

Women in this period were admired for their innocence, their
refined, delicate nature and dainty physique, not for their intellect
or physical strength. It was generally accepted that men who were
superior in physical strength were also intellectually superior. It
was a man's duty to protect the weaker and more sensitive sex, and
it was a woman's duty, acknowledging her inferiority, to be guided
by his superior judgement and accept his authority. This inequality
between the sexes was given institutional recognition in the law.

   An Act of 1806 decreed that a woman's property should auto-
matically pass to her husband on marriage, and that any income
she had would also become his property, so a wife had to rely on
her husband's generosity and good nature. Before marriage, a lady
remained in her father's house under his jurisdiction and inferior
to sons; when she married she promised to obey her husband. He
was entitled as her father had been to discipline her and punish her
if she disobeyed him. In short women were deemed incapable of
running their own lives, and controlling their own property.

   If women were regarded as generally inferior to men, there was
one respect in which they were superior — that of morality and
goodness:

> '(Woman was) given to man to be his better angel, to dissuade him
> from vice, to stimulate him to virtue, to make home delightful and life
> joyous...in the exercise of these gentle and holy charities, she fulfils

her high vocation. But great as is the influence of the maiden and wife, it seems to fade away when placed by that of mother. It is the mother who is to make the citizens for earth...and happy are they who thus fulfil the sacred and dignified vocation allotted them by Providence.' (2)

This ideal of woman – a mixture of purity, duty and domesticity, dominated in nineteenth century middle class society. It was exemplified by Queen Victoria, a dutiful and virtuous young wife and mother. Following her lead, large families were popular in all classes. It was a wife's duty to provide her husband with children, particularly sons to whom he could pass on his property. Sex was a duty; no respectable woman could possibly take pleasure in it. Women's pleasure was in motherhood but again women had few rights. In the case of a separation, the custody of children was automatically given to the father. In 1837, Mrs Norton, who had suffered at the hands of a brutal husband, fought a famous case to win custody of her children. This was only possible because she was a woman with many influential friends, and even so she was only awarded custody until the children were seven years old.

The middle classes were obsessed with respectability and the chastity of women. A lady's reputation depended on a strict adherence to the established codes of respectable behaviour. She must be above suspicion, without any slur on her character. A man had to be confident of the chaste and pure nature of his wife before and during marriage so he could be sure the children to whom he passed his property were his legitimate heirs. Of course, men did not have to follow the same rules. During the Victorian period the number of prostitutes grew and concern about this and the increase in venereal disease was expressed in Parliament. Mayhew estimated that by the 1860s there were 80 000 prostitutes in London and their clients must have included many upright and respectable citizens. The purity of the ideal woman depended on the contrast with these fallen women. The Divorce Act of 1857, which gave the middle classes access to divorce, clearly embodied the double standards implicit in middle class morality. A man could divorce his wife for adultery but a woman needed further grounds such as cruelty.

Given such views about the capabilities and delicate nature of womankind, men thought it necessary to protect them from what could shock, corrupt or harm them in any way. Of course work was out of the question. Marriage and motherhood were suited to the 'natural' talents of women; they were the only desirable and socially acceptable careers for women. It was only the unfortunate, those without private means and without a father or husband to support them, who were forced to earn a living. There were few options for such women; they might earn some kind of living with their needle, more rarely with their pen, but most commonly, as a governess in someone else's house. *Women were kept apart from the 'real world' of business and the professions, they were confined to the domestic sphere in a state of financial and physical dependence.*

A woman's place was in the home where she could display the wealth that had been earned by men. The middle classes acquired large houses, filled with ornate and expensive objects, to announce their new wealth, and it was here, dressed in extravagant and cumbersome clothes, that women were expected to spend most of their time in the company of their female relatives. *Even within the house middle class women aspired to be idle much of the time.* Although a wife was expected to run the house, the servants took the major burden of housework and looking after the children. The number of servants in a household was a status symbol in itself. The greater the number of servants, the more luxurious the lifestyle, the less the mistress of the house had to do and by implication, the greater the wealth of her husband.

Apart from supervising the servants, women were not expected to do anything 'useful' except, perhaps, a little charity work, a few 'good works' for the local needy. They filled the long hours with leisure activities such as embroidery, painting, music and the reading of long novels. In addition, there were the delights of shopping, the demands of her toilette and maintaining her wardrobe, the round of social calls and gossip! Women were not expected to engage in serious conversation; it would be considered 'unwomanly' to discuss science or politics. The world in which most women moved was so narrow and their social circle so restricted they had little to talk about apart from the latest fashion in bonnets and the latest local gossip. Finding a husband was a major preoccupation for all single women and their mothers, because as we have seen it was the only 'career' for a woman. Much energy and time was devoted to the pursuit of eligible husbands for daughters and friends, for the fate of the old maid was not an enviable one!

Women did not indulge in any vigorous or strenuous activity because of the supposed physical weakness of the female form and no girl wished to appear robust and healthy! A gentle stroll, protected from the harsh effects of the sun by bonnet, veil and parasol, was considered adequate exercise for a lady. Indeed, some women found themselves incapable of even this activity and were confined to their homes and chaise-longues, suffering from recurrent bouts of ill-health. The lifestyle of the middle class woman was not a healthy one — lack of exercise, poor diet, and many pregnancies were just some of the problems.

What a picture of the middle class woman emerges! Hemmed in by social restrictions and moral attitudes, condemned to a life of subordination to men — 'the more doll-like and delicate, the more empty-headed and useless the better!' — they led a life of tedious ease.

Corsets and crinolines: the subordination of women in fashion

By the 1830s the fashionable styles of dress emphasised the different roles of the sexes. Women's dress had become much more extravagant and restrictive. After forty years of relative freedom, the small waist had returned to fashion and it was made to look even smaller by the addition of wide sleeves and large skirts. At first, numerous petticoats were worn to swell the skirts and the demand for larger and larger skirts led to the introduction of the crinoline in 1857. This metal frame was much lighter than the petticoats and as a result skirts reached enormous proportions. The vast skirts survived until the late 1860s when the fullness was shifted to the back and the crinoline was replaced by the bustle, and women's clothes were bedecked with all manner of bows, flowers, flounces and frills. What do these styles tell us about the position of women and attitudes to them?

These styles exemplify what Veblen termed *conspicuous consumption* and *conspicuous leisure* — the ability to buy expensive goods and at the same time indicate that the wearer was not expected to earn a living. The extravagant use of fabric was a straightforward *display of wealth*. One writer recorded in her diary that 'Lady Aylesbury wears forty-eight yards of material in each of her gowns'. (3) Apart from the cumbersome nature of the garment, the expensive and fragile fabrics used in fashion such as silks would make it *unsuitable for working in*.

At a time when many families were climbing up the social ladder, there was great preoccupation with status, and fashionable clothes were an immediate and convenient sign of person's social position. The wearing of fashionable clothes was an important part of a middle class woman's role. It served as a means by which a man could display his wealth and status. Prestige accrued to a man who supported an idle wife and provided her with expensive clothes, in the same way as it would to a man who owned any other form of expensive property. *It was not in her own right that women acquired status through dress but as the 'property' of a man.*

The degree of extravagance in a lady's dress signified her marital status and her position in relation to men. A single woman was expected to dress in simple styles such as a white muslin evening dress decorated with fresh flowers. Her simplicity of dress expressed her innocence and purity, and also indicated that she had not yet found a husband to provide for her. Extravagant dress raised suspicions about a young lady's character: was she an extravagant spendthrift likely to ruin her future husband, or had she improperly received costly gifts from a man? Married woman could dress in a much more ornate fashion. Married women took social precedence over single women. They had achieved the goal to which all women aspired. It was their duty to display the status of their husband and so their costume could be much richer than that of a single woman, even if as in all other spheres they were expected to show obedience to their husbands!

Dress was also an important indicator of gentility or social standing. Of course, the rules of fashion were set by the richest people in society and reflected their wealth and lifestyle. Those wishing to associate themselves with high social standing were forced to follow those rules. Many women tried to maintain a wardrobe and style of dress beyond their means, and which was designed to suit a lifestyle quite different from their own. Not all middle class households were able to achieve the *ideal* life of leisure for their womenfolk. Necessity might compel a middle class woman to help with the housework, or seek paid work. There was a conflict between the need to work and the need to appear genteel. But the crinoline became almost universal wear, and was even adopted by servants, despite its obvious disadvantages for anyone wishing or needing to be active. In the context of the clutter of Victorian houses, the crinoline for servants was a disaster. Some ladies forbade their servants to wear it while on duty. Nevertheless, it rapidly became popular. *The Times* reported in 1857 that 40 000 tons of Swedish iron ore had been imported for crinoline manufacture, and cheap non-steel crinolines were sold in every little draper's shop. The

cheap ones made from buckram and split cane produced a very
inferior result.

The quality of clothes, and the type of fabric used were obviously
indicators of wealth, but it was not enough merely to be able to
spend and follow fashion. A lady was not only expected to follow
the rules of fashion, a *real* lady also appreciated the subtleties of
good taste and was familiar with the complex *etiquette of dress*. The
middle class endorsement of social mobility had not been totally
accepted. All classes continued to attach great importance to good
breeding. *Good taste* was the taste of the established and dominant
classes; knowing the rules was still the mark of true status, the
mark of gentility.

A *real* lady knew what combination of colours, fabrics, trimmings,
garments were within the bounds of good taste; she knew what
were the appropriate forms of dress for each social occasion and
time of day. This was not so for those trying to climb the social
ladder; they needed guidance in order to produce the effect of
gentility. During the nineteenth century many books were written
on etiquette in general, and the etiquette of dress in particular −
for example, *The Art of Dress or The Guide to the Toilet* (1839).
New women's magazines were also a useful source of information.
The Englishwoman's Domestic Magazine, first published in 1852,
served the needs of the middle class market. It gave advice on
household management (the publisher was Samuel Beeton, husband
of the famous Mrs Beeton), how to hire servants, on dressmaking,
on problems concerning marriage and courtship, and on problems
of etiquette. It also provided information on fashion, bringing the
first fashion reports from Paris. As the century went on, more and
more magazines included advice on the etiquette of dress, answering queries on all matters of taste, and as styles became more
elaborate and changed more rapidly more and more space was
devoted to fashion. Cynthia White in *Women's Magazines 1693−
1968* wrote: 'For... women ignorant of Society's modes and manners
the women's magazines proved an indispensable guide'. (4)

So, women's dress acted as a status symbol for male relatives in
the sense that it demanded expenditure and thus indicated wealth;
it could convey 'taste' and thus served to distinguish the genteel
from the vulgar; and its styles implied that the wearer lived a life of
ease far removed from the necessity of work.

Women's dress was not merely a symbol of leisure in its impracticality, it actually enforced leisure by its restrictive nature. In this

way, it promoted and perpetuated certain conceptions of women which shaped both the ideas of men and of women themselves. *Women were supposed to be weak, fragile and empty-headed. How did clothing contribute to this impression?*

First, the corset, worn to produce a fashionably small waist actually *physically weakened women*. Veblen wrote:

> 'The corset is. . .(an instrument of) mutilation for the purpose of lowering the subject's vitality and rendering her unfit for work. It is true the corset impairs the personal attractiveness of the wearer (i.e. when naked), but the loss suffered on that score is offset by the increase in reputability which comes of her visibly increased expensiveness and infirmity.' (5)

The Victorian corset has been compared to the Chinese practice of foot-binding as a means of implying status through the severe physical restriction of women. When tightly laced, the chest was constricted to such an extent that a woman could not breathe properly. The resultant shallow breathing was attributed by some doctors to an *anatomical* difference between men and women. Men apparently breathed abdominally whereas women breathed thoracically! This constriction of the chest must at least partially explain why so many women of the time were subject to attacks of breathlessness and fainting fits. However, despite damage to their health, many women persisted in wearing corsets throughout pregnancy and periods of ill-health. For though excessive lacing was condemned, it was considered bad taste for a lady not to wear a corset; she would be considered immodest if not immoral. The adjectives 'straight-laced' and 'loose' were used of morals as well as bodies. A woman who did not restrain herself physically was assumed to be incapable of moral restraint!

Secondly, there can be little doubt that fashionable dress with its huge skirts, large shawls which could be eight feet across, bonnets which blinkered a woman's vision, and tight gloves and shoes made it *very difficult for a woman to move about freely*. The combined weight of outer clothes and underwear alone must have caused many women to lose what inclination they might have had for activity.

Although the crinoline, worn from the mid-1850s, reduced the number and therefore the weight of petticoats, it had its own problems of manoeuvrability as it held out the voluminous and heavy skirts. Simple acts like passing through doorways, sitting down or getting into a railway carriage became complex operations. A later development, the '*sans flectum*', was advertised as bringing many advantages over the ordinary crinoline, not only in looks. Apparently it also allowed a lady 'to ascend a steep stair, lean against a table, throw herself into a chair, pass to her stall at the opera...without embarrassment to herself, or provoking the rude remarks of others'. Presumably none of this was possible before. No wonder great ladies preferred to remain seated in their carriages when shopping and have the assistants bring out goods for their inspection.

Fashionable dress created a barrier between the fragile lady and the possible dangers of society! The crinoline kept a physical distance between a lady and her companions, as did gloves which were never removed in public even to shake hands. The bonnets and veils worn until 1860 sheltered her from unpleasant sights and unwelcome gazes.

Fashionable dress also made great demands on a lady's time. Etiquette demanded that she should change her clothes and attend to her toilette several times a day. Even with the help of a maid, this in itself was time-consuming but there was also the selection, purchase and upkeep of a fashionable wardrobe. This demanded

A Splendid Spread –

Fig. 5.2 Cartoon 1850 (Mary Evans Picture Library).

not only wealth but the commitment of time and energy. Even if servants took the burden of cleaning, laundering, ironing and repairing (which was not always possible in the less affluent households) ladies still had to keep abreast of the latest styles, choose fabrics and trimmings, visit the dressmaker for several fittings, supervise the maintenance of her clothes and, of course, choose what to wear! All this kept women occupied for many hours, preventing them from using their time, energy and talents more constructively. So whilst women were expected to devote themselves to fashion, talk of ribbons, new styles and whether to wear the blue taffeta or the pink was taken as evidence of the frivolous nature of women.

In these ways dress contributed to a particular image of women, an image associated with the wealthier classes and to which the less well-off aspired. The success or failure of women in conforming to this image, and the values implicit in it, determined to some degree the social status of their families.

Little women in perspective

We have been discussing the dress and lifestyle of *ladies*, the wealthy and leisured women of nineteenth century society. They represented only a minority of the population. The upper and middle classes made up about one-quarter of the population and many households included in that group would not have sufficient means to achieve the ideal lifestyle and form of dress for their womenfolk, although they constantly strived towards those ideals. But what of the others, the majority of women, who belonged to the working class?

There is a stark and striking contrast between their lives and those of the rich. The Industrial Revolution had created the material basis for the standard of living of the middle class. It had also created a great demand for labour and in the first half of the century women and children had been drawn into factories and mines as cheap labour. The reports of Lord Shaftesbury testify to the long hours and the terrible conditions in which many women and children worked, always for substantially less pay than the men. These women were not 'protected' from the harsh realities of life! The Shaftesbury Commission, reporting on the employment of women and girls in mines, gave evidence that young women and girls worked below ground, doing the same kind of work for the

Fig. 5.3 Opulence and extravagance in the 1850s.

same number of hours as men and boys. There were many reports of women working stripped to the waist alongside the men. 'Their dress, when they come out of the pit, is a kind of skull cap which hides all the hair, trousers without stockings, and thick wooden clogs; their waists are covered.' (6) In the textile mills, women worked long hours near dangerous machinery, sometimes up to eighteen hours a day. They then returned to the closely packed slums of the new industrial towns. Social reformers such as Shaftesbury were able to bring about reforms. In 1842 an Act was passed forbidding the employment of women underground in mines. In 1844 the Twelve Hour Act limited the hours a woman could work to twelve hours a day and, in 1847, the working week for women was limited to fifty-eight hours! These reforms obviously improved the lot of working class women as did the rising standard of living during the nineteenth century. Nevertheless, women had to work incredibly hard in factories, workrooms and in their homes. They had to be physically tough and strong and they certainly had no time for genteel arts or adorning themselves. Their dress was simple − a skirt, shawl and blouse (and very occasionally trousers, when work demanded it, much to the horror of respectable society) and clogs in the North or boots in the South.

It was on such women that the lifestyle and dress of the middle class lady depended. Their labour was needed to produce wealth in the factories, to take over the drudgery of housework and to produce the clothes a lady wore. It is perhaps ironic, the extent to which a lady's finery depended on the exploitation of her poorer sisters. The vast quantities of fabric needed for the huge fashionable skirts were produced by the cheap labour of women in the textile towns. Large numbers of women and girls were employed in the dressmakers and allied fashion trades such as millinery, button making, lace making, etc. These trades were notoriously badly paid and the conditions of work very poor. A Royal Commission reported in 1843 that many girls in these trades died of consumption and overwork. Before the invention of the sewing machine in the 1850s, girls damaged their eyesight by sewing often through the night to complete vast orders of fashionable mourning to be delivered at short notice. The demands for rapid delivery of the ornate fashions of the period put almost unbearable pressure on the girls working as seamstresses. Sweated labour of this kind was more difficult to control than factory work and conditions did not improve for workers in these trades until the turn of the century.

Middle class women depended on the labour, the physical strength and endurance of others for their own life of luxury, and it was the extent to which they themselves, their lifestyle and their dress differed from those on whom they depended that determined the status of their husbands and families.

THE BEGINNINGS OF CHANGE

Within the confines of respectable Victorian society there were women who wished to break out of the legal, economic and social restrictions which surrounded them, and out of the fashionable clothes which physically imprisoned them. The process of reform was long and slow for not only did laws have to be changed but the barriers of prejudice in a society convinced of man's mental and physical superiority had to be overcome. Nevertheless, some women were prepared to challenge the prevailing view of women and their role in society, and to reject the dictates of fashion and respectable dress. Let us first examine the changes which brought social liberation and then the attempts to develop a freer form of dress for women.

Towards emancipation

In order to improve the status of women in Victorian society, reform was needed in the law, in the provision of education and in the sphere of employment. Legal discrimination against women existed in marriage, in property rights and, of course, in their access to the vote. In the field of married women's property, social reformers had some success; in 1870 a law was passed giving women the right to possess their own earnings and in 1882, the Married Women's Property Act returned to women the right to keep their own property after marriage. The struggle for the vote met with less success. The first regular suffrage committee was set up in 1855 and from the 1860s onwards women like Millicent Fawcett and later the Pankhursts worked steadily for the vote for women. In 1867, John Stuart Mill's proposed amendment to the Second Reform Bill to introduce equal voting rights was defeated. But by the 1880s it was said that about half the MPs in Parliament were in favour of limited female suffrage but they could not agree on the extent. At this time not all men had the vote and so an extension of the franchise to women was fraught with problems for the major parties. However, women were given some limited voting rights in local elections through two Acts in 1888 and 1893. Some women were content with the financial changes and this minimal voting power. Others, however, continued to struggle for the vote and the means to exert influence on the lawmakers. To further the cause of women's suffrage and to increase pressure, the Women's Social and Political Union was founded in 1903. Their campaign was peaceful in the years until 1908 but the Union became frustrated by their lack of success and the intransigence of the new Liberal government. The suffragettes embarked upon a militant and some-times violent campaign; they chained themselves to railings, broke windows, slashed paintings, went on hunger strike, and of course Emily Davison was killed when she threw herself under the King's horse. This campaign seemed to harden attitudes against them; they were condemned as 'unwomanly', irrational and hysterical. At first it seemed that their efforts were to no avail. It was the upheaval of the First World War and the part women played in the victory which seemed to bring about a change of heart.

The second half of the nineteenth century did bring access to education for middle class girls. On the whole, women had been educated by governesses in the home but from 1850 onwards schools were opened for young ladies. The first was Mrs Buss's North London Collegiate School in 1850, followed by Cheltenham Ladies' College in 1853. Many more followed. The curriculum of these schools included the conventional feminine skills of needle-work, drawing, singing and dancing, but academic subjects were also included and could be taken for public examination. Perhaps because they modelled themselves to some extent on public schools for boys, the curriculum also included sports. Girls were introduced to a range of physical activities including calisthenics, hockey, netball, tennis, fencing and skating. This obviously had great signifi-cance for the improvement of girl's general health and fitness but also signalled a shift away from the view that women were passive, feeble creatures. Girls and women began to enjoy physical activity and by the end of the century sport had become a very popular leisure pursuit for upper and middle class women. In addition, women were competing in international tournaments in sports such as netball, hockey and golf. This taste of education in schools led to a demand for higher education. Separate colleges were established for women; the first was Girton College, Cambridge in 1869. It was followed by Newnham College and, in London, Bedford College. Education was not regarded as a virtue by many, and quite often as a positive disadvantage in relation to marriage opportunities. 'Blue stockings' were the subject of scorn and ridicule, and it was even suggested that education was 'unnatural' for women and that too much might prevent girls from having children in later life!

Having gained her education, the middle class girl sometimes wished to pursue a career other than marriage. What opportunities were there? In the past, there were only two respectable professions for a gentlewoman — that of governess or seamstress — and it was only those who were forced by economic circumstances who took such work. The others, as we have seen, on the whole had to be content with a sheltered and often tedious existence. Two strands of protest emerged about the lack of useful employment for middle class women. Some like Florence Nightingale rebelled against the strongly held Victorian conviction that women could be of little service outside the home. She rejected the comforts and tedium of the drawing room and polite society. Her work tending the sick and injured in the Crimean War won the respect of many, and she was able to establish nursing as a respected and respectable profession. Elizabeth Garrett Anderson fought for the right of women to practise as doctors in this country. Both these women showed extraordinary courage and determination in the face of great opposition and prejudice. They, and others like them, shared a new confidence in women's abilities and they fought hard to develop opportunities for their talents to be used. But pressures for greater employment opportunities were also coming from other perhaps less confident women, those seeking 'genteel' employment. Many middle class women, without sufficient income to support themselves and trained only for the career of marriage, faced a life of poverty if they failed to find a husband. The 1851 census showed that almost a quarter of women were unmarried and eighteen per cent of those were under thirty-five. There was a surplus of women, and the numbers of them forced to support themselves continued to multiply. Anxious letters to women's magazines reflected this growing problem which continued into the twentieth century. It was for the benefit of such women that *The Queen* and *The Lady* ran their 'Women's Employment' and 'How to Live' columns. (7)

Changing circumstances did help to create some new career opportunities for some of these women. After the outbreak of the Crimean War in 1854, women did begin to work in spheres hitherto exclusive to men, such as in large retail shops. (8) The invention of the telephone and typewriter opened up new employment possibilities for women. In 1870, when the Post Office took over the telegraph system, it engaged women as telephone operators. Women were employed in increasing numbers in commercial offices in the last decade of the century, and the Civil Service, having taken its lead from private business began to employ women as typists in 1888. The introduction of compulsory education in 1870 provided more opportunities for women to become teachers.

By the end of the nineteenth century a new type of woman was to be found. A 'woman with views', she was concerned about her rights and social freedom; she was more active and sporty than her Victorian predecessors and more conventional contemporaries, and more likely to have a career. *These career girls needed more practical clothes than the fussy and extravagant fashionable styles of late Victorian and Edwardian fashion. Where did she find them?*

Aesthetic gowns and bloomers: new dress for women

Victorian clothes had come under attack on both medical and aesthetic grounds, and for their general impracticality. (9) The first attempt to provide an alternative came from America in the form of Bloomerism. Mrs Amelia Bloomer gave her name to a style of dress consisting of a short skirt worn over ankle length trousers, inspired by traditional Turkish costume and renamed 'bloomers'. This style was first illustrated in the newspaper of her husband and Mrs Bloomer, an active campaigner for women's rights, adopted it as a more practical form of dress. However, when she travelled on her lecture tours wearing 'bloomers' she met with criticism and ridicule. She was the subject of numerous cartoons on both sides of the Atlantic. Her ideas found very little favour in England – the great majority of women were too conventional to even consider wearing such an 'indelicate' costume. By the end of the 1850s Mrs Bloomer herself had given up wearing it.

A group of painters, the Pre-Raphaelites, unintentionally provided another alternative to fashionable dress. The Brotherhood, as they were known, was founded in 1848. (10) They were opposed to the Establishment style of painting and sought to create a new art which projected ideas but which was also faithful to reality. This concern with reality required the convincing depiction of the folds and drapery of their subjects' costume. Rossetti, a member of

Fig. 5.4 Amelia Bloomer.

the Brotherhood, was particularly interested in medieval themes, and he found it necessary both to research and re-create the clothes of the period. His wife and model was a skilled seamstress and was able to make up the clothes for him. In 1854 he painted his wife wearing these very simple clothes with no corset or crinoline at the time when small waists and crinolines were the height of fashion. His wife began to wear these dresses in everyday life. Compared to the restrictions of the corset and the difficulties of managing a crinoline, they were easy and comfortable to wear. Other painters in the group created clothes based on the costumes of the Middle Ages, the Renaissance and Antiquity. Women in their circle adopted these styles and continued to wear them until it became the established style of this radical artistic circle.

Artistic, or Aesthetic dress as it was later known, began to

flourish more generally in the 1870s. Although it remained a minority fashion, it was adopted by those who wished to link themselves
with the prestigious and avante garde artistic set and it even had
some influence on the designs of Parisian fashion houses such as
Worth. The demand was such that Liberty's of London began to
produce Aesthetic gowns in their workroom. The styles made in
soft draping materials were medieval or classical in their inspiration
and therefore were very different from the tightly fitted bustles and
trains of the day. The popularity of Aesthetic dress was certainly a
reaction to the brash products of manufacture and to the crude
aniline dyes used since 1859 in the production of fabric. Liberty's
chief part was to import soft oriental fabrics so different from the
stiff silks, thick woollens and hard cottons of mainstream Victorian
fashion.

A more conscious and direct attack on contemporary fashion
came from those advocating a change to more healthy and hygienic
dress for women. The Rational Dress Society was founded in 1881
with Viscountess Haberton as president. Its aims and principles
were set out as follows:

'The Rational Dress Society protests against the introduction of any
fashion in dress that either deforms the figure, impedes the movement
of the body, or in any way tends to injure health. It protests against the
wearing of tightly fitting corsets, of high-heeled or narrow-toed boots
and shoes; of heavily weighted skirts, as rendering healthy exercise
almost impossible; and of all tie-down cloaks or other garments impeding
the movement of the arms.

'It protests against crinolines or crinolettes of any kind as ugly and
deforming. The object of the R.D.S. is to promote the adoption,
according to individual taste and convenience, of a style of dress based
upon consideration of health, comfort, and beauty, and to deprecate
constant changes of fashion that cannot˙be recommended on any of
these grounds.' (11)

Viscountess Haberton tried to promote the wearing of a divided
skirt but even other members of the Society found this too extreme
to follow her example. In retrospect, many of the reforms they
proposed seem over-cautious. For example, they suggested that
ladies' underclothing should be restricted to a *maximum of seven
pounds*! What would these ladies have thought of the complete sets
of clothing worn by women today which weigh only two or three
pounds?

The Society exhibited examples of practical and comfortable

Fig. 5.5 Aesthetic Dress.

dress wherever they could. In 1884 it participated in the International Health Exhibition. The exhibition was primarily concerned
with improving conditions in English domestic and industrial life
and so the greater part was devoted to topics such as drainage and
anti-pollution, however there was quite a large section on Hygienic
Dress which drew considerable interest. Another exhibitor in this
section was Dr Jaeger, a German physician who advocated wearing
wool, rather than vegetable products such as cotton, next to the
skin. He argued that animal fibres absorbed and allowed perspiration
to evaporate in a way vegetable fibres could not. He produced a

range of knitted woollen underclothes and outer clothes. An agency for his 'health' clothes was opened in Regent Street in 1884 and devotees included George Bernard Shaw and Oscar Wilde, whose wife was an active campaigner for dress reform.

We have seen that the complaints about fashionable dress came from vocal minorities amongst the well-to-do of society, not least because it was only the rich who could afford such clothes. However, there were other activities associated with wealth and leisure which produced some further if limited changes in women's fashionable dress. Those activities were travel and sport. Travelling had been the pastime of the rich but in the nineteenth century, the growing middle classes who wished to spend some of their newly acquired wealth began to discover its pleasures. Opportunities for travel increased with the development of new modes of transport. Rail travel was comparatively fast and comfortable and people were now able to travel quite long distances with ease. The first horse-drawn omnibus in London in 1829 and the first underground train service in 1863 provided new forms of transport for the urban middle classes. Towards the end of the century, the bicycle appeared and later the automobile and aeroplane. As a consequence, more people began to travel to visit friends, to go shopping and for pleasure. More people took holidays in this country and to the continent. Cooks organised their first tour of Switzerland in 1863. Photographs of intrepid Victorian travellers picture ladies perched on the backs of camels in Egypt, and walking across glaciers in Switzerland, clad in fashionable bustles. In this country, the seaside resort was gaining in popularity. Queen Victoria had made outdoor pursuits fashionable by her example. She had thrown herself into highland life at Balmoral and the activities of the Queen and her family were detailed for the benefit of its middle class readership by the magazine, *The Queen*. Obviously women were beginning to feel the need for more practical dress.

Sporting activities grew in popularity as the century progressed. By the Edwardian period, young ladies were actively pursuing a variety of sports — walking, climbing, cycling, riding, yachting, automobilisation, tennis, cricket, roller-skating, etc. However, there was no necessary connection between the increase in activity and the development of comfortable dress. Mrs Peel wrote in the 1880s:

'For tennis we wore long skirts with bustles, washing shirts with stiff linen collars, ties and mannish straw hats. The meeting place of shirt and skirt were hidden by a Petersham belt and kept in place at the back by an ornamental safety pin stuck through the belt.' (12)

Until the development by Burberry in 1904 of the 'Free Stroke Coat' with the pivot sleeve and adjustable skirt, ladies had to play a very modified form of golf because their clothes inhibited the swinging of the clubs.

Nevertheless, changes in women's dress did take place to accommodate these new activities. Special clothes for sport were exhibited at the International Health exhibition, including cycling wear. Costumes for the Ladies Cycling Tourist Club were made by Mr T.W. Goodman, a tailor of Albemarle Street. The costume consisted of a Norfolk jacket and a long skirt covering knickerbockers with tweed hat to match. At first, tricycling and, later, bicycling were the pursuits of the rich who were taken by carriage to a park such as Battersea Park where they would mount their bicycles for exercise, in the same way as they had taken exercise on horseback. By the mid-nineties, cycling had become tremendously popular. Hyde Park was opened to cyclists and William Whiteley sold a consignment of five hundred bicycles in a matter of days. The need for greater mobility meant that baggy knickerbockers or bloomers were worn by many women and girls, although often they were concealed under long skirts. Where Mrs Bloomer and Viscountess Haberton had failed the bicycle had succeeded. The degree of liberation should not be overestimated, for many women and girls remained excessively modest, and bloomers were one means of preserving that modesty. Describing the cycling costume, Mrs Ballin wrote in 1885: 'Lined with flannel it is worn over woollen combinations and flannel body instead of stays, to which the knickerbockers to match the dress are buttoned...of course these unmentionables do not show but a lady clothed in this way is better able to face the risks of accidents.' (13) Others were less cautious and modest, Gwen Raverat recalls cycling in 'baggy knickerbockers over frocks and over our frilly drawers. We thought this horribly improper but rather grand...'. (14) Perhaps the bicycle brought as much social liberation as it did freedom of dress, for it provided mobility and a welcome release from constant chaperonage for the Edwardian girl.

Both the tennis costume with its stiff collar and tie, and the cycling costume with its tailored Norfolk jacket and matching hat owe much to the men's fashions of the day. The attempts to produce more practical ladies' sportswear seem to have resulted in

Before going for a spin Miss Jenny is very careful not to forget to put in her glove a few Poncelet's Pastilles. She can avoid all risk of cold by keeping one in her mouth now and then when riding.

LISTEN! YOU WHO COUGH, TO GOOD ADVICE, **PONCELET'S PASTILLES.**

Poncelet's Pastilles are most Agreeable to the Taste. They Prevent and Cure Coughs, Colds, Bronchitis, Hoarseness, Throat Irritation, &c., when all other remedies have failed. Their Action is Immediate.

1s. 1½d. PER BOX OF 100. OF ALL CHEMISTS.

Wholesale Depot: FASSETT & JOHNSON, 31 & 32, Snow Hill, London, E.C.

Fig. 5.6 Practical cycling costumes 1899 (Mary Evans Picture Library).

a peculiar hybrid of traditional female attire in combination with the more uncomfortable aspects of men's clothes. Another style undoubtedly inspired by menswear was the 'tailor-made'. Two couturiers claim credit for making this sporting costume popular – Henry Creed and John Redfern. Henry Creed lays claim to making the tweed suit popular for travel and sport when he made the Duke and Duchess of Alba suits from the same tweed fabric. John Redfern had a draper's business in Cowes which became the centre of the yatching world. The rich were taking to yachting in a big way and Redfern began to cater for their needs. He developed a ladies' tailoring section where he produced tailored yachting suits. In 1885 he was commissioned to provide a travelling suit, yachting suit and riding habit for the trousseau of Princess Beatrice. A variety of sporting outfits were becoming essential parts of an Edwardian lady's wardrobe. Fashionable clothes were divided into

Fig. 5.7 The Edwardian tweed suit.

two categories — those for town and those for country and sports-wear. The former remained ornate and luxurious but sportswear took on the practical and serviceable appearance that the dress reformers had craved.

It was therefore to fashionable sportswear that the new career girl turned for the practical styles she needed. They were reproduced in cheaper fabrics and in simplified form. The 'tailor-made' worn with a stiff collared shirt and tie, and straw boater became the uniform of the 'New woman'. It was not really so emancipated; the waist was tight and the skirts and underskirts were still long and trailed in the mud. *But the severe masculine style gave it an efficient no-nonsense look which expressed the attitudes of women who were determined to show they were the equals of men and wanted to be treated as such.*

References

1. Courrèges *The Guardian* (1979).
2. White, C. (1970) *Women's Magazines 1693–1968.* (Michael Joseph) 42.
3. Adburgham, A. (1964) *Shops and Shopping 1810–1914.* (George Allen and Unwin) 91.
4. White, C. (1970) *Women's Magazines 1693–1968.* (Michael Joseph) 52.
5. Veblen, T. (1931) *The Theory of the Leisure Class.* (New York: Random House Modern Library).
6. Extract from 'First Report of the Children's Employment Commission, Mines' *Parliamentary Paper 1842.* In: *Victorian Culture and Society* (1975), ed. E.C. Black. (Harper and Row) 172.
7. White, C. (1970) *Women's Magazines 1693–1968.* (Michael Joseph) 151–181.
8. By 1914, one hundred out of the three hundred assistants employed by Peter Robinson were women.
9. Beale, Dr Lionel 'The laws of health in relation to the mind and body' 46 and Mrs Merrifield *Dress as Art* (1850) 105–106.
10. Members of the Brotherhood, included Millais, Rosetti, Hunt and Watts.
11. Newton, S. (1974) *Health, Art and Reason.* (John Murray).
12. Adburgham, A. (1964) *Shops and Shopping 1810–1914.* (George Allen and Unwin) 33.
13. *ibid.*
14. *ibid.*

6 Into the Twentieth Century

Edwardian Splendour

The attempts to bring about the emancipation of women and reform their dress had met with only limited success by the turn of the century. Although new opportunities existed for middle class women in education and employment, they were taken up almost exclusively by single women. Only a few penetrated the higher professions – medicine, the Civil Service, and university teaching. Most opportunities were in shop work, clerical work, nursing, and teaching in elementary schools and these jobs brought little in terms of status or income. For upper and middle class families, status was still achieved by ensuring that both mother and daughters did as little arduous and useful work as possible.

The respectable working class man preferred his wife not to work outside the home. For many families this was not possible, and of course most single girls had to work. In the North there was industrial work: women were a vital source of labour in the textiles industry and women still did heavy labouring jobs at pit heads and coal tips in some parts. However, the alternatives to poorly paid industrial work were few, and in many cases worse. Women tended to be concentrated in those areas of work with very poor conditions and poor pay for example the sweated trades such as dressmaking, millinery, sack-making and box-making. In these trades women worked in their own homes or workshops and were paid derisory sums for very long hours. Of course, domestic service provided employment for many working class women but the conditions were disliked and when given the opportunity during the war, many women left as soon as they could for other work and did not return.

As women entered the twentieth century, they still did not have the vote; they could not be awarded a degree from Oxford or Cambridge; they were excluded from certain professions; and they were discriminated against in the law and in social attitudes. Although some things had changed much had remained the same.

This was certainly true of dress. More practical styles had been developed for sport, which had been adapted for working dress, but mainstream Edwardian fashion brought little relief from restrictive or extravagant dress. The figure was still corseted, now moulded into an S-shape with bosom pushed forward and hips thrust back. The styles remained ornate. The fabrics were light-coloured fragile lawns and chiffons. A lady was still hampered by a trailing bell-shaped skirt, rustling petticoats, huge hats, boned collars, gloves and by the complex etiquette of dress. Although the ideal image of woman had changed from the demure girlish figure of the Victorian period to that of the mature woman supposedly favoured by Edward VII, ladies were expected to be decorative appendages to male existence. This description of a tea-gown, that very Edwardian garment, reveals a great deal about Edwardian fashion and the women who wore it.

'For any woman making her round of country house visits, the tea-gown is quite as important an item as the tailor-made costume. Indeed one might almost say more so, for certainly gorgeous variety at the witching hour of tea is more appreciated by the returning sportsman as he stretches his tired limbs in the depths of a luxurious armchair than the neat cloth suits which achieved a general grunt of approval when the women joined the guns at lunch in the coverts. It gives a man a sort of luxurious feel of being an Oriental Pasha, as he lies in his chair, smoking the ever present cigarette, to see himself surrounded by graceful houris clad in gauze and gorgeous draperies, shimmering with rainbow colours...(the following creation) would suggest dreams of houris when viewed through the blue cigarette smoke after a long day with the partridges.

'The long plain fourreau of maize Liberty soft satin is cut somewhat on Empire lines and has a little bodice of maize chiffon crossed at the breast and held by two bands of satin. The full sleeves of the chiffon are simply tied at the elbow with maize velvet ribbon. Over the satin robe is a long sleeveless coat of coarse filet net, edged all round with a narrow band of sable or mink fur and embroidered all over with a large pattern of conventional roses in every shade of brown and copper in heavy silks interspersed with brown and copper iridescent tube sequins at intervals. The rich colouring of autumn is expressed in this beautiful but simple gown, while the note of symbolism which is one of the most subtle fascinations of the tea-gown finds utterances in the brown faded roses of the silk embroideries.' (*Country Life*, September 1907.) (1)

The image of the Oriental despot and his houris is hardly one which suggests emancipation for women. The influence of the

Fig. 6.1 Edwardian splendour.

Orient and the Middle East was strong in fashion and art, not least in the work of Bakst and his designs for the Ballet Russe, and the fashion designer Poiret.

But at the same time as some women were enjoying lunch with the guns, or the witching hour of tea on the country estates, others were chaining themselves to railings and struggling to bring about the emancipation of women. It was as their campaign entered its militant phase in 1908 that a marked change in fashion occurred. Poiret's introduction of the straight silhouette is sometimes hailed as the beginning of modern fashion, and he claimed to have liberated women. The style was in fact a curious combination of liberation and restriction; it freed the waist to follow a more natural line but the legs were shackled by a hobble skirt. Although the silhouette looked more like the line of a man's suit, it was still a hampering line. It was created for the wealthy and privileged and, as in the past, indicated that the wearer would find it impossible to do anything other than look decorative.

However, the hobble skirt did bring some benefits for women. It made underwear simpler and put an end to the Edwardian petticoats with frills and flounces. In its most extreme and fashionable form, the hobble skirt almost immobilised the wearer, but the active middle class woman could adapt the style by inserting discreet pleats or slits. The close-fitting nature of skirts inevitably made them shorter, and the 'trotteur', a walking skirt of above ankle length was very popular. Many women may have *wanted* to look 'shackled' and in need of protection, but they also *needed* more freedom. But the most significant changes in women's dress in terms of freedom and practicality were to come during the First World War.

Women at war

The First World War changed British society. How did it affect women? How did it affect their dress?

When war was declared in August 1914, many people thought it would be over by Christmas. The British would teach the 'hun' a lesson and life would return to normal. Of course, the war was to drag on and make tremendous demands on the nation, and the longer it lasted the more it affected women. In the early days, a wave of enthusiasm for war swept the country and although there were objectors, jingoistic fervour took hold of many people. Men volunteered in their thousands to serve King and Country, and women were eager to do their part. The suffragettes called off their campaign against the Government and supported the war effort. They, like other women, were eager to encourage men to fight and handed out white feathers to young men not in uniform. Some women volunteered to fight abroad or to serve as nurses. In the early days many such offers were turned down by the military authorities, and the employment of women was resisted in many quarters by trades unions, male workers and employers. But it was in the fields of both employment and voluntary service that women were to play such a vital role in the life of the nation and on the battlefields. It was their success in these fields which changed attitudes to women and opened up the way to greater equality.

At first the war led to a decline in the employment of women, as the trades in which they were traditionally employed (textiles, dressmaking and food) suffered setbacks. Almost half the women employed in dressmaking and millinery were thrown out of work or put on short time as fashionable ladies patriotically turned their attention away from new clothes and fancy hats. From the earliest days the upper and middle class women had been organising relief and hospital work, raising funds, making bandages, and caring for the wounded. As prices rose and the hardship of wives left behind by volunteer husbands increased, these ladies organised charity work for those in difficulties. The First Aid Nursing Yeomanry (FANYs) had been formed in 1907 in anticipation of war and ladies with their own mount volunteered. Similarly, the Voluntary Aid Detachment (VADs) were formed in 1909 for home service in case of an invasion. Because the work was unpaid, they relied on middle class volunteers, many of whom were ill-qualified for the work which they eventually had to undertake. Nor did the upper class women confine themselves to welfare work; they also formed uniformed groups like the Volunteer Reserve. The uniform designed by this group for themselves provided the basic model for the uniforms of the women's services formed later in the war.

The employment of ordinary women began to pick up in 1915, not only as wartime demand stimulated their traditional trades, but also in the 'substitution' of women to free men for military service. They began to work in jobs previously thought unsuitable for women. Some merely took over their husband's work in a family business and worked as blacksmiths and even chimney sweeps, but others were recruited into such jobs as ticket collectors, railway porters, postwomen, delivery girls, and van drivers, and into the Police Service.

The trade unions were opposed to the employment of women in factories; they feared eventual loss of jobs for men and lowering of wage rates. Through agreements with the unions, where women did take over men's jobs they were paid less than men. Nevertheless, the advantage of working in 'men's jobs' was that on the whole women received higher wages than those paid in the trades normally associated with women. London bus conductresses were one of the two groups of workers to get equal pay; the other was women welders. The bus conductresses earned £2 5s a week (compared with the 11s 7d average industrial wage for women before the war). This enabled a woman to support herself in some comfort and wages like this and the increased personal freedoms attracted many women out of domestic service.

This trend continued with the entry of women into munitions.

Fig. 6.2 Women workers loading sacks of coke at the South Metropolitan Gas Works, London (Imperial War Museum).

The shortage of shells, and the heavy casualities at the front which led to universal male conscription in 1916 created more opportunities for women. The workers in munitions were soon predominantly female. Although they worked long hours in dangerous conditions, it was the wages that attracted many women into the work. In the dangerous workshops a woman could earn up to £5 a week with overtime. This new affluence allowed the working class woman to buy better food than before the war, and indulge herself in the purchase of fashionable clothes. Middle class society was shocked by reports that such girls were buying themselves fur coats. This experience changed the expectations of working class women about their conditions of work, their pay and the goods they wanted to buy.

Fig. 6.3 Bus conductress (Imperial War Museum).

The deteriorating situation in 1916 brought pressure to admit women to two other crucial areas on a formal basis: the land and the armed services. Farmers had not responded to attempts to encourage the employment of women but in 1917 the Women's Land Army was formed and women were directed to farms and forestry plantations. Although not as well paid as some other war work, many girls volunteered and went off to a physically demanding outdoor life in their breeches and boots. The women's sections of the armed services also came into being in 1917. There was still some doubt about women's ability to take command and 'to keep their heads' and women were employed as back-up support for the fighting men as clerks, typists, cooks, drivers, messengers and mechanics.

In civilian life there was an increased demand for women to work as typists, clerks and secretaries in commerce but also in administration. These jobs were not to disappear like so many of the others after the war; the independent 'business girl' was to survive and prosper in post-war society. She had the means and independence to enjoy the lifestyle of pre-war bachelors:

> 'The war-time business girl is to be seen any night dining out alone or with a friend in the moderate-priced restaurants in London. Formerly she would never have had her evening meal in town unless accompanied by a man friend. But now with money and without men, she is more and more beginning to dine out.' (2)

New social patterns for women were beginning to emerge.

The business girl could not only afford to go out in the evening but also to live away from home and the authority of her parents. These new freedoms were being enjoyed by women of all classes – munitions workers, land girls, nurses and women serving in the armed forces – many of whom were living away from home in camps, hostels or lodgings. Women recounted with pleasure their wartime escapades and adventures – trips to Paris Plage, flying in aeroplanes without permission, taking their boyfriends out in military vehicles, going out with officers and being found 'in the bushes'. The freer association of the sexes, away from the supervision of family and neighbours may have caused the rise in the rate of illegitimate births. However, moral standards were beginning to change, and unmarried mothers were not treated as harshly as in the past. In the munitions industry in particular, they were well-cared for and allowed to return to work after the birth of the baby. Increasing concern for the unmarried mother and the welfare of her child was reflected in the establishment of the National Council for the Unmarried Mother and Her Child in 1918 which sought to reform the laws concerning illegitimacy, and to improve the help available to women.

Although the war did bring benefits to women in terms of employment and new freedoms, it also brought hardship and un-happiness to many. Many women were left to bring up families and run the home alone, and others close to the war were brought face to face with the appalling carnage it involved. Perhaps some of the most harrowing experiences were those of the nurses and VADs who nursed the wounded. Many came from middle class back-grounds and had led very sheltered lives, yet not only were they nursing men but men with horrific wounds. The VADs who had very little training had to nurse men with limbs blown off, suppu-rating wounds, dysentery, severe shock, and those suffering the effects of mustard gas. They were all too familiar with the cost of the war in life, and some recounted how sadly they watched the battalions marching to the front knowing only too well how few would return. In her autobiography *Testament of Youth*, Vera Brittain records the hardships she encountered as a VAD, and the loss of a brother and so many friends in the war. But she also is terribly proud of being able to do something useful, even though it involved the giving up of her much longed for university education:

> 'Nothing would induce me to stop what I am doing now, and I would never respect myself again if I allowed a few physical hardships to make me give up what is the finest work any girl can do now....'.

After the war, Lloyd George acknowledged the enormous contri-bution women had made to the ultimate victory: 'It would have been impossible for us to have waged a successful war had it not been for the skill, ardour, enthusiasm and industry which the women of this country have thrown into this war'. This praise was extended to women from all classes.

The contingencies of war had forced men to change their attitudes. In the first place they had to concede to the necessity of women's labour, not only to replace men drawn into active service but to expand the labour force for the war effort. Secondly they had to acknowledge that in the event women proved themselves capable of doing the same work as men and doing it well. Moreover, it was not only 'tough' working class women who proved themselves.

'Ladies of leisure' showed they too could face hardship and hard work with courage and determination. They were not totally weak and in need of protection. *The basis on which equality had been withheld from women was being undermined.*

The involvement of women from all classes in employment or voluntary service, and their removal from the domestic sphere, began to change social conventions. The finer points of proper behaviour for women began to disappear. Chaperonage was abandoned, women could dance more than one consecutive dance with the same partner without causing a scandal, they began to smoke and wear make-up. Women could now go out to restaurants, dances and the cinema with friends. They experienced a taste of the freedom previously enjoyed only by young men and were reluctant to relinquish it.

New freedoms in dress

To what extent did women's dress reflect these new freedoms and in what ways did it contribute to it?

The war years 1914—18 is a very short period in our study of women's dress but it is one in which women's dress changed quite considerably and in which the foundations for a much freer dress for women were laid. During the war women's dress changed as both a consequence and a mark of their changing role in society and acceptance of that role.

At first there was very little change in fashionable styles. It has been suggested that fashion reflected the view that women's 'mission in life was to be elegant and gracious; to soothe and inspire the tired warrior when he came home'. (3) But in 1915 when it became obvious the war was not going to be over with the speed that had originally been anticipated and it became apparent that women would be called upon to take an active role, the hobble skirt disappeared and was replaced by a shorter, fuller skirt. As the war went on women became increasingly active. Not only did the war increase the female labour force by about 1 345 000 but fewer led lives of leisure even amongst those not involved in paid employment. If not contributing to voluntary work, more middle class women were forced to look after at least their homes and families!

The many women working in factories or replacing men in other work needed practical and comfortable clothes. They wore uniforms, or overalls which were designed to be serviceable and protective rather than decorative. Pamphlets issued to factory workers advised against the wearing of stiff and tight corsets, and heavy skirts which restricted movement and could be dangerous. Women were encouraged to wear caps to cover their hair to prevent injury. Some women began to cut their hair short, but many retained their 'crowning glory' despite the problems of keeping it clean and free from lice. Although it was considered daring at first, during the war it was accepted that women workers should wear trousers for rough tasks. Many photographs show women delivery girls, mechanics and munitions workers in trousers and boiler suits and, of course, land girls in their breeches. Trousers, the symbol of masculinity, were no longer completely taboo for women, but were considered suitable in *certain* circumstances. This opened the way for trousers to be worn as leisure-wear and fashion in later decades, as women enjoyed the freedom and comfort of such garments.

The war brought large numbers of women into uniform for the first time. Apart from those of the nurses, the uniforms worn by women in the Police Service, on the railways, trams, etc., and in the armed services, were very similar to men's uniforms in fabric and style. They were fairly bulky but comfortable, and worn with a fairly short skirt. The style acknowledged women's need to move about unheeded. They played down the 'feminine' aspects of appearance.

Of course, the world of fashion continued to produce luxurious and extravagant styles, particularly in Paris. The war certainly did not involve all women, or women all of the time. There was still a demand for feminine and attractive clothes. There were still plenty of tea-gowns, evening dresses and pretty dresses in the shops. However, on the whole, clothes became easy-fitting, even shapeless. They tended to be bulky but they were much freer than any previous fashionable clothes. Some fashionable styles resembled uniforms, obviously representing a trend to greater simplicity and comfort in civilian clothes as well as reflecting the mood of wartime.

As we have seen, the war brought comparative affluence to some women workers and they were able to afford fur coats and some fashionable clothes. The simpler styles represented a move away from the extravagant elitism of fashion of former times, and were *wearable*, not just a form of display.

During the war, large numbers of women were brought into the work-force, not because it was thought to be a good thing for women or that it would bring them confidence and independence, but because their labour was needed. New demands were made on women and in order for those demands to be met, dress styles had to change. The benefits of clothes designed for work or as uniforms were incorporated to some extent into civilian dress and fashionable styles, which themselves were changing to accommodate women's new activities. In periods like the First World War, it seems that rapid changes in dress are precipitated by changing social and political needs rather than the creative force of particular individuals.

References

1. Stevenson, P. (1980) *Edwardian Fashion*. (Ian Allen) 11.
2. *Daily Mail* September 1915.
3. Ewing, E. (1974) *A History of Twentieth Century Fashion*. (London: B.T. Batsford).

7 Women between the Wars

Substantial changes had occurred in the position of women and in their style of dress during the First World War, but were these changes to last? In fact, the years between the wars saw moods of both progressivism and conservativism in relation to both the roles and dress of women. The flapper with her boyish looks and emancipated habits is the dominant image of a twenties woman, but the thirties brought a reassertion of traditional values and a return to elegant and feminine styles. How can we explain these social and fashion changes?

THE TWENTIES

One of the dominant factors affecting women in this period was the loss of so many young men during the war. This had created a substantial imbalance in the population, particularly in the younger age groups. In 1921, in England and Wales, for every 1000 men between 20 and 40 years of age there were 1172 women. The situation was made worse by the lack of employment opportunities for men. After a brief post-war boom, there were a million out of work by 1921 and figures remained high throughout the twenties. Many young men went abroad to the colonies in search of work. This imbalance meant that some women had to face the fact that they would be denied the possibility of marriage and motherhood, the traditional sources of both financial security and emotional satisfaction. What alternative ways of living were there?

At first sight it seemed that women were set for political and economic equality at the turn of the decade. They had been given the vote and the right to stand for Parliament before the end of the war. However, the vote was restricted to women over thirty who were householders themselves or married to householders. The vote on equal terms with men was delayed until 1928, and even then some men feared the effects of the numerical domination of women on the electoral register. The Sexual Disqualification (Removal) Act of 1919 promised equality of opportunity: 'A person shall not be disqualified by sex or marriage from the exercise of any public function, or from being appointed to or holding any civil or judicial office or post, from entering or assuming or carrying on any civil profession or vocation'. (1) The war had made the employment of single women from all sections of society acceptable and in 1921 71 per cent of all single women were employed. Now the professions were open to women; they could become barristers, solicitors and engineers and in theory all 'top posts' were within their reach. However, when the war ended, men had returned to claim back their jobs and women workers were dismissed. The spirit of the Act had been undermined by the Government itself when it had ordered the dismissal of thousands of women from their war-time occupations in government service, but also when it required women employed in the Civil Service and in teaching to resign their posts on marriage. It was generally assumed, not least by women themselves, that the returning heroes had a superior claim to employment. The single working woman was accepted but not the working wife!

After the war, many women were forced back into the poorly paid jobs in textiles, clothing retailing and domestic service which were traditionally regarded as women's work. But there were also some significant changes and new opportunities for single working women of working and middle class origin. Despite the economic problems of the twenties, and the high rates of unemployment in some areas, there were some expanding industries which provided new employment opportunities. There was a general expansion in the service and light industries, and particularly in fields such as electrical engineering there was a growing demand for women workers. Women had been used as cheap labour for repetitive assembly work during the war and this pattern continued in the twenties in such 'new' industries. There was also a growth in employment opportunities in the expanding worlds of banking, insurance, and commerce, and in the Civil Service and local government. Typing and clerical work were now becoming primarily identified as women's work and so women were able to take advantage of the overall increase in clerical work, even if their rates of pay were well below the male rate for the job.

There also had been a shift away from the employment of working class girls and women in domestic service. Although there was still a tremendous demand for domestic help, and over a million women were still employed in such work, over four hundred thousand women had refused to return to it after the war. After the freedom of war-time factory work − the regular hours, good rates of pay and companionship of fellow workers − some women were reluctant to return to the long hours of domestic drudgery under the critical eye of the mistress. Many preferred to seek employment in factories, shops or even offices. This meant that many suburban housewives and daughters had to take on the burden of domestic labour in their own homes.

Although the single working girl was part of twenties life, it is important to remember that about two-thirds of all women in the twenties were still largely concerned with domestic work either in their own homes as unpaid help or as employees. Society still regarded women as *homemakers*. So natural was this role for women that 30 per cent of single women were classified as 'not gainfully employed'. Magazines like *Good Housekeeping*, first published in 1922, emphasised the virtues and importance of domesticity. It also stressed a new 'professionalism' that women should bring to housework, with the aid of the new electrical labour-saving devices now available to the middle class housewife. For many, whether middle or working class, a woman's place was still in the home.

During the war there had to be a reassessment of attitudes to women and their role. This questioning of traditional attitudes was to continue in the atmosphere of change which was so pervasive in the twenties. There were new developments in science, technology, transport and the arts; there were new products to buy and new ways of advertising and selling them; there were new forms of entertainment, new places to go and new things to do. There was also a sense of social liberation and change especially amongst the young, an urge to defy the 'stuffy' conventions of pre-war social behaviour.

The image we get of the 'Roaring Twenties', the 'Jazz Age', is one of youthful exuberance and hedonism, personified by the 'Bright Young Things' and of course the flapper. The younger generation seemed to have a social dominance they had never had before. The popular press of the twenties delighted in recounting tales of 'orgies' (a favourite twenties word) and escapades of the Bright Young Things, and the middle-aged and the middle class were suitably shocked.

'Their morals were lax and promiscuous, their manners at the best casual and the worst abominable. They live on cocktails, never answer letters, wreck borrowed cars, make apple pie beds for honoured guests in historic houses, spend their nights in night clubs, and mock and ill-use their parents.' (Lady Violet Bonham Carter.) (2)

The Bright Young Things were obviously a minority, members of the extremely wealthy Mayfair set. Their behaviour was wild and unruly, even childish. But they had their imitators and they shared with many others in Britain a passion for dancing, cocktails, fast cars, energetic and daring sports, and a fascination with sex. All these things had implications for women and the way they were regarded.

Since before the war, both high society and the population in general had been experiencing the influence of American culture. The field of entertainment − music, dance, the cinema and night-life − is just one aspect of that influence. An important change for the wealthy, which was partly the consequence of their changing financial position as well as new social customs, was that evening entertainment was becoming increasing public. They were entertaining less in their own homes; cocktail parties were replacing banquets and receptions. The young in particular frequented smart cocktail bars and night clubs. The strict social etiquettes did not apply, they could dance to the early hours with energy and abandon to the music of black entertainers. The less well-off could also enjoy the exhilaration of the Black Bottom or the Charleston, or the seduction of the Tango at the new 'palais de danse' that were springing up everywhere. They could listen to bands like the Dixieland Jazz Band and sip their ice-cream sodas. Men and women mixed freely and the new equality of social relations established during the war continued. If they wished, women could smoke in public, they shared the same slang as men, perhaps even got 'blotto' on cocktails! Partners could now hold each other with 'familiarity' but women remained at a disadvantage. The shortage of partners meant that a young lady might be invited to a party on the condition that she brought her own partner, and at dance halls women had to dance together or hire the services of a male 'taxi-dancer'.

Despite such problems, many young women seemed determined to enjoy life. They had joined men at work and they were not going to be left behind at play. They, too, enjoyed the thrills of riding around on motorbikes, or going for a spin in a car. After all, the flapper took her name from the flapper bracket of a motor cycle. The glamorous heroines of novels and films were portrayed as drivers, not just passengers. For instance, the promiscuous and ill-fated Iris Storm, heroine of the novel, *The Green Hat*, committed suicide at the wheel of her motor car. The growing availability of motorbikes, second-hand cars and cheaper new ones meant that cars were losing their exclusive image; they were no longer only playthings for the rich.

In the suburbs, young men and women threw themselves with great energy and enthusiasm into sports like tennis and golf, the more wealthy enjoyed skiing and the more daring flying. Energy and daring were admired in both sexes. Women became sports

Fig. 7.1 Lady motorcyclists 1925 (BBC Hulton Picture Library).

'personalities' like Suzanne Lenglen who was the centre of attention at Wimbledon, not least because of her revealing and more practical tennis clothes designed by Patou. Her style was to revolutionise tennis clothes for women. Others wanted to prove they could do what men could do, like Gertrude Ederle who swam the Channel, and pilots like Amy Johnson, the solo flier who proved that an ordinary girl from Hull could do better than the ordinary 'next man'.

Men felt challenged by the modern girl. She no longer needed his protection: she could earn her own living, she could drive, she could beat him at tennis, but perhaps most alarming — she now knew all about sex! In the twenties there does seem to have been a heightening awareness of and interest in sex. It was discussed in intellectual circles, discussed in the courts, written about in novels and in the newspapers, and displayed on the cinema screen. Sex was no longer a taboo topic.

The work of Freud and Havelock Ellis stimulated a new frankness about sex in intellectual circles. Freud's ideas had been used in the treatment of shell-shocked soldiers in the First World War, and some of them were to become popular in a simplified or modified form. For example, the popular misconceptions of his ideas about repression were used to suggest those who repressed their sexual impulses could become mentally ill. Now, sex was good for you! Havelock Ellis' study *The Psychology of Sex* led to the consideration of sex from a woman's point of view. Questions were raised about what Ellis termed 'the erotic rights of women' and the ability of men to satisfy those demands. Marie Stopes' book, *Married Love*, dealt with the issue of a wife's enjoyment of sex and gave practical advice on how maximum pleasure might be achieved. Such topics obviously shocked and horrified many people but in *some* circles at least it was acknowledged that women could and should enjoy sex without this being evidence of a totally depraved character. In addition, perhaps for the first time, men who had been brought up in a society which assumed a man had to keep his impulses in check, now found their sexual confidence challenged by the fear of being 'inadequate'. The popular press cruelly exploited this issue in their coverage of the case of Lord Inverclyde who was divorced for failing to consummate his marriage to a beautiful actress in musical comedy.

The cinema was enormously popular and directors like Griffiths and De Mille lost no opportunity to depict sex and display nudity on the screen even if it was usually under the guise of criticising the excesses of some earlier period. The love scenes of the twenties now seem ludicrously torrid. The absence of sound meant that all amorous emotions had to be expressed by the pouting of lips, rolling of eyes, and writhing of limbs. The predatory female was to be found represented on the cinema screen if nowhere else. Theda Bara, a quiet respectable woman in real life, created the vamp in her film *A Fool There Was*. The female vampire was sexually attractive and immoral; she could bring total ruin to a man caught in her web of seduction. Heavily made up to give the impression of smouldering passion, the vamp appeared in costumes frequently inspired by spiders' webs. Stars like Gloria Swanson portrayed women who knew about sex and were strong enough characters to show men who was boss. But not everyone was in this mould; there was the innocent Mary Pickford and the playful tease, Clara Bow, both looking not for independence but romance. Cinema was becoming one of the major forces in moulding women's ideas of how they should look and how they should behave, and of course, how men should look and behave.

A new male hero was also emerging. One of the most popular books of the decade was M.C. Hull's *The Sheik*, the tale of a girl raped by an 'Arab' who actually turns out to be English. The forceful lover became the new heart-throb, portrayed in the movies by Rudolph Valentino. Dressed either in riding breeches or in the costume of a ruthless 'sheik' and usually carrying a whip, he 'strode through reel after reel, hurling women about as though they were sacks of potatoes and smacking them on the bottom'. (3) It seemed in the world of popular fiction and cinema that however emancipated a woman might seem, all she really needed was to meet a *real* man who could show her who was boss and into whose powerful embrace she would eventually surrender herself and, what is more, enjoy the consequences.

This focus on sexual matters created anxiety amongst the older generations about declining moral standards. Ideas about sex were changing but there was no wholesale sexual revolution in the twenties. Although some women did take lovers and the Bright Young Things included sexual promiscuity as part of their creed, sexual liberation was much more a cultural stance than a reality for most young women. Certainly their social habits, interests and appearance represented a stance of defiance and disregard for their elders' views but the average girl was much more of a 'chum' or a 'sport' than a seductress, more of a Clara Bow than a Theda Bara in her relationships with men. There is no evidence to suggest there was a widespread change in sexual morality; in fact illegitimacy rates fell during the twenties and there was no adequate means of contraception available to single women. Those single girls who did become pregnant had to pay the social costs as in the past.

There were, however, significant changes in sexual attitudes as far as married women were concerned which had important consequences for the way marriage and the role of women were viewed. A new sexual equality was accorded to women in divorce; the Matrimonial Causes Act (1923) gave women the right to divorce their husbands on the grounds of adultery alone. The double standard of morality was no longer embodied in the law. Although the revised prayer book was rejected by Parliament in 1928, some clergy used some of the revisions to allow emancipated brides to omit the wife's vow to obey her husband in the marriage ceremony. But perhaps the most important changes for women were those affecting their role as mothers. They were given equal guardianship of their children in 1925 and the right to legitimise a child by subsequent marriage to the father.

In the twenties there seems to have been a fundamental change in attitudes to family size. The birth rate fell sharply in the twenties, 46 per cent of women married after 1920 had only one or two children and the trend to smaller families was noticeable in all classes. Dr Marie Stopes, whose book *Married Love* gave advice to women and men on how the sexual pleasure experienced by women in marriage could be increased, also argued that it was important for the health of the mother that children should be spaced. In her second book, *Wise Parenthood*, she gave practical advice on contraception and she founded the first birth control clinic for working women. Inevitably, there was a great deal of hostility to her work. She was accused of undermining marriage by giving women a licence to be unfaithful to their husbands, of 'purveying a beastly and filthy message', but by the end of the decade 'family planning' for *married* women had become acceptable. Birth control became widely used; one survey showed that of women married between 1925 and 1929, 61 per cent had used some form of birth control. Women were at last released from incessant and involuntary childbearing and some could look forward to a healthier and longer life than their mothers.

In the twenties, however, much had remained the same for women. The majority were still concerned with domestic work;

few reached senior positions in employment; and women were paid substantially less than men doing similar work. But if we compare women in the twenties with their demure and passive counterparts from the Victorian period we can see just how much things had changed. Single women from all social classes had more opportunities for employment and financial independence; women in general had greater social and political equality; they were more active, fitter and stronger; and they were having fewer children. They also looked very different!

Short skirts, short hair and lipstick

After the war there seemed to be a return to longer more feminine styles but this was not to last:

> 'I think we were trying to be feminine after the war worker in trousers and uniforms but the pendulum quickly swung back. Soon the heroine of every novel was described as "boyish"... Hems went down nearly to the ground in 1923 but were up to the knees by 1925, and the waistline wandered high and low but throughout the twenties bosoms and hips were definitely *out*. A lovely figure meant a perfectly straight figure and the slightest suggestion of a curve was scorned as fat. The ideal woman's vital statistics would probably have been something like 30−30−30.' (4)

Although knee-length skirts were only fashionable for a maximum of four years and were most popular with the young, ankle-length skirts have never again been generally worn by women for daywear. Not everyone could or even wanted to achieve the 'ideal' figure described by the Duchess of Westminster but the tubular silhouette was characteristic of the twenties and influenced many who were far from young and highly fashionable. (Fig. 7.2) The extreme of twenties style was the short, straight sleeveless, V-necked chemise dress worn with a net cloche over short hair. For not only were women's clothes changing − many women now had short hair and wore make-up.

To what extent did dress reflect or create women's sense of emancipation?

It has been suggested that these changes in women's appearance were a *consequence* of the changing role of women in society. Now that women worked alongside men they ought to look less fussy

Fig. 7.2 Short hair, short skirts and tubular silhouette.

and feminine. Whether the changes in employment for single women and the changes in social attitudes to women actually *produced* these stylistic changes or not, it is clear that these styles resulted in much greater freedom of movement for those wishing to work or engage in active pursuits than other fashionable styles to date.

Women were no longer encased in stays or corsets, although some women wishing to achieve the perfect tubular figure flattened out their curves by wearing a brassiere (at this point designed to minimise the breasts rather than make them prominent) or a corselette. Petticoats were replaced by 'slips'; women were no longer weighed down by numerous petticoats or concealed under the layers of underwear which had previously been thought necessary for both warmth and decency. The use of crêpe de chine and its cheaper imitator, rayon, had reduced the weight of underwear to ounces. The use of light fabrics such as silks, rayon and jerseys, simpler styles and the general reduction in the amount of clothing worn meant that the clothes of a woman in the twenties probably weighed one tenth of those of her Victorian counterpart. *This fact alone must have given her a sense of physical freedom and pleasure in activity which had been denied to her pre-war sisters.*

Short hair and simple hats brought freedom from the anxiety of keeping a huge or elaborate hat pinned to an equally elaborate hairstyle:

> 'Women cut their hair and everybody said "How practical!"'...The woman who had experienced the comfort of being able to take off her hat at any moment without the apprehension about the state of her hair, or more disorder than could be put to rights by merely running a comb through it, instinctively realised that here was a passport to freedom in daily life which she was not going to let go.' (5)

The convenience of short hair has been appreciated by many women ever since the bob, the shingle and Eton crop of the twenties.

Simpler, more practical and convenient styles were emerging for the active woman. The designer Chanel said 'I make fashions women can live in, breathe in, feel comfortable in and look younger in'. (6) Her style was the antithesis of the extravagance and restrictions of Victorian dress. She introduced 'functional' elegance into daywear with her simple jersey cardigan suit. Her use of cotton, rayon, jerseys and costume jewellery represented a further move away from the traditional elitism of fashion, its opulence and extravagance. Such fabrics and styles made fashion practicable for the ordinary woman with an active rather than leisured lifestyle.

In addition, they were crucial factors in the development of mass-produced ready-to-wear fashions which were to free women from the necessity of making their own clothes, choosing fabrics, attending for fittings, etc., and which gave women the convenience of buying good quality fashionable clothes off the peg!

During the twenties, as the activities of young men and young women became more similar, as they worked in the same offices, shared the same sports and same entertainments, there was some convergence in their styles of dress. It was not just that girls looked 'boyish' or less 'feminine', the appearance of young men changed too. 'It may almost be said that sex is departing from modern clothes, which are becoming interchangeable. Many women wear plus-fours, pyjamas, and dinner jackets, while their suits follow closely the lines of a man's.' (First published in 1927.) (7) Women did borrow men's styles. There was a brief trend amongst the more daring of women for wearing men's evening jackets, lounging pyjamas appeared for evening and beachwear. The tailor-made, often made by a man's tailor, was still very popular − particularly with career women. But if women's hair was getting shorter, some men were wearing their hair longer; hairstyles for some young people became almost identical. The silhouette for men and women, particularly for casual wear became very similar. If women wore tubular garments, men wore wide skirt-like plus-fours and Oxford bags. Knitwear was popular for both sexes in bold patterns and colours. The rising popularity of golf meant brightly coloured Fair Isle, Argyle and other diamond and check-patterned cardigans, sweaters and matching socks were to be seen at the clubhouse and used for casual wear.

The stiff formality of menswear was gradually being undermined and some men envied the liberation in dress that women had achieved. In 1929 the Men's Dress Reform Party was formed. Their aim was to make men's dress more attractive but also more comfortable and hygienic. They particularly disliked the tight collar and trousers which they thought were too hot in summer and concealed the natural line of the limbs. The party suggested re-placing trousers with shorts and boots with sandals. These views were regarded as eccentric by most of the population but there was a growing informality, a desire for comfort, and a trend towards less sober clothes for men. As their dress became more similar it brought some degree of emancipation for both men and women.

However, a new difference in the appearance of the sexes was growing in popularity, one which reasserted the different roles of the sexes and which was not so liberating for women. It was now commonplace for women to wear make-up. In the Victorian period it had been considered immoral to 'paint' one's face and many older people still subscribed to this view. But now women could be seen everywhere pouting at their compact mirror in an attempt to achieve the desired cupid's bow with the aid of lipstick and dabbing at their noses with a powder puff. The advent of Hollywood and its stars had made the open use of cosmetics acceptable but it also brought a new bondage for women, that of trying to look like someone else. Millions of women were confronted by particular images of femininity, and of beauty, and these images could be achieved partly through the use of cosmetics, adopting a particular hairstyle or colour, and plucking one's eyebrows in a certain way. Every woman, no matter how plain, could improve herself by looking a little bit more like a particular heroine of the screen, and it became her duty to do so. From the twenties onwards, cosmetic and toiletries companies were eager to encourage women in such self-improvement, and to supply them with the 'necessary' tools.

So did women really want to look like men?

It may seem a little contradictory that at a time when there was a shortage of men that women should adopt a style which is widely interpreted as 'boyish'. Some writers have suggested that because of the 'close companionship' experienced by men during the First World War, women now had to compete with men for the affections of men. This kind of explanation reflects the preoccupations of the twenties concerning male sexuality, and the fashion for 'Freudian' explanations. Although the look of women did change there is no reason to believe that they looked less attractive as women to the young men of the day. The silhouette was youthful, and its slimness was in marked contrast to the maternal amplitude of the mature figure fashionable at the turn of the century. Perhaps this is not surprising given the emphasis on youth and activity in the twenties, and the apparent decline in the popularity of motherhood. It is probable that young men found the slim, lightly-clad girls attractive in the same way that similar styles in the sixties were seen as attractive. After all, never before had so much of a woman been visible. Legs, arms, chest and back were all revealed by the wearers of the slinky sheath dresses with shoestring straps which were popular in the late twenties. Short skirts exposed more of the female leg to view, and the popularity of beige-coloured stockings gave the illusion of bare legs. (Apparently beige, rather than schoolgirlish black stockings were considered more sexy!) Fine rayon stockings replaced thick woollen and cotton ones, at much lower price than silk.

The new cult of sunbathing was making swimwear and sportswear much more revealing. Attitudes to the sun and the suntan were changing. In Germany the cult of nudism, exposing the body to the sun and air, was becoming popular. The effects of the sun were seen as health-giving. In Britain, sun treatments were being used to help cure tuberculosis and rickets. Sunbathing became a holiday pursuit; it became fashionable for the rich to take their holidays in the south of France and to acquire a deep tan. Previously, of course, all ladies wished to preserve the whiteness of their skins; now a suntan became a status symbol and woman needed garments in which to get maximum exposure and then show it off. By the end of the decade, women were to be seen in tight-fitting jersey swimsuits and shorts.

It is clear that there had been a radical change in standards of decency and modesty for women during the twenties. This change must be seen as part of the general change in attitudes to sexual matters and in social behaviour, in particular those affecting women. Women obviously no longer needed layers of cumbersome clothing to act as a barrier between them and the social and physical worlds they inhabited. They were no longer the passive and modest sex!

However, it would be misleading to place all our emphasis on explanations that attribute changes in women's appearance to changes in their role and social attitudes. The design of their clothing was without doubt influenced by developments in the arts and other spheres of design. Knitwear provides one straightforward case in point. Patterned knitwear clearly shows the influence of Art Deco and Cubism, and Schiaparelli's *trompe-l'oeil* effects such as fake bows were obviously inspired by Surrealism. However, the general tubular shape of women's clothes, the disappearance of the curvaceous feminine silhouette is in accord with clean lines of trends in interior design, furniture and architecture.

Finally, it would also be wrong to give the impression that everyone subscribed to the views outlined above or adopted the styles described. Although access to fashionable styles was gradually expanding and the means of disseminating fashion were becoming more powerful, some people chose not to follow the fashions of the day and many could not. For example, Queen Mary chose to ignore changing hemlines and shifting waistlines and stuck resolutely to her own particular style of long, figure-defining dress and toque hat. In poorer districts, old women were still to be seen in the dark-coloured long skirts, mantles and bonnets of the previous century. There were those excluded by poverty, wives and daughters of the one million unemployed among them, who found it hard enough to clothe themselves and families without worrying whether hemlines had dropped or risen.

Important changes had occurred in the position of women and

their style of dress. Some were to last uninterrupted until the present day, but others were reversed as the decade changed and the world experienced the effects of the Wall Street Crash and a drop of nearly half in the volume of world trade.

THE THIRTIES

The thirties were dominated by the Depression, unemployment, higher taxation and cuts in government expenditure at home, and by the rise of Fascism abroad. The shock of the Wall Street Crash in 1929 marked a shift in mood from the gaiety and progressivism of the twenties to the conservative, even reactionary values which dominated the greater part of the thirties.

How were women affected?

By 1931 unemployment in Britain had risen to almost three million, and an average of 14 per cent of all insured workers were unemployed throughout the thirties. Britain was divided between those living in areas of high unemployment in the North, in Wales and Scotland and those enjoying relative prosperity in the South. Obviously women in different parts of the country were affected in different ways, as were women from the different social classes. In areas of high male-unemployment, men found it difficult to retain their self-respect and position as head of the family, especially after the introduction of the 'Means Test'. In order to draw the dole, a man had to prove he had no savings left but the greatest indignity was that the earnings or savings of any member of his family had to be deducted from his allowance. This meant that many men found themselves living off their wives and children. There was work available for women: either the traditional low-paid work such as taking in washing, charring, baby-minding or — for the younger ones — the new industries, particularly in areas like the South and Midlands. In 1931, the census revealed that 37 per cent of the female population between fourteen and sixty-five were in paid employment but it also showed that the rate of employment peaked between the age of eighteen and twenty. Eighty per cent of eighteen-year-olds were employed but only 65 per cent of twenty-one-year-olds. After the age of twenty-five, the rate dropped to 37 per cent. Young unskilled women were the cheapest form of labour; older women found it much harder to get employment, and there was still a substantial number of older women who needed to earn their own living.

The shortage of work for men created a growing hostility to working women, and particularly to married ones. Women teachers in areas of high unemployment were particularly resented. Although they had suffered a cut in wages they still received much more for themselves than an average working man had to keep his family on. The rule that married teachers had to resign their posts was strictly enforced even though their husbands might be unemployed. Married women also suffered under the cutbacks in Government spending in 1931. A change in the regulations meant that 134 000 women had their unemployment benefit withdrawn before the end of the year. The old idea that if a woman was married then her husband would provide sufficient income for her needs was re-affirmed. Women were either workers *or* wives. But as the economic depression deepened they were encouraged increasingly to think of themselves as the latter! The more liberal attitudes which had made it possible for women to enter medicine, dentistry, law, and accountancy were now out of fashion. The small but steady increase in women entering such fields came to a halt, and in many cases actually declined. The acceptance of the professional woman which had been at best precarious was now undermined.

There was increasing pressure on women to think of their role as primarily one of daughter, sweetheart or wife. The media addressed to women encouraged them to see marriage as their primary goal and the only real means to happiness. Hollywood was producing a predominantly, though not entirely, sentimental diet of romance for the thousands of film-goers in this country. Women were represented as achieving happiness (and financial security) through falling in love. The climax of many films was a marriage. The tremendously popular Fred Astaire and Ginger Rogers musicals consisted of a series of very enjoyable dance routines and songs performed in glamorous settings, with the participants wearing beautiful clothes, and the plot involved the hero and heroine overcoming a series of obstacles before the film culminated in a blissful union. Popular fiction for women provided a similar escape into the world of romance and glamour where love and riches were for once within reach. Women were encouraged to live the life of their screen idols vicariously through the pages of the film magazines.

There were a growing number of publications aimed at the

middle classes which placed women firmly in the home. Daily papers now had a 'Woman's Page', concerned with woman's role as housewife, but more important in the drive to get women back into the home was the growth in number and popularity of magazines for women.

The emphasis of these publications is clear from their titles – *Good Housekeeping* (1922), *Woman and Home* (1926), *My Home* and *Modern Home* (both 1928), *Wife and Home* (1929), *Everywoman's* (1934), *Mother* (1936), *Housewife* (1937). Three magazines published in the thirties were to become the first mass circulation magazines for women – *Woman's Own* (1932), *Woman's Illustrated* (1936) and *Woman* (1937). All had much the same message:

> 'A man's enduring love was the only important thing in a woman's life; and if you did not find the whole absorbing world of shopping, cookery, knitting and bringing up children sufficient to occupy your time and talents, it could only be because there was something the matter with you.' (8)

Women were encouraged to see themselves as 'professionals' within the home, technicians able to wield all kinds of electrical labour-saving equipment. Such tools were largely restricted to the suburban, middle class housewife and they enabled her to take over many if not all of the tasks done by servants in the past. Magazines also encouraged her to raise the standards of comfort in the home and to improve its style by buying 'tasteful' furniture and carpets, and by the food she provided. However, being a wife was not just being able to run a home efficiently and economically (an increasing concern in the thirties); she must also maintain her husband's interest in her as a 'woman'!

Magazines portrayed marriage as a love affair, a perpetual honeymoon. Women had to work hard to keep alive the romance in their marriage. The first edition of *Woman's Own* contained an article entitled 'Looks do count after marriage' which warned the young housewife that she would 'deserve all the unhappiness that is coming to her' if she serves her 'lord and master' his breakfast wearing a dreary dressing gown or old frock. The message was clear in the magazines and in songs – 'It's your duty to be beautiful. Keep young and beautiful if you want to be loved'.

However, according to *Woman's Own*, beauty is not 'perfection of features but a certain loveliness which is born of a healthy mind

Fig. 7.3 Hikers at Euston station before leaving for the country 1935 (BBC Hulton Picture Library).

and a healthy body, plus a fastidiousness about one's toilet'. The twenties' preoccupation with sex seems to have been replaced by an obsession with the virtues of fresh air and exercise. Sport remained tremendously popular throughout the thirties, particularly group activities. The Women's League of Health and Beauty was founded by Prunella Stack. Its aim was to bring fitness to wives and mothers in a *graceful* and *womanly* way. All over the country, women participated in demonstrations in village halls and congregated in their hundreds for displays at Wembley Stadium. Hiking was another very popular pursuit, and in a uniform of shorts, open shirts and carrying rucksacks, train-loads of earnest young people set off to the countryside to enjoy the benefits of fresh air. Sunbathing and holidays became increasingly popular for those who could afford them, and the suntan became established as a status symbol.

By the late twenties, women's chances of marriage had improved. Boys who were at school during the war were now of marrying age and the steady flow of disillusioned fortune seekers back from the Empire, and the political refugees fleeing the rising tide of Fascism in Europe during the thirties, added to the number of available men. However, the emphasis on the romance of marriage and the role of women in the home did not produce more stable marriages or a rise in the falling birth rate – quite the reverse in fact. There was a substantial increase in the number of divorce petitions, perhaps because people's expectations of connubial bliss were now much higher. In 1937, the Matrimonial Causes Act paved the way to more liberal divorce laws. It introduced three new grounds for divorce in addition to adultery. These were desertion for a period of three years, cruelty, and incurable insanity.

In spite of pressures for women to return to their traditional role of wife and mother, the birth rate fell to its lowest point in peace time. This decline cannot be attributed to the high rate of unemployment and awful poverty in which many families lived, as the smallest families were found not among the poor but the middle classes. There was great anxiety in official circles about this and the Government tried to encourage middle class families to have more children by introducing tax relief for second and subsequent children. It seems that in this period of the expansion of private house building and the growing availability of consumer goods and cars, many middle class couples were more concerned about their mortgage payments, the acquisition of modern labour-saving equipment and furniture for their homes, and enjoying the new leisure pursuits of drives in the country and holidays, than having a large family. A large family was now seen as a financial burden, a cause for pity rather than a source of pride, and the middle classes were able through their knowledge of contraception to avoid such a burden on their overstretched resources.

The reassertion of the domestic role for women did not reverse all the advances made in the twenties for women. Women had smaller families and health and fitness was a primary concern. But there was a narrowing of women's lives. They were discouraged from taking an active role in life outside marriage, except while young, and encouraged to see success in life in terms of romance and marriage. A major preoccupation for a woman was making herself attractive first to potential suitors and then her husband. The 'natural' sphere of the woman was domestic and her sources of satisfaction were individual or 'personal' – that is, in personal relationships and improvement of self.

Were these changes in attitudes reflected in dress?

Masculine and feminine

It seems that the return to more traditional attitudes to the roles of men and women, the breadwinner and the little woman in the home, is paralled by a return to stereotypically more masculine and feminine physiques and styles.

> 'In order to be fashionable in the thirties, every man tried to look like a strong and masculine athlete...His face was clean-shaven and had a healthy outdoor look; his chest was broad and well-built, his shoulders square and muscular, and his general appearance was bold and manly.' (9)

For those lacking the necessary physique, tailors used all kinds of tricks of shaping and padding to give the desired effect.

For women there was a return to a more curvaceous 'feminine' silhouette. Although the fashionable figure remained slim, girlish rather than maternal, the waist had returned to its natural position and the curves of the breasts and hips were visible again. Later in the decade, the fashion for wider, squarer shoulders emphasised the small waist and slim hips. Longer skirts for daywear, full-length dresses for evenings, soft fabrics, and softer, wavy hairstyles completed the more womanly and elegant image of the thirties.

In the thirties a clear distinction between day and evening wear developed. In the past the wearers of fashion had been wealthy and led a life of leisure so there had been no need for day wear to be particularly practical, or to reserve luxurious or extravagant styles for evenings or special occasions. Increasingly, during the era of the Depression, women of all kinds were leading busy and active lives, either in employment or running homes without the aid of servants. There was also a mood of restraint in contrast with the hedonism of the twenties. Thirties' styles for women seem to have been a compromise between practicality and romantic femininity. For day wear, smart suits or dress and jacket were popular, often worn with a fox fur draped round the shoulders. The image was one of respectable and restrained elegance – 'Everyone began to look like well-paid secretaries'. (10) There were also many overtly fussy and feminine styles – dresses made from georgette, crepe de chine, or printed rayon, with draped or cowled necklines, large collars and full sleeves. These styles were

Fig. 7.4 'Everyone looked like a well-paid secretary'.

less practical and, like the platform-soled shoes which became fashionable at the end of the decade, hampered women's movement to some degree.

However, despite the return to the feminine, more mature styles, some of the advantages of twenties styles were retained. Although

Fig. 7.5 Glamorous eveningwear.

skirts were longer, the soft fitted shape was created by the use of the bias cut. This allowed freedom of movement without bulk, as the costumes of dancer Ginger Rogers demonstrated. Underwear was also decreasing in quantity and becoming progressively lighter. Boned corsets were replaced for the majority by corsets or suspender belts using the new two-way stretch elastic. Slim bias cut slips and cami-knickers were the height of fashion but young women were starting to wear 'briefs'.

The almost fanatical belief in the therapeutic effects of sunlight and fresh air, and the passion for outdoor activities, produced a new category of daywear 'casual' clothes. As more people sought the benefits of the sun, on the French Riviera or in a British holiday camp, there was a demand for more revealing clothes − swimsuits for women in figure-hugging jersey had more scooped away at the back and sides, bare-backed sundresses became popular, and shorts were popular at the holiday resort as well as for hiking and cycling. There also began a trend for going hatless, and although hats were still an essential part of proper attire for town wear, the gradual demise of the hat had begun.

The display of the suntan may have inspired one of the innovations of the thirties − the backless evening dress. Eveningwear was glamorous and sexy and was actually worn across the social spectrum for a variety of occasions from debutantes' balls to dances at the local dance hall. Generally, the style of eveningwear and the aspirations of those who wore it were in tune with the romantic and escapist tendencies which dominated the films and popular songs of the period. Hollywood films and the publicity pictures of the stars fostered the notion of glamour. Stars like Jean Harlow and Joan Crawford helped to create the demand for glamorous eveningwear and influenced the styles. Perhaps because many of the stars had been ordinary girls themselves once, they seemed to provide a more accessible role model for the aspiring beauty than the society ladies. In the right frock perhaps you, too, could marry a millionaire, or be swept off your feet by a Clark Gable or Gary Cooper!

References

1. Branson, N. (1975) *Britain in the Twenties*. (Wiedenfeld & Nicolson) 209.
2. Waller, J. (1977) *A Man's Book*. (Duckworth).
3. Nicholls, Beverly (1970) In: Seaman, L.C.B. *Britain between the Wars*, ed. L.C.B. Seaman (B.T. Batsford) 59.

4. Duchess of Westminster, a debutante in the twenties. In: Ewing, E. (1974) *History of Twentieth Century Fashion.* (London: B.T. Batsford) 92–3.
5. Hamilton, M.A. In: Adams, R. *A Woman's Place.* (1910–1975) 97.
6. Chanel. In: Ewing, E. (1974) *History of Twentieth Century Fashion.* (B.T. Batsford) 100.
7. Waller, J. (1977) *A Man's Book.* (Duckworth) 47.
8. Adams, R. *A Woman's Place. (1910–1975)* 125.
9. Waller, J. (1977) *A Man's Book.* (Duckworth).
10. Heinman, M. and Branson, N. (1970) *Britain in the Thirties.* (Wiedenfeld & Nicolson) 104.

8   Wartime and Post-war Women

When war was declared in 1939, women's lives were again to change dramatically. The demands of war brought changes in their role in society and in their appearance, as it had done before. However, there were some interesting contrasts with the First World War which produced differences in the appearance of women both during and after the war. There is a striking contrast between the post-war images of women in the form of the twenties flapper and fifties blond bombshell. *When women had taken an active role in both wars why was it that a boyish silhouette and liberating clothes followed one, and a curvaceous figure and restricting clothes followed the other?*

WOMEN AT WAR AGAIN

The Second World War disrupted the daily lives of everyone in Britain. Essential goods were rationed; all men aged 19 to 40 were called up except those working in essential industries; married couples were separated; children were evacuated from cities, and women were drawn into the war effort. Unlike the First World War, when hostilities were largely confined to the continent, the civilian population suffered not only the deprivations and hardships of a wartime economy but also found themselves under attack. During the first three years of the war, more civilians died than service personnel and half of them were killed in London.

As in the First World War, women were called upon to replace the conscripted male workers. In 1939, women under the age of 40 were categorised as 'mobile' or 'immobile'. The immobile were those women with children under 14, the old and workers already employed in essential work. The others were encouraged to go wherever they were needed into 'reserved' occupations like engineering, farming, medicine, munitions, shipbuilding and administration, or into the Women's Auxiliary Forces. Initially, women volunteered for war work, some persuaded by government appeals and others out of sheer necessity.

In the first years of the war, married women were considered to be fully occupied looking after their homes. It is perhaps ironic that women such as servicemen's wives were designated as immobile and therefore were not included in employment schemes, when many of them were desperate for work. In 1939 the lowest grade in the services (man or woman) was paid two shillings a day (10p), a proportion of which was sent to the wife, plus a grant of twenty-five shillings (£1.25) a week for a wife with two children. Other workers were earning from three to ten pounds a week. The serviceman's wife often could not manage and had to take whatever part-time or homework she could find. *However, later the resource of married women's labour had to be tapped in a more systematic way.*

In 1941 a Ministry of Labour survey revealed a shortage of two million workers in the Armed Forces and the munitions industry. Until 1941, women could volunteer and choose what contribution they wanted to make as in the First World War. From now on they were to be conscripted. Although a survey at the time showed that 97 per cent of women thought that women should make a contribution to the war effort, many felt less than enthusiastic about being conscripted themselves. In practice it was only single women between the ages of nineteen and twenty-four who were conscripted but 'mobile' married women were 'directed' to certain kinds of work. Both forms of command had to be obeyed; those failing to comply were fined and some conscientious objectors were even imprisoned. Both married and single women could find themselves being sent away from their homes and separated from their families.

By 1943, 57 per cent of the work-force were women, and these women came from all sections of society. Ninety per cent of all single women and 80 per cent of all mobile married women were working. In April of that year, the Minister of Labour, Ernest Bevin, found it necessary to tap the reserve of labour of women with children or other domestic commitments. Many 'immobile' women now had to register for work, and in July the age limit for registration was raised to fifty-one. Bevin was accused of conscripting 'grannies'.

Domestic commitments, even the care of children, were no longer to be considered a woman's first priority. More nursery provision was provided during the war than ever before or since. If the First World War established the practice of single women working, during the second it became commonplace for married women to work outside the home. Of course it was extremely hard for married women who had to combine two previously separate occupations. After long shifts in factories and night-time duties in the Civil Defence, they had to do the housework, queue for food and take care of their children and other dependent relatives. In many cases there was the additional strain of air raids, and of separation from their husbands and possibly their evacuated children.

Women's magazines of the period were concerned with providing comfort and advice. That advice could include how to cope with problems of separation, or the directives of the Ministry of Food or Labour translated into a form which related to women's everyday lives, be it how to make the most of food coupons, the 'make do and mend' policy, or encouraging women to offer themselves for employment. The covers of magazines like *Woman* and *Woman's Own* now often had glamorous-looking girls in uniform on the front. Women's magazines had taken on a new role, that of directly transmitting the wishes of Government to women.

> 'Throughout the war, women's magazine editors, Government ministers and officials met regularly in the Holborn offices of the Periodical Proprietors' Association. This close cooperation between rival editors and relevant ministries in translating social and economic policies affecting women into prescriptions, proscriptions and practicalities has never been attempted on such a scale again.' (1)

The role women were encouraged to take by magazines and government propaganda was not necessarily different from their peacetime role. Many found themselves doing the familiar work of cooking, cleaning, nursing and clerical work, even in the Forces. There were less than half a million women serving in the three women's services – the ATS, the WRNS and WAAF in 1943 and the larger proportion of these were volunteers rather than conscripts. Churchill disapproved of women taking up arms so women were not called upon to handle a lethal weapon unless they specifically expressed a willingness to do so. Many women felt frustrated by this and the most romantic, if one of the most dangerous jobs, was performed by the women who operated the anti-aircraft batteries. These were the only women officially entitled to fire weapons.

Despite official opposition, many women did train with guns, particularly those in the Home Guard who wished to be able to defend themselves against possible invaders.

However, as well as the support work which might not be so different from the kind of work women did in civilian life, women did take on a whole range of technical and scientific work such as overhauling torpedoes, communications work of all kinds, air traffic control, plotting the routes of allied and enemy aircraft and ships, and all kinds of electrical and mechanical repairs. Women were also exposed to considerable dangers – for example, the nurses who accompanied the fighting forces, the women who operated the searchlights for enemy aircraft and automatically became targets themselves and, of course, the anti-aircraft gunners.

Many married women found themselves directed into Civil Defence in which they took active and often dangerous roles as air raid wardens, fire-fighters, and ambulance drivers. In the cities, women had to deal with the chaos and devastation of bombing raids, the human misery they caused and the constant threat of personal injury.

After the First World War, women who had done 'men's work' had been largely replaced by men; now women were called upon again to become bus conductors, drivers, pilots and do a whole range of industrial jobs as welders, shipbuilders, mechanics, munitions and armaments workers, and heavy labouring work as navies. Despite the evidence of women's abilities during the 1914–18 war, it was anticipated that where women were substituted for men in most industrial work it would take three women to do the work of two men. But women proved once again that they could equal men when given the opportunity. In 1943 the Ministry of Information issued examples of record production by women; for example, a woman employed as a welder in a shipbuilding firm could produce thirty feet a day more than the men on similar work.

Government propaganda and glamorous posters lured women into industrial work. The reality was far from glamorous. The factories were noisy, dirty, and had very few and very poor facilities for women. Women were required to work long hours; in munitions and the aircraft industry eleven- or twelve-hour shifts were common. Women found they had to fight for reasonable working conditions, decent washing facilities and the provision of overalls, etc. They also found they were paid substantially less than

Fig. 8.1 Woman at work in an armaments factory 1940 (BBC Hulton Picture
Library).

men, in many cases for exactly the same work. In engineering,
women were paid 75 per cent or less compared with men and in
metal work half as much as men. In the case of industrial injury,
women received less compensation – their limbs apparently were
worth less!

Although it was recognised that without the efforts of women and the versatility they had shown, the war could not have been won, there was still no acceptance of equal pay. In 1944, Churchill described the women teachers' request for equal pay as an 'impertinence'!

The war was not all hard work or suffering. For some it was a time of excitement, dances and, unlike the First World War, a surplus of partners. During the latter years of the war when there was an increase in the foreign troops based in Britain, as well as the British troops and airmen, there were many opportunities for having a good time. Dances and social events were held in aircraft hangers, village halls and all sorts of unlikely places, in towns and in isolated country areas near bases. Women were taken by the bus-load if necessary, and thoroughly enjoyed themselves:

> 'We all made dates we could never possibly keep, and had the time of our lives, never expecting war could be such fun. There was no question of settling down with anyone, just the sheer enjoyment of dancing with soldiers from different nationalities in different styles. We recut our mothers' dance dresses, wore as much make-up as we could and loved every minute of it.' (2)

The GIs, in their smart uniforms, were the most glamorous. An influx of 'handsome', immaculately dressed and comparatively affluent men was a very exciting event in rural Britain and many of them enjoyed living up to their image as brash, generous and sexy. They brought fresh foods (flown in to their bases), cosmetics, nylons and chocolate into a deprived and shabby Britain. The GIs, and the American way of life, symbolised everything that was glamorous. Many girls were seduced by that image.

For many women it was, as the quotation implied, 'good clean fun', but as in the First World War there were shifts in patterns of behaviour and morality. Tremendous strains were put on relationships by extended separations and by people being thrown into new and different situations. Under such pressures, people behaved in ways they would not have dreamed of before the war. Women now frequented public houses, a thing unheard of in the past. Married women went to dances and on dates with men-friends. People married after an acquaintanceship of only a few weeks and under the threat of immediate separation, or became sexually involved outside marriage. The figures for venereal disease and illegitimate births increased. In one survey in Birmingham, it was suggested that about half the babies born to married women in the first half of 1945 were illegitimate. Moral attitudes were still condemnatory, particularly amongst the better off. It was still commonplace in working class families for an illegitimate child to be passed off as a younger brother or sister of the mother and to be brought up by its grandparents.

Despite the boom in marriages in the first year of the war, the birth rate fell for married women. In the period between Dunkirk and the end of the Blitz, the number of conceptions fell to its lowest recorded level. However, by 1942, the birth rate shot up to the highest number recorded for eleven years and continued to rise to a peak in 1947. It is difficult to say why women had more babies, after 1942. It may have been loneliness and the need to restore a sense of family life. It may have been to avoid conscription, a serious fear of many, or an attempt to put a relationship with a man on a continuing basis.

Although two important trends were started during the Second World War − the employment of married women and the demand for equal pay − many aspects of women's position in society remained unquestioned. During the war, women, − and, in particular, sex symbols − were regarded as morale boosters for troops. Troops were visited by film stars, and pictures of Betty Grable, were popular 'distractions' for men. Throughout the war, the Windmill Theatre put on nude shows for the residents of London, for servicemen on leave and foreign troops. Perhaps more romantic was Vera Lynn, the 'Forces' sweetheart' who reminded the servicemen of their wives and sweethearts waiting at home to welcome them back.

How did women look?

What is interesting about the Second World War is that the clothes that women wore were influenced not only by designers, or the roles women had to play, but by government regulation. For the first time in recent history there were government restrictions on the making of clothes and the access of the individual to clothes. Fashion was brought to a standstill and the choice of clothes was very limited.

In the early months of the war it was still possible to buy clothes, even expensive clothes, from Paris. But by the sixth month, prices had risen by 25 per cent and clothes were becoming more difficult to obtain. In 1940 the Limitation of Supplies Order banned the production of 'inessential' goods and cut down the production of many others by between 33 and 75 per cent, so that all raw materials and labour could be concentrated in the war industries. In the case of the clothing industry this meant that much of its productive capacity was turned over to the production of government supplies such as uniforms, parachutes and dungarees. Corset factories were turned over to more essential goods like chinstraps for helmets and parachute harnesses. This left only a limited workforce and limited capacity for the production of goods for civilian requirements.

So that the reduced supplies were distributed equitably, the Government intervened and introduced rationing for essential goods such as clothing and food. In order to obtain goods, the customer had to present both money and the requisite number of coupons. Each individual was issued with a book of coupons each year. At first, sixty-six coupons were issued per year but this dropped to forty-eight and then to thirty-six in the last year of the war.

For an adult woman, the following number of coupons were required for each item:

Utility tweed suits	18
Coats	14
Jackets	11
Woollen dresses	11
Dresses in other fabrics	7
Skirts	5
Pyjamas	8
Stockings	2

As the war went on and the number of coupons were reduced, goods became harder to obtain and Britain became shabbier and shabbier. Rationing continued until 1949.

At first, points were awarded to garments irrespective of quality, but in the autumn of 1941 the Utility Scheme was introduced to control the quality and price of goods. This was to ensure that the goods obtained with coupons were of serviceable and durable quality. Detailed specifications of the standard to which cloth should be made were drawn up and 85 per cent of cloth was manufactured to those standards. The production of clothes were regulated by

The Making of Clothes (Restrictions) Order. These regulations were also known as the 'austerity' restrictions because their purpose was to economise on materials and labour. They set limits on the amount of fabric to be used for each garment, the length of the skirt, the number of pleats, pockets, buttonholes, and the amount of trimming which could be used. Embroidery and sequin decoration were barred. These restrictions obviously affected the styling of clothes. Designers such Norman Hartnell, Hardy Amies and Michael Molyneux created utility clothing (stamped with CC41) for the Board of Trade, which followed government restrictions and guidelines. The 1942 Order also limited the number of styles any manufacturer could produce, further limiting the choice of the consumer.

In general, the styles produced were square-shouldered with straight or frugally pleated skirts reaching just over the knee. The look was functional and even militaristic. Many of the suits and coats looked like the uniforms which were to be seen everywhere and the dominant colours were dusky blues, bottle greens, burgundies and reds and blacks.

There were cloths and clothes not controlled by utility regulations, and about 15 per cent of cloth was produced for the free market. They were of better quality and designers and manufacturers had more freedom with these clothes. They were not, however, exempt from purchase tax and were not sold at controlled prices like utility clothes. So the rich could still obtain couture, but it was in very limited supply — as some of these 'free' goods were produced for export — and it was expensive. By 1943 a pre-war nightie priced 25s (£1.25) would cost £13 14g (£14.70) coat and skirt would cost £42. This price increase was far in excess of the 31 per cent rise in the cost of living and the rise in the average wage from £2 13s 3d (£2.66) in 1938 to £4 16s 1d (£4.80) in 1945.

However, even the 'free' clothes did not differ significantly in style from the utility clothes. With the majority of people struggling to look decent, and many others in uniform, flashy smartness had become a cause for mistrust rather than admiration. In the atmosphere of national unity, good taste and distinction in dress were considered inappropriate. As in the First World War, civilian dress was strongly influenced by military styles.

Dress was not only influenced by government restrictions and the wartime mood. Women, once again, needed clothes which were appropriate to the new conditions in which they lived and

Fig. 8.2 Military influence in fashion. Airforce blue suit from Debenham and Freebody.

worked. They needed clothes which were durable, practical, comfortable and easy to move in. They wore trousers, dungarees, and boiler suits at work and many women, becoming accustomed to the advantages of wearing trousers, now wore them for other occasions. The siren suit, a one-piece zip-up suit, designed to be worn by both sexes in air raid shelters was extremely popular. (The garment in modified form reappeared as a highly fashionable form of evening-wear years later.) Other popular and practical styles were turbans and headscarves originally worn in factories to protect the hair, and hooded capes.

But in addition to being patriotic and practical, women wanted to look attractive. They did not accept readily either the shortages or the drabness of wartime clothes. A solution to both these problems was sought through improvisation. The Government's 'make do and mend' campaign encouraged women to cut down old clothes and remake them, to make skirts out of trousers, to reverse collars, to shorten sleeves, to make a pillowcase into baby clothes and unravel sweaters and re-knit them. Clothing exchanges were set up where repaired clothes could be swapped. The stocks of clothes for renewal were swelled by the millions of second-hand garments sent from the United States and the Commonwealth.

Women tried to supplement their wardrobe and make it more attractive by using non-rationed goods to make clothes. Blankets were dyed and made into coats; pillowcases and lace were made into blouses; net curtains and butter muslin were made into wedding dresses; parachute silk was used for making underwear and evening-wear.

With so many women in boiler suits and uniforms, and in the absence of attractive clothes, hairstyles and make-up became even more important to women wishing to look 'feminine'. Ironically, the use of lipstick, powder and face creams were at their most desirable when their production was most restricted. The Limitation of Supplies Order had cut down the provision of raw materials for the cosmetics and toiletries industry to 25 per cent of its pre-war level, as the two basic materials petroleum and alcohol were needed for war supplies. Famous companies like Yardley had their factories turned over to the production of aircraft components and sea-water purifiers. Cosmetics manufacturers were able to produce only one quarter of their normal output. The production of essentials like soap was severely curtailed and was rationed. There were even restrictions on the absolute basic — bath water!

Fig. 8.3 Women in the Land Army 1941 (BBC Hulton Picture Library).

Obviously cosmetics were regarded as a luxury, and even *Vogue* stressed that women should look as if they worried less about their faces than what they had to face. They advised 'natural' beauty aids like exercise to tauten the figure instead of corsets. But the production of cosmetics was not completely banned; their importance to morale was recognised, even in the women's services. But with standard products being in such short supply, substitutes had to be found and these were often very inferior. The WAAF issued a lipstick which 'was like dry chalk to put on though it looked like garish enamel or greasepaint. It had a bitter taste and we waited for it to dry with our mouths open.' (3) Local chemists and individuals experimented with home-made versions. Women were advised to use lemon juice, potato flesh, or egg white for toning the skin, egg yolk as shampoo, and vegetable oil was recommended as a foundation for powder. As foodstuffs like eggs were in extremely short supply and rationed, it seems odd that they could be spared.

Many women working in factories had to keep their hair tucked out of the way under headscarves or caps with perhaps only a curl or two peeping out. But for the evening, hair was washed with home-made shampoo. Women tried to make themselves more glamorous by using pungent perms or peroxiding their hair like the film stars. One very popular style was rolling the hair round a stuffed stocking. As well as home hairdressing, salons flourished – some staying open until midnight to cater for shift workers. For women with a small amount of money to spend on themselves, but with very little to spend it on, having their hair set was a welcome luxury.

Another luxury which was much harder to come by but in great demand, was stockings. When women had darned and redarned their stockings, and supplies began to fail altogether, they had to resort to complicated methods of simulating stocking legs. Shoe polish mixed with face cream was one experiment. Other women tried commercially produced dyes and drew a seam up the back of the leg with an eyebrow pencil. These stains were generally streaky and marked clothes. No wonder girls would do almost anything to get stockings and nylons, and no wonder the GIs who could obtain cosmetics and nylons from home were so popular!

Despite the war, their work and the shortages, some young women were determined to make the most of themselves and the opportunities for enjoyment. Even after long hours at work, they flocked to dances and socials.

> 'At a Hereford factory...the office became a beauty parlour until the coach arrived straight after work to take the girls to the dances. "We washed our hair at lunch time, set it in steel clips...several people went to have their eyebrows plucked by colleagues, or painted their nails." ' (4)

Of course, many women were too busy and too tired to bother with looks or dances, but perhaps all were longing for a time when they could indulge themselves in attractive clothes and cosmetics when shortages and rationing would be at an end.

OLD LOOK, NEW LOOK

The period after the war can be seen as a return to traditional feminine roles and styles of dress. *Why, after the hardships and triumphs of the war, did women apparently go meekly back to the role of wife and mother?*

There do seem to be important differences in women's experiences during the two wars. In the first, women wishing to prove themselves, contributed willingly and enthusiastically. The Second World War lasted longer and had wider ranging effects on the civilian population; they suffered greater deprivation, and of course, although many women did volunteer their services, many others were conscripted or directed to work. This aspect of compulsion and control was also apparent in dress. Although, once again, people appreciated the need for such regulation and restriction on dress, they often found the effects irksome and depressing and, as we have seen sought to mitigate the effects if possible. Dissatisfaction must have been fostered to some extent by the popularity of cinema as a form of entertainment. The stars still appeared in glamorous and luxurious clothes with beautiful make-up which women *wanted* to emulate. How dowdy they must have felt in comparison to Betty Grable or Ginger Rogers!

Another important difference is that after the war, although more men had been killed than women, there was not a serious imbalance in the population like that after the First World War. There was no great surplus of women — in fact, by 1951, the numbers of each sex in the age groups up to thirty were equal.

Return to the home

After the war, the annual marriage rate went up and after demob-
ilisation a very large number of young couples settled down to
family life. The age of marriage dropped and in the fifties 75 per
cent of English women were married before the age of twenty-five.
But not only did women marry, they returned to the home. The
Minister of Labour, Ernest Bevin, was determined that unemployment should not follow this war as it had the first. Demobilisation
took place slowly and there was no immediate sacking of women.
Male unemployment was avoided but this must have been due in
part to the way in which two million women workers left their
jobs. By 1947, the number of married women workers had been
reduced very rapidly to 18 per cent. Despite the fact that two-
thirds of women said they would like to stay on in work (answering
an AEU survey of over 200 factories just before the end of the war)
it seems that when men were demobilised the old feeling that
women really ought to make way for the men returned. Perhaps
more important, firms who had organised shifts to suit women now
stopped doing so and many wartime nurseries were closed down.
Or, perhaps it was just a reaction against the restriction, the
regimentation and institutional nature of wartime life that made
'home life' seem particularly attractive, and of course the freedom
of 'being your own boss'.

The role of housewife and mother acquired a new status and the
term 'career woman' seemed to become a term of abuse. The
newly elected women MPs (there had been a record number elected
in 1945, and a record number of women candidates in the 1951
election) presented themselves at every opportunity as voicing the
'housewife's point of view'.

The baby boom of the post-war period seemed to carry all
before it and back into the home. In 1947, 881 025 babies were
born in a single year compared to an average 580 413 in the thirties.
Even after the immediate post-war boom had slowed down, the
parents of the fifties went on having more children than their own
parents had. Another interesting aspect of this renewed enthusiasm
for parenthood was that it was the better off and better educated
who tended to favour larger families. This was the reverse of
previous patterns. The small elite of graduate women were, it
appeared having more children than the non-graduates. They made
it clear that, for them, motherhood and housework were not a
second-class occupation but a profession.

Academics, government and commercial interests all gave support to the view that women's place was in the home. Dr John Bowlby in his book. *Childcare and the Growth of Love* (1953), popularised the notion of 'maternal deprivation'. He argued that the first five years of a child's life were crucial and without a mother's constant care the child would grow up emotionally handicapped and incapable of forming deep relationships. His original research was conducted amongst children brought up in institutions but it started a whole new school of child-rearing methods. Women who took his advice as it was put across in books and magazines became afraid to leave their babies at all.

Educationalists like John Newsom writing in 1948 had also expressed views which implied that woman's place was in the home, and pleasing her man was to be her priority:

'In many girls' grammar schools the more intellectually able pupils take a second foreign language while the less able are allowed to take domestic science, forgetful of Samuel Johnson's dictum that "a man is better pleased when he has a good dinner on the table than when his wife talks Greek".' (5)

On the whole, women's magazines in the fifties supported this view. The view expressed by *The Lady* that 'It was a great loss to the nation when women with expensive training were not allowed to use it after marriage' was the exception. The mass circulation weeklies took the opposite view; they positively discouraged women from trying to combine the roles of wife and worker. There was an increasing emphasis on articles concerned with 'getting and keeping your man', and articles concerned with domestic matters.

When rationing finally ended in the early fifties a whole new range of consumer goods flooded the market. An intensive selling campaign directed at women began and as magazines began increasingly to depend on advertising revenue, these interests began to influence the content of magazines. Whilst exploiting and reinforcing the traditional feminine roles of wife and mother, advertisers wished to influence women in *their role as consumers*, chief spenders of the family budget.

Consumerism flourished in the social and economic environment which had developed in the fifties. The social reforms introduced by the post-war Labour Government and the economic prosperity of the fifties led to a new sense of security. It seemed that the deprivations and hardships experienced during the Depression and during the war were to become things of the past.

The Welfare State as we know it today had been established. The National Health Service was introduced in 1948 and provided not only hospitals but also the free family doctor system, child care clinics, dental services, etc. Pension provision was improved and National Assistance extended to include the handicapped, deserted wives and unmarried mothers. There was also an expansion in educational provision which introduced secondary education for all and provided greater access to higher education. Indeed, in the fifties people were better housed, better educated and better cared for when they were sick or old than ever before. People felt protected from poverty and the consequences of ill-health or misfortune.

This sense of security was developing at a time when people were also experiencing a considerable increase in their spending power. During the fifties the economy seemed to be booming. Productivity was rising, labour was in great demand, wages and spending power rose. Average weekly wages rose from £6 8s (£6.40) in 1950 to £11 2s 6d (£11.12½) in 1959. Although prices were also rising, people enjoyed a rising standard of living and the security of full employment. Consequently, social patterns changed and there was a great rise in consumerism, a boom in home ownership and a great increase in the number of holidays taken abroad.

During the first six years of the fifties, the amount spent in British shops increased by almost 50 per cent. The sales of one type of goods rose *six* times as fast as other consumer outlays and this was the sales of electrical and durable goods. These goods represented a new lifestyle to which many British people aspired – the world of pop-up toasters, refrigerators, vacuum cleaners, washing machines and gramaphones, the world of American-inspired convenience equipment which people had seen pictured on the cinema screen, in magazines and then on television. When hire-purchase restrictions were lifted in 1958, these goods became available for a small payment per week. It was to women that many advertisers made their appeal.

Women's magazines carried an increasing amount of advertising material in the fifties for goods ranging from nail polish to floor polish, cake mixes and cookers to setting lotions and corsets. Many advertisements implied that success as a woman, wife and mother lay in the ability to be a discriminating consumer − the ability to choose the *right* washing powder or gravy browning. But there was also an increasing emphasis within the editorials and articles on providing information and advice to women in their role as consumers. To some editors like Mary Grieve, editor of *Woman*, this role appeared to be of great significance in women's lives, almost their *raison d'être*:

'A very great part of a woman's life is spent choosing, buying and preparing goods for her own and her family's consumption...An immense amount of her personality is engaged in her function as the selector of goods....'.

It was as important to her as a career:

'Success in this function is as cheering and vitalising to her as it is to a man in his chosen career, failure as humiliating.' (6)

But her role as consumer did not create independence like a career. Her ability to consume was based on her financial dependence on her man, and her aims were to provide a pleasant home and good food to please him. A woman's ability to consume reflected her husband's wealth and status, not her own!

Had things changed at all since the Victorian period?

Although there was so much value put on marriage and family life, ironically during the fifties there were more broken marriages and homes than ever before. In government circles there was anxiety about the family and a number of supportive organisations were set up to safeguard it. The Children's Act of 1948 set up a network of support and care for children without parents or guardians and to help families with problems. The increase in divorce was causing particular concern and Marriage Guidance Councils were given government grants to aid their work in trying to bring about marital reconciliation.

Women were not, it seems, totally satisfied with life in the domestic sphere. By 1957, 33 per cent of married women were working and by 1961 over half of the women in employment were married. Why did women begin to drift back to work? It may have been out of boredom, the frustration of having only children to talk to, or it may have been the desire to have more money to spend on the new consumer goods. However, many returned part-time so that their work did not interfere with their domestic commitments which remained the priority. They were able to return to work in this way because once again there was a demand for female labour. In the latter half of the fifties there was a boom in the economy, full employment and vacancies to be filled. The Government encouraged immigration from the Commonwealth and encouraged women to return to work. The Ministry of Education put out appeals for trained teachers to 'Come back to teaching'. The Ministry of Health was short of 48 000 nurses and urged hospitals to accept married women part-time and to arrange shifts which would enable them to work and fulfil domestic obligations.

The forties and fifties saw a reassertion of old moral values after the uncertainties of the war. It was not a permissive age, quite the reverse. The majority of young people believed in premarital chastity, and falling in love seemed to lead inevitably to marriage. Birth control was difficult to obtain for the unmarried, and anyway 'nice girls didn't'. It seems that, like the Victorian period, restrictive clothing was part of a girl's moral armour:

> 'The would-be seducer of the fifties had to reckon with an armoury of uncooperative underwear which stood between him and his objective. The nylon stocking was still suspended from a constricting girdle of unyielding firmness, a fortification virtually impossible to bypass without active collusion, and preferably plenty of time. Unpremeditated impulses were often frustrated by such hurdles.' (7)

However, ideas about female sexuality were changing. The Kinsey Report shocked people in Britain. As a study of the sexual behaviour of Americans, his report called into question all kinds of beliefs about class and sexual behaviour and the differences between the sexes. He found that whereas men are at their most potent early in life, the sexual capacity and enjoyment of women are at a peak in their thirties. He challenged notions of slower sexual arousal in women, natural chastity and requirement for serious emotional involvement.

New images of sexuality were being promoted in the media. Heroines were no longer always virgins for whom marriage was the end of the story. Alongside the pure, irreproachable, high class virgins represented by stars like Grace Kelly and Deborah Kerr, a new, playful, sexy heroine was appearing, a woman with an obvious sexual appetite. In Ian Fleming novels, the heroines were portrayed as high class, glamorous and willing to enjoy sex without commitment. Stars like Marilyn Monroe and, later, Bridget Bardot became 'sex symbols'. Both were considered models of feminine desirability, but the antithesis of 'a lady'.

> 'Both appeared as nearly naked as possible ... and both were obviously walking wriggling and giggling embodiments of Dr Kinsey's findings. Not only did they enjoy, indeed relish, healthy sexual appetites, they made it obvious that they would satisfy them where and when they felt like it, on their own terms.' (8)

Sex was fun but this image was in conflict with the image of domestic fidelity and bliss pictured in women's magazines. Women felt conflicting pressures to be both a wonderful wife and a seductress. In the past these two roles had been strictly separated.

NEW LOOK WOMEN

After the war it seems that women longed for glamour:

> 'As the last guns rumbled out and the last all-clear sounded all the squalor and discomfort and roughness that had seemed so fitting for so long began to feel old-fashioned...I wanted to throw the dried egg out of the window, burn my shabby curtains and wear a Paris hat again. The Amazons, the women in trousers, the good comrades had had their glorious day...Gracious living beckoned once again.' (9)

The New Look certainly recaptured that sense of glamour, elegance, and luxury for which Anne Scott James longed. It also reasserted a kind of femininity reminiscent of the Victorian period in its restrictiveness and its explicit extravagance.

Mrs Ridealgh, a Labour MP and Ex-regional controller for the Board of Trade's 'make do and mend' campaign was outraged, as were many others, by the post-war fashions from Paris:

> 'Utterly ridiculous, stupidly exaggerated waste of material and manpower, foisted on the average woman to the detriment of more normal clothing...Our modern world has become used to the freedom of short sensible clothing...The New Look is too reminiscent of a caged bird's attitude...I hope our fashion dictators will realise the new outlook of women and will give the death blow to any attempt to curtail women's freedom.' (10)

The New Look was characterised by a tight-fitting bodice narrowing into a closely defined waist and then blossoming out into a long full skirt. The figure was gently curved, with rounded unpadded shoulders, a rounded bosom, full hips possibly padded or stiffened with pleats and a small waist created by the reintroduction of the 'waspie' corset. In the days of post-war austerity, continuing short-ages and rationing, it was extraordinarily extravagant. After the freedom of the siren suit and dungarees, it was cumbersome and restricting. Those women who wore it, and they did in their millions, were making a statement that freedom of movement, economy, practicality all came second to looking romantically feminine and sexually attractive. In that way the role women wished to take in society found visual expression.

The fashions of the fifties continued to reaffirm this 'ultra-feminine' and glamorous image. The styles of high fashion were elegant, sophisticated and mature. The silhouette remained softly curved, the waist became less clearly defined and skirts were either long and very full, or pencil slim giving an effect rather like a hobble skirt. Eveningwear was extravagant and glamorous, strapless boned tops with full bouffant skirts were popular or tight sheaths moulding the body. For daywear, tailored suits, coats and dresses were popular, all worn with carefully chosen matching hats, gloves, scarves, jewellery, shoes and bags.

There was still considerable formality in dress for most occasions in Britain in the fifties. Although it was now permissible not to wear a hat for some occasions, gloves were worn even with an informal cotton summer dress. Young girls wanted to look mature and sophisticated. Women wanted to appear well-groomed and elegant, with carefully chosen clothes, immaculate make-up, beautifully manicured hands, and not a hair out of place. The look was epitomised by the outstanding model of the day, Barbara Goalen. Her image was one of impeccable taste and elegance, a mature woman of 'class'.

The status symbol aspect of fashion was still much in evidence in the fifties. The style of dress implied an elegant and leisured existence, given the costly and restrictive nature of the ideal and the time and energy necessary to choose and coordinate the clothes and accessories. A fashionable woman still needed a large and varied wardrobe; there were still quite strict ideas about what clothes should be worn for what occasion and there was pronounced seasonal differences in dress.

'As late as 1959, *Vogue* could run a feature on "Clothes for the Occasion", defining what the smart woman would wear for a lunch

Fig. 8.4 A return to feminity with the 'New Look'.

Fig. 8.5 Barbara Goalen − fifties' elegance.

date, a lunch party, racing, a committee meeting, a garden party, cocktails, dinner, the theatre, a dance and wedding. Every one of them was different. It couldn't happen today.' (11)

Women still bought 'spring suits', 'summer coats', 'winter hats' and so on.

The popular fashions of the day, that is, fashions not created by couture designers but coming from another source such as cinema, also projected the image of 'femininity' and restriction, if not elegance. The New Look was mirrored in the full dirndl skirts worn especially by the young though not exclusively, which were often padded by numerous petticoats usually made from stiffened nylon. Dior had brought back the curvaceous figure to high fashion but, even during the war, the curves of the pin-ups had been admired. In the Fifties breasts seem to have become an obsession for both men and women. The cinema was still a very popular form of entertainment and the 'sweater girl' look popularised by stars like Lana Turner and Jane Russell must have contributed to this preoccupation. The breasts had to appear both large and prominent and this affect was achieved by a bra which had two projecting cone-shaped cups which were usually stiffened with whorls of stitching.

Many though by no means all of the stars of the screen were 'well-endowed'. It has even been suggested that some of these actresses 'made' their careers on the size of their breasts rather than any talent for acting. This may, however, be an unfair transference of the qualities they were asked to portray on the screen in 'dumb blonde' roles, rather than an accurate description of the individual. Nevertheless, their breasts were an important part of the allure of actresses like Marilyn Monroe, Jayne Mansfield (whose breasts were insured for a million dollars) . . . Sabrina and, in Britain, Diana Dors. These stars were of course all 'blondes', and it is said that three out of ten brunettes dyed their hair blonde in the fifties. Blonde or not, no woman wished to be considered flat-chested. Those who felt that nature had not endowed them sufficiently tried to increase their actual size by buying bust improvement creams and devices advertised widely in the press, or by wearing padded bras and underwired cups. As a result of the desire for prominent breasts, a slim waist and curving hips, women's underwear was once again complicated and uncomfortable − a blend of stiff materials, bones and elastic. All women wore 'foundation' garments − a bra, a corselette, a roll-on or a suspender belt. As we saw above, these garments appeared like a form of armour to some people.

Another fettering fashion of the fifties, and one in which they appeared to delight, was the stiletto-heeled shoe. Millions of women teetered around on these narrow heels which were sometimes four inches high, and forced their toes into the pointed winkle-picker fronts. The overall effect, like that of the Chinese bound foot, was to make women less able to move about but it made their legs look slimmer, their feet smaller and made women sway when they walked (and, of course, welcome an arm to lean on!).

To complete the picture, bouffant hairstyles became popular. The most exaggerated form was the beehive. Long hair was set on rollers (a recent import from the continent), back-combed to give it height and bulk, and finally stiffened with lacquer to give the appearance of candy-floss.

Dior claimed to have brought back 'the simple art of pleasing'

Fig. 8.6 The blonde bombshell.

and the fashions of the fifties do seem to have stressed once again a passive and decorative role for women. They were creatures to be looked at and enjoyed rather than workers or active participants in the business of life.

However, fashion was not so extreme as it had been in the past; women did not give up all the gains they had made in society or in dress. Alongside these formal and feminine styles there were alternatives. Inspired by styles from the United States and Italy, there was a growth in 'casual' clothes. Tapered slacks and chunky sweaters became popular. Young people started to wear jeans. The trend towards more relaxed and practical dressing began, and became more pronounced in the following decade.

References

1. Ferguson, M. (1983) *Forever Feminine*. (Heinemann).
2. Mimms, R. (1980) *Bombers and Mash*. (Virago).
3. *ibid* 157.
4. *ibid* 175.
5. Adams, R. *A Woman's Place (1910–1975)* 165.
6. White, C. (1970) *Women's Magazines 1693–1968*. (Micheal Joseph) 146.
7. Lewis, P. (1978) *The Fifties*. (Heinemann) 43.
8. *ibid* 53.
9. Wilson, E. (1980) *Only Halfway to Paradise* (Tavistock) 83.
10. Adams, R. *A Woman's Place (1910–1975)* 160.
11. Ewing, E. (1974) *History of Twentieth Century Fashion*. (London: B.T Batsford) 167–168.

9   Equality at Last? Women in the Sixties and Seventies

When Betty Friedan described the models of femininity and domesticity which held sway in fifties' America she wrote:

> 'Each suburban wife, as she made the beds, shopped for groceries, ate peanut butter sandwiches with her children, chauffeured cubs and brownies, lay beside her husband at night, was afraid to ask even of herself the silent question, "Is this all?".' (1)

A decade or so later, women were no longer afraid to ask; many aspects of women's roles were brought into question. By the mid-seventies, their sexual role, their roles as wives and mothers, as pupils and workers, their status in society and, of course, the way they should look, all had been subject to reassessment and change.

Did women achieve real equality in the sixties and seventies? Did the styles of dress really represent a break with old models of femininity, and reflect new roles, and new attitudes to women?

First of all it is perhaps necessary to point out that the changes which affected women were not isolated changes but one aspect of the changes affecting society as a whole. The sixties were experienced by most people as a period of change and, by many, change for the better. It was a period of optimism. The economic boom of the fifties *appeared* to continue; people's wages and standard of living continued to rise, they worked fewer hours and had longer holidays. Some people even suggested that the class structure in Britain was withering away and a new classless society would emerge. People were encouraged in this view by the popularity of 'working class' stars like Michael Caine, models like Twiggy, photographers like David Bailey, artists like David Hockney, and of course pop stars like the Beatles. However, there was no evidence to suggest any real change in the structure of power and privilege in Britain. A further source of optimism was a belief in the power of science and technology to produce a better society. As leader of the Labour Party, Harold Wilson promised a new Britain 'forged in the white heat of a technological revolution'. People delighted in the prospect of automation, new domestic technology, new drugs, new architecture, new roads, etc.

The sixties and early seventies were also a period of discontent and protest. There were a number of important protest movements – the Civil Rights Movement in the United States, Campaign for Nuclear Disarmament, the anti-Vietnam demonstrations, the various student protests all over Europe and America, the Women's Liberation Movement and the Gay Rights Campaign. There was considerable pressure for political and social reform, but there were also reactionary groups like the racist National Front (established in 1966) and anti-permissive groups such as the 'Clean up TV Campaign' (established by Mary Whitehouse in 1964).

The 'swinging sixties' were not the universal triumph of permissive or liberal values that is sometimes claimed, although many important reforms were achieved. In the conflict that was waged between those who wished to maintain the status quo, to preserve traditional values and standards of behaviour and those wishing to bring about change, it was the latter who gained the upper hand on certain issues. In the case of women, many of the changes brought new opportunities and new freedoms but others brought new discontents, new criticisms, and not only from the 'traditionalists'. Not all the changes were as beneficial or liberating as they had first appeared. Disillusionment led to pressure from some women for further changes in the seventies.

Young women and girls were obviously also involved in the 'Youth Revolution' of the sixties and seventies. Young people were developing their own styles of dress, their own ways of behaving, their own values and beliefs which were seen as distinct from and in many ways in conflict with the adult world. (See Chapter 8 for a fuller discussion of these issues.) Youth became a dominant force in music and fashion, and this dominance had implications for all women young and old, in terms of what kind of woman was considered beautiful or sexy.

Let's look in more detail at how these wider changes affected women.

THE SEXUAL REVOLUTION

There was a growing atmosphere of permissiveness in the sixties and patterns of behaviour did change, especially although not exclusively among young people. Relatively high wages meant that young people were no longer financially dependent on their parents.

Some could even afford to live away from home and away from parental restraint. Phrases like 'the single girl' and 'bachelor girl' were coined to describe the growing number of young women living in flats or bedsits, women who were not someone's daughter or wife and who were certainly not spinsters or old maids.

The notion that sex was fun had begun to take root in the fifties. In the sixties the freedoms enjoyed by young women meant that they also found themselves under increasing pressure to have sex and to have it often. The double standard remained, however, and women found they were still labelled as tarts if they had sex on the same terms as men. But equally, they found themselves criticised if they refused to have sex — they were old-fashioned, frigid or 'tight'. As Anna Coote remarked: 'You were damned if you did, and damned if you didn't!' (2) Women could not win!

Sexual freedom brought new pressure and anxieties. Women now felt that they ought to enjoy sex. They felt guilty if they did not, it was *their* fault. They worried about whether they were good in bed. Then, of course, there was the problem of contraception. Until 1965 it was almost impossible for single girls and women to obtain contraception. Illegitimacy rates rose — 4.7 per cent in 1955, 7.7 per cent in 1964 and 8.4 per cent at the end of the sixties.

It was in 1965 that the Brooke Advisory Clinic began to supply contraceptives to unmarried women, and they were followed later by the more cautious and conservative Family Planning Association. Attitudes to abortion also began to change in the sixties, particularly after the thalidomide disaster and an epidemic of German measles which resulted in the birth of many handicapped children. It was also argued that the rich had had access to medically safe abortion through private health care for years but this facility had been denied to the less well-off who suffered at the hands of back-street abortionists. In 1967, David Steele was able to get government support for his bill to reform the abortion laws.

The availability of contraception and, later, abortion was tremendously significant; they were hailed as the cornerstones of women's liberation. For the debate about a woman's right to have control over her own body was really a debate about women's role in society. The security that real control over fertility provided changed women's attitudes to sex itself but it also had great implications for the relationships they could have, and for their work and careers.

A woman could now embark on sexual relationships without the fear of producing an unwanted pregnancy which could hurt other people as well as herself, or which could interrupt her career. Sexual relationships outside marriage became more 'acceptable'; by 1970 people no longer felt obliged to keep the fact that they were lovers a closely guarded secret. An active sex life could now be combined with a career as it became acknowledged that it would not inevitably lead to children.

The Pill, which had become widely available by the end of the decade, did bring women greater sexual freedom, and in many cases pleasure. However, in the seventies some women began to feel it was not without its disadvantages. Side-effects were discovered and there were scares about high-dose pills. Some women felt that although it gave them more freedom, it put their health at risk whilst it relieved men of any responsibility for contraception. Women were expected to 'get themselves on the Pill', and if pregnancy did occur, to 'get themselves an abortion'.

It was also felt that even though sex was more freely and more safely available, it was still based on the old patterns of male dominance. Attitudes to women had not changed in the sense that women's bodies were for men's enjoyment. Women were not men's equals but their playthings – they were 'dolly-birds' or 'chicks'. These attitudes were found amongst the reformers and political activists. The Black Power leader Stokely Carmichael is given credit for the now infamous remark that the only position for women in his campaign was prone!

During the sixties there was a trend towards removing the regulation of sex from the public to the private domain. In 1957 the Wolfenden Report had suggested that individuals should have the right to make their own choices about morals and sexual behaviour in private without fear of the law. Changes in the law concerning homosexuality in 1967 reflected this view, as did the changing approach to censorship and pornography.

During the sixties, there was a growing liberalism in approaches to what adults could see in the theatre, cinema or in the arts. Censorship of the theatre was abandoned by the end of the decade. Television, however, and the BBC in particular found itself under attack for its portrayal of sex from the 'Clean Up TV Campaign'. Such protesters seemed to be in the minority. Commercial interests were not slow to take advantage of the permissive mood and to exploit interest in sexual material. There was a tremendous growth in the number of strip joints and sex shops. 'Soft porn' became available at every newsagent, and in the seventies there was an increase in the number and circulation figures of magazines featuring hard-core pornography.

However, shots of semi-clad women, women in demeaning poses or shots which had the aim of sexually stimulating the onlooker were not confined to such publications. When it was clear there were profits to be made from nudity and sex, tabloid papers like *The Sun* and *Daily Mirror* began to include photographs of women wearing very little, accompanied by suggestive captions as a daily feature. The 'quality' papers also accepted illustrations for their supplements which featured shots of naked women or women in suggestive poses as part of articles and advertisements. Advertisers had been quick to jump on the bandwagon. Rum, cars, aftershave and foreign holidays are just some of the products which were promoted by using pictures of women to give them an image of sexual glamour.

By the late sixties, some women were beginning to object to the way women were portrayed, and the way in which women's bodies were used to sell goods. They argued that it encouraged both men and women to see women as 'sex objects', there for male pleasure and approval rather than individuals with feelings and desires of their own. These feelings were given public expression when a group of women protestors disrupted the Miss World contest in 1970. The same year Germaine Greer had written:

> 'The universal sway of the feminine stereotype is the single most important factor in male and female woman-hatred. Until woman as she is can drive this plastic spectre out of her own and her man's imagination she will continue to apologise and disguise herself, while accepting her male's pot belly, wattles, bad breath, farting, stubble, baldness and other ugliness without complaint...Is it too much to ask that women be spared the daily struggle for superhuman beauty in order to offer it to the caresses of a subhumanly ugly mate?' (3)

American femininists had ritually burned their bras, and were imitated by British women. The bra was obviously a symbol of the way in which clothes are used to reshape women's bodies and the way in which women are oppressed by the pressure to look feminine and 'sexy'. Some women stopped wearing bras as a protest against the stereotype of femininity Germaine Greer describes, but the protest backfired to the extent that it gave the press another excuse for photographing women's bodies and drew attention to women's breasts. Genuine attempts were made to adopt a non-sexist style of dress and these attempts, as we shall see later, had a widespread influence on women's clothes.

Women rejected not only the need to transform themselves for male pleasure, but also to reject the submissive and passive role they were expected to play in sexual relations. Women began to be concerned with their own sexual pleasure and fulfilment. For some femininists, this meant a rejection of heterosexual relationships. But for *Cosmopolitan*, a magazine aimed at the single career girl, it meant having sex as often as you wished, with whomever you liked. Practical advice about contraception, venereal disease, and how to achieve orgasm was given in much the same tone that women's magazines had used in the past to give tips on home decorating or how to make a light sponge cake.

What had started in the sixties as 'a strange stirring, a sense of dissatisfaction, a yearning that women suffered' (4) had erupted into the Women's Liberation Movement by the seventies. In the United States, the women's movement had modelled itself to a large extent on the Civil Rights Campaign in which many women had been involved. They used the technique of 'consciousness-raising groups' which had been used to give black people a sense of identity and shared struggle. Now such groups were used by women as a means of sharing the feelings of resentment, humiliation and injustice which the way they were treated had aroused. The groups served to show that these feelings and the situations which provoked them were not just personal or individual as most women experienced them − they were common problems for all women. It was recognised that radical changes in society and in the attitudes of both men and women would be required to overcome these problems, but these groups provided support to their members as they tried to bring about change in their own lives and in society as a whole.

Women's groups were being formed in Britain by the late sixties and the first National Women's Liberation Conference was held in 1970. During the early seventies a number of women spoke out and published books on the nature and causes of women's oppression. (4) They questioned the taken-for-granted image of femininity, and showed it to be a social and cultural construct. They described and criticised the discrimination against women in education, employment, the law, trade unions and in social relations, and in particular they deplored the subordination of women within the family. As we shall see, equal pay and equal opportunities were important demands but it was recognised that equality with men could not be achieved without radical changes in men's attitudes to work, child care and family responsibilities.

Although in the early seventies the term 'women's libber' was frivolously applied to any woman who asked her partner to do his share of the housework, and the term 'male chauvinist pig' to any man who refused, the new wave of feminism did provide a climate in which women and their role in society was an issue not only for intellectuals and feminists but also for 'ordinary' men and women.

Marriage and the family

How did the permissive attitudes of the 'Swinging Sixties' affect marriage and the family, and women's roles within them?

Patterns of marriage and family life did change. Along with a trend towards increased sexual experience amongst teenagers, there was a trend towards earlier marriage, especially amongst young women. For the first time they were outnumbered by young men, and so had a better chance of marriage than any previous generation of women in recent times. And marry they did. It is ironic that at a time when women were beginning to have more sexual freedom, so many young women were so eager to tie themselves down at a much younger age than their predecessors. The number of teenage marriages increased.

Not only did young people tie themselves down in marriage, there was a baby boom. It reached a peak in 1964 but remained high until the early seventies when it fell back to the level it had been in the fifties. Perhaps the boom reflects the optimism felt in the sixties, but it seems oddly out of step with the fashionable 'bachelor' girl image of the decade.

Although marriage and children were a popular option for women during the sixties, by the seventies the marriage rate began to decline and the divorce rate had risen sharply. There was a certain disenchantment with both marriage and the family. The hippies were experimenting with alternative collective styles of living; psychiatrists like R.D. Laing represented the family as a repressive institution; and, of course, femininists were critical of both institutions in so far as they were seen as oppressing women. New liberal sexual attitudes meant that cohabitation was becoming accepted as a prelude or alternative to marriage. In fact, in some circles marriage became unfashionable.

The number of divorces rose from 37 785 in 1965 to 58 239 in 1970, and to 120 052 in 1975. The Divorce Act of 1969, when it was incorporated into the Matrimonial Causes Act of 1973, made divorce easier than ever before. 'Irretrievable breakdown' became the only necessary cause for divorce, and couples simply had to establish that their marriage was not working by living separately for two years in order to obtain a divorce. Blame no longer had to be attached to one partner.

In addition to more permissive attitudes and the liberalisation of the divorce laws, the changes in the social security system may also have contributed to the growing number of divorces and separations. In 1966, National Assistance had been replaced by Supplementary Benefits. Supplementary Benefits were based on a means test and were payable to those not in full-time employment. They were intended to bring income up to an adequate level and the actual amount was calculated on a scale according to the number and age of children plus a rent allowance. These reforms meant that women who previously could not leave their husbands because they felt they had little chance of receiving maintenance and because they had no means of support for themselves or their children, now had a real alternative to living in an unsatisfactory marriage.

One striking feature of the sixties and seventies was the growing number of single-parent families. The rise in the number of illegitimate births and the growing number of separations and divorces contributed to this. By 1976 they represented 11 per cent of all British families, and the majority of these consisted of a mother and her children.

Education and employment

What kind of life was education preparing girls for? What employment opportunities were there for women?

The 1944 Education Act had brought particular benefits for girls, as secondary education was now received as a right and no longer depended on parental consent. The number of girls staying on into the sixth form increased and in some schools at least girls were encouraged to choose GCE subjects which would be useful to a career. By the sixties more girls were going on to further and higher education. According to Robbins, the percentage of girls continuing their education after 18 had risen from 1 per cent in 1942 to 8 per cent in 1962. From the mid-fifties the applications for university places from both sexes were rising.

Although it was now accepted that a girl should be prepared for a career, it was also assumed that she would marry and that she would at least interrupt her career to have children. For those entering higher education, teaching was a popular choice of profession; over half went to Teacher Training College in the early sixties. There was a great demand for teachers but it was seen as the ideal career to combine with marriage. It may have been this assumption that women would have a shorter or interrupted career that resulted in the lack of change in the position of women in the main professions, despite equality of educational opportunity. At the end of the sixties 90 per cent of nurses were female but only 15 per cent of practising doctors; women comprised 75 per cent of all primary school teachers but only 40 per cent of head teachers; and although nearly half of all university students were female, less than 2 per cent of university professors were women.

However, women's labour was in great demand during the sixties and seventies, and an increasing number of women entered the work-force. The structure of British industry was undergoing substantial changes. The manufacturing sector was declining, with the number of those employed falling from eleven million in 1960 to nine million in 1970. But there was a corresponding growth in the service industries which ranged from banking and insurance to catering and entertainment. This changing structure led to a growth in those areas of employment which were regarded as women's work, namely clerical work, lower professional and technical work, and unskilled labour in the service industries, but it did little to upgrade the type of work women did and wage levels still lagged behind those of men. In 1970, women formed 70 per cent of service workers, 67 per cent of clerical workers, but only 7.5 per cent of executive and managerial workers!

Another important feature of women's employment at this time was the increase in the number of married women who worked. Not only had the number of married women returning to work gone up but they were returning to work earlier after having children. The trend continued throughout the sixties and seventies until in 1979 married women represented 26 per cent of the work-force and outnumbered single women two to one. Many of these married women worked part-time.

The patterns of employment which were established in the sixties raised two crucial issues as far as women's emancipation was concerned. The first was the continuing inferior status and pay of the majority of working women. The second was the way most women were expected to carry the dual burden of work inside and outside the home.

The issue of equal pay had been raised many times. Some workers like teachers had already achieved equal pay but the vast majority of women were paid substantially less than for similar kinds of work. Public attention was drawn to the issue once more when there was a strike of women machinists at Ford's in Dagenham who wanted their pay upgraded. It became the first issue around which feminists organised in establishing the Women's Liberation Movement in Britain. The Secretary of State for Employment, Barbara Castle, held discussions with the strikers and later announced her intention to start negotiations for implementing statutory equal pay.

The Equal Pay Act became law in 1970 and was to be fully implemented by 1975. Under the Act, women were to be paid the same rate as men if employed in like work and they were to enjoy equal terms and conditions of employment. However, the delay in full implementation gave employers time to find means to circumvent the Act. Some employers produced new job specifications for male workers, or new gradings; others segregated workers so that no comparison could be made. Although officially supporting the principle of equal pay, some male trade unionists resisted pay changes which would have narrowed differentials.

It became obvious that equal pay would not solve the problems of equality for women at work. Second class jobs and status at work belonged to women by custom, a custom which was rationalised by ideas about what interests women and the argument that they have shorter working lives. But these views affected everything from training for jobs to the size of the pension a woman would receive. As well as finding difficulty in practising certain professions, in getting to the top of their own line and exerting influence within unions, women found they were discriminated against in ordinary transactions such as buying a house or insurance, and entering hire purchase agreements. Society was organised around the principle of the supporting male breadwinner; women were generally poorer and had lower status than men.

Feminists pointed out that there was a chain of discrimination which prepared girls for second class jobs and status. It began in early childhood with the toys young children were given and the behaviour patterns they were encouraged to adopt. Feminists criticised the way girls were given dolls, soft toys and 'domestic' toys like miniature irons, cookers, tea-sets, etc. − toys which emphasised a rehearsal of the mother's role − or nurses' outfits instead of doctors'. Boys, on the other hand, tended to be given more active and technical toys such as cars, trains, chemistry sets, microscopes, or building sets of various kinds. It was argued that girls were encouraged to be less adventurous, to stay neat and clean whereas boys were allowed to explore and be independent.

At school, femininists found evidence that the organisation of the curriculum tended to direct girls towards certain kinds of examination subjects and consequently limited their choice of career. For example, in some schools girls took domestic science whereas boys took technical subjects like technical drawing or metalwork. In some girls' schools there was only minimal provision for the teaching of science subjects. In other schools, science subjects like physics were identified as boys' subjects and girls tended to choose or were encouraged to choose arts subjects like English literature or a foreign language.

A White Paper on Equality for Women was published in 1974 and the Sex Discrimination Act was passed in 1976. Under this legislation, girls were to be offered maths, physics and engineering on the same terms as boys, and boys were to be offered domestic science. Employment agencies, training organisations, professional organisations and employers were forbidden to discriminate on the ground of sex, as were banks, hotels and housing bodies − in fact any institution or company offering facilities for entertainment, recreation, refreshment or travel. The precedent for anti-discrimination legislation had been set by the Race Relations Acts of the sixties, and so the Sex Discrimination Act did not meet with much resistance. Although the legislation was far from perfect in the view of many feminists, it did give official recognition to the principle of equality for women, even if it was left mainly to the individual to fight for that equality in courts of law,

However, this legislation did not give women equality in so far as their dual role was concerned. Women were greatly disadvantaged in their careers by the heavy burden of domestic work and child care which they carried in addition to paid employment. The majority of working women had to combine work with family responsibilities. In addition to their own work, their domestic chores of washing, ironing, cleaning, shopping, cooking and looking after the children, they were often still expected to have a meal ready for their husband when he returned from work.

This situation led to resentment and marital discord. A number of suggestions were put forward by feminists in an attempt to remedy this such as pay for housewives in order to raise the status of housework; others campaigned for workplace nurseries, for playgroups and play schemes to ease the burden of child care, and most feminists encouraged members of their households to take an equal share in housework and child care. Most women did the best they could with little help from the state or employers.

Working wives changed the lifestyle of many families. Many women worked in order to provide a second income, an income which could buy 'luxuries' like a car, or fitted carpets, to help buy a house, or pay for a holiday abroad. Not surprisingly, sales of electrical goods rose, particularly labour-saving domestic equipment such as washing machines, refrigerators, etc. In addition, all kinds of 'convenience' foods became popular, particularly frozen foods and 'easy care' clothes which could be drip-dried and did not need ironing.

It is perhaps ironic at a time when there was a massive growth in the so-called service industries and in women's employment, that women were required more and more to serve themselves. The laundry was replaced by the lauderette, waitress service was replaced by self-service cafes and restaurants, and in many shops from grocers to clothes shops customers were expected to serve themselves.

The sixties and seventies were a period of transition for women; new roles were emerging alongside traditional roles. Women's magazines reflect the uncertainty and the conflicting views about women's roles. One significant feature was the decline in popularity of the mass circulation women's weeklies like *Woman's Own* and *Woman*. Throughout the fifties, sales had boomed whilst they served up the old themes of finding your man, marriage and motherhood, and features about royalty. In the sixties sales fell and continued to fall; some titles disappeared altogether. IPC commissioned an American psychologist Dichter, to study *Woman's Own* and report on its performance in relation to present and future requirements. He pointed to the emergence of a 'new woman' − 'the kind of woman who can combine, adjust and compromise femininity with independence and personal fulfilment with family responsibilities. . . .'. (5)

Dichter argued that magazines should take account of the changes affecting women such as increased education, change in employment patterns, exposure to the media. Some editors were sceptical about the extent of the change:

'The goals of the average girl are still to find a man to love, to set up house, and to lead a happy married life. Women's lives may have been changed by affluence but women are still women underneath and the things they care about have not changed.' (6)

Some magazines did continue with more of the same old themes but IPC did try to innovate change. It launched a new kind of magazine *Nova* which advertised itself as taking an 'intelligent' approach to women's publishing. At first it tried to avoid the traditional subject matter of women's magazines but later it did include them, although they did try to treat them in a new way. For example, *Nova* broke new ground in its treatment of sex. Vague generalisations and innuendo were replaced by facts and expert opinion supplied by prominent medical figures. *Woman's Own* also tried to respond to social and economic changes. It replaced its condemnatory attitude to working wives with a more positive approach. In the early seventies it was to run a five-page special on 'How to get the Right Job at the Right Time'. It also began to deal with more controversial subjects like lesbianism and transvestism in its features on sex education.

Estimating the extent of changes affecting women was very difficult, as was the pacing of change within magazines. Dichter may have overestimated the degree of change as *Nova*, in fact, failed. *Spare Rib*, an overtly femininist magazine, was launched in 1972. Its explicit aim was to bring an end to the repression and exploitation of women. It has refused to compromise in order to increase its circulation and in comparison with many women's magazines it has a tiny readership (about 30 000). The magazine which most successfully captured the market of the young independent woman was another magazine launched in this country in 1972 – *Cosmopolitan*. It combined an emphasis on a career with features on health, fitness, taxation and mortgages, and finding your man.

To summarise, women's lives did change in the sixties and early seventies but the image of fun and freedom for women had masked to some degree the continuing inequalities and in some cases had made matters worse. Perhaps it was the contrast between the 'image' and the reality which stimulated the new wave of feminism.

Let's look now at the clothes women wore, the ideals they sought to emulate, and assess to what extent their appearance contributed to or reflected the changing position of women at this time.

Minis, maxis and unisex

The mini was the outstanding fashion of the period in much the same way as short skirts had been in the twenties, and the 'dolly-bird' was the sixties equivalent of the flapper. Although the mini was a widespread and influential style causing even establishment figures like the Queen to shorten her skirts, it did not represent all fashion throughout the sixties or into the seventies when it was still popular. The mini was certainly part of the youthful look which dominated fashion for both men and women for much of the period, but like many other features of women's dress at the time, the youthful look was a reflection of the preoccupations of society at large and not something particular to women.

In addition to the influence of 'youth', there was an emphasis on science and technology, an interest in space travel, and a fascination with new and synthetic materials in all spheres of design. In clothes such interests found expression in the futuristic designs of Courrèges and Cardin, in the use of plastics and metals by designers like Paco Raban and John Bates, and the increasing use of all kinds of synthetic fibres from PVC to crimplene. Of course, when confidence and interest in these areas began to wane, when hippies, for example, sought alternative lifestyles and dress, a return to natural fibres was in keeping with their idealisation of archaic and traditional styles of dress.

Developments in the arts, like Bridget Riley's Op Art were used as a direct source of ideas for textile and fashion design. Later the influence of drug culture and interest in the East brought psychedelic and oriental patterns into fabric design. Political and protest movements also had an impact on dress. For example, the wearing of army surplus and bits of uniform was initiated as an anti-war, anti-military gesture.

But let's turn our attention now to women's dress, and to how these and other changes can contribute to our understanding of women at this time. The styles of the sixties and early seventies certainly appeared to bring greater physical freedom to women. As in the twenties, clothes seemed to become *less restricting but also less substantial*. Once again, the straight unwaisted silhouette dominated. Although bell-shaped skirts continued into the sixties, the trend away from the clearly defined waist had been started by Givenchy who introduced his sack dress in 1957. By the sixties the sack had been converted into 'the shift' and loose-fitting unwaisted dresses dominated. Women were no longer required to have a voluptuous figure as in the fifties and John Bates defined the perfect figure as a 'narrow body, perfect square shoulders, long legs and small bust'. (7)

Skirts had begun the decade just at the knee, standard skirt lengths were 25 inches or 26 inches long, but by 1966 skirts of 18 inches in length were mass-produced and many young women wore them even shorter. Not everyone wore such extreme skirts but the middle-aged and even more elderly women wore their skirts above the knee.

The shortness of skirts led to a focus on the legs, with patterned and decorated stockings. Seamed stockings began to lose popularity, and looked very dated. As hemlines rose it became impossible to avoid the display of stocking tops and suspenders. Morley had produced thick woollen tights for winter wear; these were now produced in a lightweight version and soon became popular with young women. Gradually they replaced a large part of the stockings market even for older women.

Underwear was also changing partly in response to changes in the fashionable silhouette and outer garments, but also because of the availability of new fabrics. During the sixties and seventies, underwear was to become less bulky, lighter in weight, more comfortable and for the young much less ornate in style. At the beginning of the sixties, Lycra (the most common of the elastane fabrics) became widely used in women's foundation garments. Lycra is three times as powerful as rubber and opened up new possibilities for lightweight underwear. Boneless, seamless lightweight corselettes were produced which were forerunners of the 'nude look' in foundation wear. This development affected mainly the older or more curvaceous woman. For, as more women changed to tights, the wearing of suspender belts and 'roll-ons' became unnecessary. This signalled not only a change in style but changes in attitudes. The wearing of a girdle had been a matter of decency, as had the wearing of proper underskirts, but now younger women preferred lightweight stretch bras and bikini briefs which gave a more 'natural' shape. Some preferred the extremely lightweight and transparent body stocking. Foundation garments were now believed by many to be harmful as they weakened the muscles by making them lazy. By the mid-seventies the girdle seemed doomed. The bra may have also seemed doomed when feminists stopped wearing them, but although some women did not wear bras regularly, others turned to the 'no bra' look of bras in soft stretch fabric moulded to the shape of the breast and which did not conceal the shape of the nipple. There can be no doubt that underwear was much more comfortable at the end of this period.

The change of style in the sixties also brought new shoe styles. The decade began with winkle-pickers and high-heels but these were replaced for the young with flat shoes often with rounded toes and straps or buckles, like children's shoes. Other comfortable trends were the popular suede Hush Puppies and desert boots. Even 'kinky boots' were usually flat or had low heels and offered protection from the weather. Young women in the sixties enjoyed a great improvement in comfort and mobility but by the seventies high-heels were returning and a forties revival brought the re-introduction of platform shoes in a grossly exaggerated form. Both young women and men clumped about in enormous platforms which made them look club-footed, and made them subject to twisted ankles. Despite being so unwieldy, they *looked* strong and stable, and of course they were worn by men as well.

Another major fashion change which brought greater practicality to women's dress was the growing popularity of trousers. They were not always comfortable — for example, the fashion for wearing extremely tight jeans — but, in general, they offered women a comfortable and practical alternative to skirts. By the seventies they had become established as standard wear for women for many occasions. Smart trousers suits were featured in couture collections and were the choice of many women wishing to look stylish. In stretch fabrics they became a popular choice with older women, combined with long tunic tops or waistcoats.

The growing acceptability of trousers was part of the growing informality of dress. The increase in holidays and leisure activities had brought with it a growing need for informal and casual clothes. Garments like the anorak, originally worn for winter sports, were becoming widespread. Young people were not concerned with the formalities of fashion which had been respected in the fifties —

they did not care about co-ordinated accessories, appropriate garments for the season, or about wearing a hat and gloves. The 'fun' image in the first half of the decade was replaced amongst the young by a studied and deliberate untidiness. Looking informal was to become the rule!

These changes of style on the whole gave women greater physical freedom but was it an image of independence and equality?

The fashions of the time certainly contributed to an atmosphere of youthful exuberance and permissiveness. The effect of short shift and smock dresses, worn with light coloured stockings and flat shoes was to give women and girls a childlike appearance. As we have seen, John Bates' definition of the perfect figure suggests at least an undeveloped adolescent figure with no womanly curves.

Jean Shrimpton had introduced the look in 1966 with her leggy, almost gawky, slimness and slightly tousled hair and big eyes, but its ultimate was Twiggy who, at six and half stone with her short hair and doll-like painted lashes and knock-kneed stance, epitomized the childlike look. Jean Shrimpton was young, but Twiggy was only sixteen when she hit the headlines and fashion pages. In the fifties models had tried to look at least twenty-five; now, not only were models young, they emphasised youth. With the popularity of cinema as a form of entertainment in decline, it was model girls like these and pop stars like Marianne Faithful who were presented as the ideals of feminine beauty. What hope was there for the over twenty-fives?

The style promoted by models like Twiggy was 'undersized' — little dresses, skinny rib sweaters (sometimes bought from the children's department to get the required fit). Some models like Twiggy had a more boyish style with cropped hair. Others like Patti Boyd presented a more feminine image with longer hair back-combed at the crown to give a raised softer effect. Make-up styles emphasised the childlike look. As in sentimental paintings of children, attention was drawn to the eyes and eyelashes. Eyeliner, mascara and false eyelashes were all widely used, and the technique of drawing in extra bottom lashes like Twiggy was common. The rest of the face was pale, the lips hardly visible under pale or frosted lipsticks.

What did this youthful image imply — a carefree, fun existence? Julie Christie, an actress who was hailed as the very image of the 'young British girl of 1966' said that 'I don't think it is the sexines in me that appeals but an air of abandonment. Men don't want

Fig. 9.1 Twiggy.

responsibility and neither do I.' (8) Was it, then, the innocence and freedom of childhood without responsibilities of earning a living or of family life? Perhaps that was what was 'sexy' – fun and freedom without responsibility.

For there can be no doubt that some of the styles in the sixties and early seventies contributed to the atmosphere of permissiveness and sexual freedom. The mini was regarded as a 'sexy' fashion — it allowed a degree of display of the body for male appraisal and approval not previously experienced in the streets. This tendency was not confined to minis. Another example would be the gimmicky

Fig. 9.2 Hot pants.

topless dresses and see-through blouses and the more widely popular 'hot pants' of the seventies. Glimpses of the body beneath were provided by crocheted dresses, all kinds of key holes, cutaways and exposed midriffs. Attention was drawn to nipples and breasts by the no-bra look of the early seventies. In the sixties, prominent zips and fastenings gave the impression that the garments would be easy to remove. Women were wearing light clothing and less of it. The feel of sixties' styles, in particular, was the opposite of Victorian or even fifties' styles when clothing had provided a physical barrier between the sexes. The sixties' styles suggest *accessibility* and *sexual availability*.

These fashions had very little to offer the older woman or the career woman and even the couture fashions looked better on young figures. In spite of the image of freedom there was very little freedom of choice even for the young. Although fashion rules had changed in the sixties, the dictates of fashion were still very strict. When the mini was fashionable everyone wore shorter skirts, like it or not, thick legs or not. There was no fashionable alternative. To be fashionable you had to be slim, have slim legs, and have straight − preferably blonde − hair. When Sassoon's straight bobs and geometrical cuts were fashionable in the mid-Sixties, no-one wanted wavy or curly hair. Girls would iron their hair and stick it down with sellotape to achieve the straight locks of Sandy Shaw or Cathy McGowan. There were really very narrow views of what was attractive. 'Never for years and years had young women looked so like each other and never before had they all looked so like Jean Shrimpton.' (9) 'If you wanted to be acclaimed as beautiful you had to look like Jean Shrimpton.' (10)

However, from 1967 onwards things began to change. New and more varied ideas of what looked good emerged in an atmosphere of social and political protest, under the influence of the hippy movement and later the influence of feminism.

One significant change was a break in the dominance of the white woman as *the* ideal of feminine beauty. In the early sixties Donyale Luna became the first black model to be featured in a glossy American magazine when she appeared in *Harper's Bazaar*. Even then there was no *black* style, most black women in the United States and Britain simply imitated the current white style. They straightened their hair or wore wigs, used skin lighteners and used make-up made for whites. But in the sixties, a growing number of black states were gaining their independence from colonial powers.

Also, the growing impetus of the Civil Rights Campaign brought a sense of pride amongst black people, and with that pride came a new pride in black appearance. The 'Afro', an unashamedly black style became popular and by 1968 the phrase 'black is beautiful' had been coined. Feminist and political activist Angela Davis projected the new kind of beauty as well as a determined and defiant political stance. What is interesting is that it was not just the emergence of a *black* style; Afros and later corn rows were copied by whites and black style led fashions. *Women's Wear Daily* wrote 'Suddenly it had become fashionable to be black. Now everybody wants to be a soul sister.' (11) Allowing for journalistic overstatement, a significant change had taken place and the total dominance of white standards of beauty had been broken. Since then, black and Asian models are to be seen in all magazines and, of course, at fashion shows.

The dress of hippies in the late sixties influenced mainstream fashion, contributing more romantic and nostalgic looks and styles based on foreign or 'ethnic' styles. The film *Dr Zhivago* had inspired the maxi coat which fitted in with the more romantic image of hippy styles, but it was not worn by everyone and those who did wear it often wore it over a mini skirt. In the late sixties, Laura Ashley's Victorian milkmaid dresses were popular, as were Biba's thirties' revival styles. So, when the midi was introduced, some people were wearing ankle-length skirts, others midis and others minis. The nostalgic look was taken into another era with the forties look in the early seventies which saw the revival of padded shoulders and platform-soled shoes worn with wide flares. There was now much more choice of skirt length and style.

Alongside the more romantic and feminine styles another trend had developed which had its origins amongst the young − that of *unisex* dressing. The dress of the two sexes did become more similar but in two rather distinct ways. Towards the end of the sixties, the influence of the hippy movement brought a change to a more flamboyant style of dress for men − flowered shirts and ties, kaftan-like shirts, velvet trousers, beads − and, of course, long hair. The changes for women had started earlier. Rather like in the twenties when women's position was changing, a freer style of dress had become popular along with a 'boyish' silhouette. But in the sixties, teenage girls started to wear boys' clothes. In particular, they wore men's jeans with the front fastening and men's shirts. They preferred the fit on the hips and front zip to the side fastening

Fig. 9.3 Hippy style.

on all women's trousers. From the mid-sixties on, the younger generation wore the same trousers be it jeans, crushed velvet bell-bottoms or cotton loons.

The older generation tended to find unisex styles deeply disturbing. Some men in authority refused to let women in their jurisdiction

Fig. 9.4 The Laura Ashley milkmaid look.

Fig. 9.5 Unisex.

or employ wear trousers. There were occasions when young men
with long hair were suspended from school and thrown out of jobs.
To some it seemed the ultimate in decadent behaviour. However,
by the early seventies it was commonplace to see young men and

women almost identically dressed with very similar hairstyles. Similar shirts, knitwear, trousers, jackets and shoes were worn, and were often purchased from the same shop. Predominantly, though, women were borrowing men's style of dress; they looked like their boyfriends, not the other way round!

Feminists also tended to borrow male styles of dress, particularly styles derived from workwear like dungarees and jeans, and heavy shoes or boots. It seemed that for women to achieve equal status in society they had to leave behind the restrictions of feminine clothes and achieve an equality in dress.

Some women found trousers so convenient and comfortable that they gave up wearing skirts and dresses altogether. For others, the unisex look was just one of the styles they wore, and they would be wearing it one day and a nostalgic style dress the next.

So far we have been looking at styles which were inspired by and worn by the young. What did the majority of women wear? The millions of women trying to run a home and do a job, the millions of women over twenty-five, how did they look?

Although the mini did affect all age groups, there was a growing division between the fashionable clothes worn by many young people and those for other sections of the population. But dress for older women was evolving and becoming less formal. The chanel suit had made a comeback in the early sixties. Jackie Kennedy in her neat hats, gloves and gabardine suits epitomised the chic European look. She appeared on the covers of magazines as much as some models. However, that style was losing ground, and women were caring less about looking neat and tailored by the end of the decade. The back-combed hairstyles of the fifties and early sixties, and the wearing of hair-pieces in the sixties had made hats less popular, and they were worn with gloves, matching handbag and shoes only for special occasions. On the whole, women began to opt for separates for everyday wear. The increase in holidays and leisure activities had encouraged the trend to more casual clothing, and particularly trousers. Older women also benefited from the more comfortable and lightweight underwear available.

Perhaps the feature which most reflected the changing position of such women, their growing involvement in work outside the home and the increasing demands on their time for home, work and leisure, was the increasing importance of easy-care. The nylon shirt and blouse were extremely popular in the sixties because they were so convenient — they could be washed, drip-dried overnight and needed no ironing. Women now wanted trousers, tops and knitwear which could be put into their washing machines, dried easily and which preferably required no ironing. They no longer wanted to be bothered with careful hand-washing, or fabrics which creased easily and needed careful ironing. The use of man made fibres went up from 31 per cent of all fibres consumed in the UK in 1960 to 69 per cent in 1977. In particular the 'easy-care' fibres showed a dramatic increase: nylon rose from 4 per cent to 21 per cent; polyesters (brand names included Terylene, Trevira, Dacron) rose from 2 per cent to 16 per cent; and acrylics (brand names included Acrilan, Courtelle and Orlon) rose from 1 per cent to 13 per cent.

The advantages of easy-care clothes for the working woman are obvious and in the sixties synthetic fabrics were considered 'modern' and therefore desirable. However, even when interest in natural fibres was revived in the seventies, most children's clothes and many clothes for adults were made in synthetic fibres or a blend of synthetic and natural fibres.

Older, and not so old women may have felt excluded from the dolly-bird image of fashion in the sixties. Whereas people were once excluded by class from participation in high fashion, it seemed you could now be excluded by age. However, as we have seen, some of those styles were not really so liberating and most women did enjoy more comfortable clothes, which were easier to care for with the convenience of washing machines. More casual clothes also reflected a growing informality of dress. By the seventies the system of precise rules about 'proper dress' for different occasions had all but broken down. Even shopping for fashionable clothes in chain stores could now be a relatively cheap and painless experience.

Many of the aspects of dress which had appeared to keep the fashionable Victorian woman in a subordinate position had been cast aside by the early seventies. As the social and political constraints which had kept middle and upper class women virtually imprisoned in their own homes have been thrown off, so clothing styles have both reflected and contributed to the growing emancipation and independence of women. A marked difference in attitude in areas like sexual freedom is clearly expressed in the dress styles of the period. But some things had not changed so much; for example, women were still expected to take primary responsibility for the domestic sphere, although *some* of the drudgery of domestic life had been removed. Also, although women were now working as a matter of course outside the home, it was still in the lower status jobs and often in a part-time capacity. The lack of 'career dressing' for women, as a fashionable style, reflected the inability of women at that time to make real inroads into men's continued supremacy in the world of work.

References

1. Friedan, B. (1964) *The Feminine Mystique.* (Victor Gollancz) 15.
2. Anna Coote speaking on Channel 4 series *The Sixties.*
3. Greer, G. (1972) *The Female Eunuch.* (Paladin).
4. Friedan, B. (1964) *The Feminine Mystique.* (Victor Gollancz) 15.
5. Dichter quoted in: White, C. (1970) *Women's Magazines 1693–1968.* (Micheal Joseph) 151–181.
6. *ibid* 221.
7. Quoted in: Bernard, B. (1978) *Fashion in the Sixties.* (Academy Edition) 64.
8. Shearer, A. 'The changing image Part III'. *The Guardian* February 1985.
9. *ibid.*
10. Anna Coote speaking on Channel 4 series *The Sixties.*
11. Keenan, B. (1978) *The Women We Wanted to Look Like.* (New York: St. Martin's Press) 176.

10   Into the Eighties

WHAT NEXT?

What happened to women after the Equal Pay and Sex Discrimination Acts? What happened after unisex? Given the economic situation in Britain in the late seventies, the deepening recession and high unemployment, one might have expected a situation similar to the thirties to develop when women returned to more traditional roles and to more 'feminine' styles of dress. Indeed, there are some parallels but also important differences.

The consensus of optimism which had dominated in the fifties and sixties began to collapse in the early seventies. Although there had been some economic problems in the sixties, the tide seemed to turn with the coal strike, the three-day week and the oil crisis. Rising inflation and unemployment destroyed the sense of security. Feelings of gloom were increased by the growing problem of terrorism, particularly by the IRA, by the growing fear of nuclear war, and by the cuts in government spending, first by the Labour government and then the successive Conservative governments. By the Eighties there had been substantial cuts in government spending on the Welfare State, housing, and education and there had been another coal strike and rioting in the inner cities. How did this change in atmosphere affect women?

A woman's place

The number of unemployed rose consistently from 1976 so that by the eighties the number of registered unemployed was over three million. The figures remained high until the late eighties and did not include those on government training schemes or those who have not registered. As in the thirties, some regions have been considerably worse affected than others. Once again areas of the North, Wales and Scotland were amongst the hardest hit but this time the Midlands and some parts of the South were also badly affected. In some communities where industries such as coal and steel were in decline there were almost no job opportunities for redundant workers or school leavers. Within the general pattern of unemployment some groups were particularly affected – the young, the old, and members of minority groups. The burden on the state of unemployment benefits produced further rounds of spending cuts including reductions in benefits. As in the thirties, society became polarised. Those in well-paid jobs enjoyed a rising standard of living while the standard of living of the unemployed and the low paid declined.

How did unemployment affect women? In the period up to the mid-seventies there was a rising demand for women workers to which women could respond. But from since 1979, the number of women with paid jobs began to fall.

Despite the decline in job prospects, women were still very anxious to work – some undoubtedly out of necessity but also because more and more women had come to think of paid work as 'normal'. It is regarded as a source of social contact and for some a source of personal fulfilment. Although unemployment may have made it more difficult to achieve their aspirations, there was little sign that women in the eighties thought it was they who had to give up work, as they had in the twenties.

On the whole, women's magazines tended to support this veiw. In her survey of women's magazines for the period, Marjorie Ferguson suggests that the working wife has become totally accepted and there are no examples of the working wife portrayed as a bad wife. (1) The new magazines appeared which aimed specifically at the working woman – *Cosmopolitan* and *Company* at the younger ones. Magazines like *Options* and the short lived *Working Woman* were aimed at the more mature woman, the latter at the high power career woman. Getting your man was now represented as only one of the goals for women; self-fulfilment and careers were also priorities. *Cosmopolitan* featured a quiz entitled 'Is he good for your career?' If your man did not achieve a high enough score, the advice was to get rid of him. (1) *Working Woman's* target readership was those in middle or top management who also have a home and love life. The articles on computers, banks airlines and management problems represented a new approach but its market of the successful business woman or executive was too narrow to sustain it for long.

Perhaps there was a tendency in the media to focus on the 'success stories' of women in professional careers. The image of the female executive found in magazine features and advertising, and the impression of their working lives, is in pronounced contrast to the way most women lived. However although women are still over-represented in the lowest paid work there were some improve-ments in the kind of jobs and rates of pay some younger women achieved, and in the lowest grades and very under-represented in management and the higher grades of many professions, things were beginning to change women were getting some 'top jobs' and the earnings of some were improving.

Attitudes to work affected motherhood. In the mid-seventies the birth rate fell and only in 1977 did births begin to outnumber deaths. This decline could be explained by a general sense of gloom or by the changing attitudes of women. It has been suggested that many women who were young in the late sixties and early seventies delayed having children and the rise in the birth rate occurred when they felt they could no longer postpone parenthood. Those women obviously carried on working longer than previous generations. Some remained at work while their children were young in order to avoid the trap of returning to dead-end and low-paid jobs as many women had done in the sixties.

If the working woman had a high media profile so did motherhood. The struggle of the infertile to have children, 'test tube' babies and surrogate mothers received a lot of media attention. The Royal Family came to forc as the 'happy family' and Princess Diana was portrayed as the 'modern mother'. The agony aunt Clare Rayner declared 'Young marriage and early motherhood are not just permitted again. They have become a perfectly reasonable choice for the intelligent, educated young woman to make...By being what she is, young and in love with life in all its aspects and proud of her parenthood (the Princess of Wales) has given women back to themselves.' Not everyone wanted this definition of womanhood back, even if parenthood did seem desirable.

The independent woman

The independent woman was certainly a popular advertising image of the early eighties financially secure, self-sufficient and attractive, able to please herself. It may not have represented a reality for many women in Britain but there is evidence of a growing desire for independence. More women were seeking careers rather than jobs and valued their financial independence. Unhappy marriages and relationships were more readily abandoned. One in three marriages now ended in divorce and, significantly, seven out of ten divorces were initiated by women. The marriage rate declined and cohabitation rates increased during the seventies. 'Living together' and single parenthood became commonplace and social stigma was no longer attached to either of these states. It was largely accepted that women should control their fertility and decide whether and when they were to have children.

Within the home, women were less willing to accept a subordinate position, especially those who worked, and were less likely to accept the traditional division of labour that occurred within the home. During the late seventies and eighties more men seemed to be helping with domestic work and child care and were to be seen much more frequently pushing pushchairs and doing the shopping. Men were much more likely to be present at the birth of their child and to be involved in looking after him or her. Whether these changes reflect any real change in the basic responsibilities is doubtful but social changes have led men to reconsider their attitudes to issues such as child care, and unemployment may have prompted some households into renegotiating domestic responsibilities.

Young women in the seventies and eighties also seemed more willing than previous generations to break with the stereotype. Although only in small numbers, young women started to break male dominance in certain fields of employment, some in the manual trades and others in areas like the City. They experimented with styles like punk which represented a rejection of 'pretty' and 'conventional' femininity.

New woman new man

The new independent woman needed a new kind of man as a partner, and by the mid-eighties there was a lot of talk about the 'New Man'. In the wake of the women's movement but also Gay Liberation, a reassessment of masculinity, and men's roles had begun in some circles. In the world of popular music, alternative images of masculinity have been created by stars like David Bowie and later, Boy George. The developments of male style within punk and subsequently New Romantics brought a new approach to male appearance, particularly the use of make-up and then flamboyant clothes. Although the 'gender-benders' were a minority even in the music scene, they stimulated a lot of discussion on gender and appearance.

For others, the 'New Man' was some one who cared about how he looked but who was also more sensitive and caring than his predecessors. In 1984, *Cosmopolitan* included in its November issue a supplement 'Cosmo Man' which its editor Paul Keers declared was aimed at the 'New Man'. The contents included articles on fashion, receding hairlines, perfume for men, 'Your body – what a woman wants', on fatherhood, as well as articles on cars, wine and work. There was a heavy emphasis on appearance compared to any other magazine for men. In a discussion on Woman's Hour, it was agreed by the speakers that men had changed. They were more caring, and traditional division between male and female tasks around the house was gradually disappearing. However, journalist Robert Elms also suggested that the notion of the 'New Man' was really a media hype with the aim of selling men more clothes, cookery books, and more toiletries like facial scrubs and tanning lotions. He felt men were being lured into the trap of time consuming and expensive indulgence in make-up and toiletries, the trap from which some women had been trying to free themselves.

Fit woman

A development in the late seventies with which men and women have been equally involved is the obsession with health and fitness. This is the product of a number of influences. Hippies had promoted an interest in alternative food such as wholefoods and macrobiotic foods and in the physical and psychological benefits of meditation and yoga. Around the same time medical research into heart disease and cancer which had reached epidemic proportions in the West, suggested that changes in lifestyle were necessary to combat these diseases. In particular giving up smoking, changes in diet, and increase in the amount of exercise taken have been recommended. Exercise was now seen as essential part of weight control and the reduction of stress, as well as contributing to general health.

Concern with health and fitness was also promoted by the media in a variety of ways. Increasing coverage of health issues and all kinds of sporting activities was given on television. The number of programmes on medical matters, healthy eating and exercise grew, and the coverage of events like the Marathon both reflected and contributed to an interest in sport. Films like *Fame* and *Chariots of Fire* with sporting themes were very popular. Women's magazines included more articles on exercise and health and some magazines entirely devoted to health or specific activities such as running were published. These articles and magazines served to promote and advertise a whole range of goods and services aimed at the fitness conscious person from running shoes, bikes and leotards to diet colas and sugar substitutes. The images of sport and fitness were used in the advertising of many other types of product.

There can be no doubt that people did become more concerned about their diet, their health and general fitness. This included concern about the environment and the effect of pollution and

Fig. 10.1 Leotards and leg-warmers.

chemicals used in food production. However it is interesting to note that the focus on personal well-being occurred when social and economic problems were acute. It is as if people retreated from the ills of society and concentrated on promoting their individual health. Indeed, it was claimed that running could promote health, solve weight problems, relieve depression, and reduce stress, a panacea for all modern ills.

For women fitness was represented as the means to achieve beauty, to increase attractiveness. Aerobics, one of the new boom sports aimed chiefly at women was connected very strongly with slimness and trimming various parts of the body. The aim was to achieve a very flat stomach, firm buttocks and limbs, but still retain a small boned 'feminine' look. Looking good became associated with hard work and even pain. Although available to anyone in theory, the fitness craze was associated with leisure and wealth. Many of the clubs and classes are expensive and only those who have the time to attend classes regularly can hope to achieve the ideal. The 'Queen' of aerobics, Jane Fonda, works out daily in her own studio. Following the example of Jane Fonda, many film stars and TV personalities have produced their own exercise and beauty manuals and tapes. They have become self-appointed experts in the field, and the implication is that you too can achieve this perfection if you try hard enough.

The glamorous woman

In the thirties the glamour of the cinema provided another form of escapism for millions, and movie stars provided important models of femininity. In the eighties there was some revival of cinema-going but television and video provided the dominant form of entertainment. One of the most prevalent themes has been the past. From *Upstairs Downstairs* to series like *Brideshead Revisited* and *The Jewel in the Crown*, some of the most popular television programmes were those which have meticulously reproduced a by-gone age. Often, though not always, they are about the well-to-do and the beautiful and the viewer is encouraged to look back on the elegance of their lifestyles. In films, too, there has been a preoc-cupation with recreating an era, as well as reviving some of the old classics, like those starring Humphrey Bogart. Furniture styles, and styles of interior decoration, advertising images, food packaging, styles of clothes, and the revival of cocktail bars and tea dances in the late seventies and eighties have all been inspired by a mood of nostalgia.

On television, the popularity of series like *Dallas* and *Dynasty* have revealed the extent to which people enjoy escaping into the world of the very rich, where domestic and romantic intrigues are played out against a background of luxurious houses, swimming pools, enormous cars and very glamorous clothes. The women are always impeccably made-up and manicured and dressed in expensive designer clothes. Stars from these series have become cult figures. Victoria Principal and Linda Evans have both published beauty and exercise manuals on how to achieve 'the look'. Joan Collins' identity has become inextricably linked with that of Alexis, the bitchy, scheming character she plays, and her style of dress on and off television is explicitly sexy and glamorous. These series do

Fig. 10.2 Joan Collins − eighties glamour.

reflect changing attitudes to marriage and women's position. The happy ending is no longer a marriage; the plots revolve around divorce, remarriage and affairs. Although the heroines of these series are wealthy, the main sources of their power are their looks, and in some cases their cunning.

If Joan Collins represents one kind of glamorous media heroine, one of the other great triumphs in the media of the eighties is the Princess of Wales. Everything she does meets with acclaim and comment in the newspapers and magazines. Why is it, in the 1980s, that a princess is regarded as so fashionable? Why is it Princess Diana and not the other members of the Royal family? Diana Simmonds, in her book *Princess Di, The National Dish*, suggests:

> 'It is because Diana is truly the modern heroine – certainly not the *Spare Rib* model, nor the career woman's heroine in the *Cosmo* mould, that she has been a popular triumph. Larger than life, and of longer standing than either of those creations of the seventies, she is the girl who took heed of the exhortation of fashion and advertising to change her body *and* her style, and she succeeded...Being a 5'10'' size 10 is the ideal for a photographic model and is thus the impossible image which every woman is taught to believe is perfection....'. (2)

Diana Simmonds regards Princess Diana as 'the disastrous heroine' of the eighties because she has chosen to adopt the dominant fashion look which is almost impossible for most women to achieve, yet she has given credence to the idea it can be achieved if you try. She has legitimised the narrow fashion and media definition of feminine attractiveness, and of course she has combined it with two good traditional occupations – fairy princess and mother.

There was still considerable pressure on women from magazines, advertising, from TV and films to conform to particular fashionable definitions of beauty. But at last a greater variety of roles and styles were open to women.

SPIKEY HAIR, MEN'S SUITS AND BALL GOWNS

As we have seen there was not a wholesale return by women to traditional feminine roles during this period from the mid-seventies to the mid-eighties, so what has happened to the way they look?

In this period we saw punks and career women, bondage wear and business suits, jogging suits and ball gowns, cross-dressing and a whole series of fashion revivals. It became increasingly difficult to isolate *one* really dominant look for women. There have been a number of 'looks' running throughout the period, various looks which do locate women in relation to the economic situation and to the range of interpretations of women's position and role in society.

Poor look, rich look

There are two styles of dressing we are bound to consider when discussing this period of economic uncertainty – the 'poor look' styles based on what has been called an 'aesthetic of poverty', and 'status dressing' based on classic styles. In the late seventies, punk and what was known as the Sloane Ranger look represented these two styles. Punk used the symbols of poverty; this was taken a stage further by the 'hard times' look, and entered the world of mainstream fashion in the form of distressed leather jackets, pre-crumpled and creased trousers and shirts, and faded fabrics. New items of clothing were made to look old and 'used', as if they had stood the test of time. They were loose and baggy and looked as if they had previously belonged to someone else. Known as the 'baglady' look, 'poor look' styles were available through high street shops. They were also found in the couture collections in 1982, in the work of designers like Rei Kawakubo ('her wrinkled cotton-coarse linen jute and knitted rag garments, all twisted, crossed over, knotted and looped') or Yoji Yamamoto's 'gruyère sweaters, ripped and slashed and worn hanging any which way'. (3)

In many ways *asexual*, these clothes did not emphasise the shape of the body beneath. They were extremely comfortable and easy to wear. They are not only a rejection of the luxury of the glamour look but also the image of femininity implicit in it. In a previous season, Lagerfeld had introduced a totally opposite style – 'the waist emphasised by breath-inhibiting patent leather corselet belts...His pencil skirts button up the back and are left undone to facilitate walking, they do not make sitting behind a steering wheel a comfortable experience...With this so-smart look go sophisticated accessories; ornate high-heeled shoes, elegant wide-brimmed straw hats...'. (4) These were opulent, non-functional styles, an overtly sexual form of dressing which implies that a woman is to be kept like an attractive accessory by someone wealthy enough to afford her. It is these kind of styles we have seen worn by the 'glamorous' heroines of American TV series but the belts and the tight, back buttoning skirts reached the high street.

The 'poor look' and its modified forms, like Katherine Hamnett's crumpled silk flying-suits, appealed to some not only because of the implicit message about the wearer's approach to femininity, but because of their apparent attitude to money and status. They are secure enough not to worry about being smart and affluent. But as Angela Carter points out: 'it is ironic that rich girls...swan about in rancid long johns with ribbons in their hair, when the greatest influence on working class girls who are holding down jobs at ludicrously low wages, would appear to be Princess Di, herself always impeccably turned out and never short of a bob. Princess

Fig. 10.3 'That's why the lady is a tramp' (photo Frank Martin, *The Guardian*, September 1983).

Di lookalikes work at the check outs of every supermarket...'. (5)

As the recession took hold and the rate of inflation soared, there was a trend back to classic dressing. At the same time as the poor look, some women were dressing in ways which implied wealth. For those who did not want the out and out luxury and blatant sexuality of the glamour look, there was the unobtrusive conventionality of the classic look. The Sloane Ranger style represented the epitome of classic and 'classy' dressing. Sales of British classics like the Burberry trenchcoat soared, as did imitations in the chain stores. Clothes and accessories with prestige labels, like Gucci scarves and shoes, were worn by those wishing to appear well-to-do in these difficult times. The style was also favoured by career women, and the yuppies, as well as by older women for whom the alternatives were too extreme.

Nostalgia

Nostalgic styles became more popular in this period. Perhaps as a reaction to the economic situation, or perhaps because people wanted something 'unique', people sought old clothing in second-hand shops and jumble sales. In the seventies some women wore a mixture of say forties' clothes with contemporary styles. In the late seventies an attempt to revive forties' styles for the mass market was not a great success. It seemed people did not want the total look but were happy to pick up odds and ends from different periods, in an individual and haphazard way. In the late seventies women also were rejecting the discipline of matching outfits, hats, gloves that was proposed, and the physical restrictions of the straight skirts and tailored jackets. However, shops like Laura Ashley were having great success bringing archaic 'country' styles to urban dwellers. At the turn of the decade, nostalgic eveningwear began to appear; long taffeta dresses with full skirts and then short 'cocktail' dresses. The former were well publicised by Princess Diana before her marriage and her wedding dress was in the same nostalgic vein. But the majority of people just did not have the occasions for wearing such garments.

After the development of comfortable non-fussy underwear in the sixties, the seventies saw a return to the glamour of sensuous traditional styles, and to the tradition of feminine seductiveness. At the top end of the market, this trend was led by Janet Reger but now in Marks and Spencer you can buy basques, suspender belts, camisoles, French knickers and cami-knickers. These styles do seem to suggest a return to overtly feminine and sexy underwear but it is only one option; these styles are sold alongside cotton boxer shorts for women and 'men's pyjamas'. A return to a more seductive femininity was also promoted by tights manufacturers. In the mid-seventies, as women chose to wear trousers more often, there was a substantial decline in the sales of stockings and tights. Pretty Polly launched a controversial advertising campaign which sought to persuade women that they would look more attractive in tights.

It seems to the observer of fashion in the Eighties that one attempted revival has followed another — the sixties, fifties, forties and twenties revivals. This is true not only of the fashion business but in the styles worn by young people. It seemed that, lacking confidence in the future, we were looking backwards for inspiration. But what are the implications of styles inspired by the fifties like those of Lagerfeld? Do they represent more variety, more fun? Or, do they carry with them overtones of fifties' femininity?

Workwear and sportswear

Casual clothes inspired by workwear and sportswear became more popular than ever before with both sexes. Workwear in the form of jeans, has obviously been popular since the fifties. But in the seventies a wider range of workwear styles were worn — dungarees, boiler suits, flying suits, lumberjack shirts and jackets. Boiler suits were even worn for eveningwear, with high heels. In the eighties, fabric, trimmings and stylistic features of workwear were being used to create fashion. Denim, cord, canvas, studs, zips, pockets, flaps, labels like 'Utility clothing', were all being widely used. Even the fabric used for Japanese farmers' work-clothes became high fashion.

In societies where the manual labour involved in manufacture and farming dramatically declined the clothes associated with such work have been adopted as leisurewear. It is ironic that workers now wear what was previously the 'Sunday best' — the suit — for work, and 'work clothes' on their days off.

As well as being nostalgic, these styles embody the image of practicality and comfort, and of being serviceable and durable, of being down to earth. This obviously fitted in with women's desire for a more practical approach to dress, although any woman who has worn a boiler suit soon becomes aware of its drawbacks!

The fitness boom spawned a whole range of dress styles. For people have not only worn sports clothes for sport but also for leisure, even for work. Indeed many people bought 'sports clothes' specifically to wear for another purpose. As a result many items of sportswear, such as trainers, jogging suits, shorts, and leg-warmers have become everyday clothes. It is interesting to note that the garments which did become popular tend to be associated with a high prestige sport or a sport which produces a desirable body type, like skiing or sailing, and dance, People wanted to look not only casual but also fit and healthy, and they wanted the image even if they were not active participants. There was a strong element of conspicuous consumption in the wearing of branded sportswear.

Sport and sportswear did promote an active image for women. Models now looked more muscular, stronger. Women were encouraged to become fitter and stronger, and there is no doubt that sportswear is both genuinely comfortable and practical. Many features from sportswear design were absorbed into fashionable styles.

Womenswear – menswear

During the sixties and early seventies women had adopted elements of menswear and men's styles in the trend for 'unisex dressing'. This trend obviously continued, and some of the looks we have discussed above were worn by both sexes or contain elements of menswear.

In the mid-seventies, the 'Annie Hall' look was created by Diane Keaton. Rather large mens' clothes were worn and the resulting image was one of 'little girl lost', not a self-confident or independent look. But by the eighties 'power dressing' had arrived and the borrowing of men's styles took on a new significance. As we have seen that in the seventies and eighties more women were taking their careers very seriously and more had ambitions to get to the top of their chosen field. Women who wanted to be accepted in a man's world and wished to be taken seriously by men, put aside the feminine wiles of dress and copied the style of their male counterparts. Many career women wore a skirt but the rest of their dress was based on the male suit, jacket, shirt blouse, and sometimes even a tie, although a bow like Mrs Thatcher was much more common. Make-up was played down, shoes were sensible and a briefcase replaced the more feminine handbag. One woman banker pointed out 'It is a deliberately negative statement; clothing is designed not to be obtrusive . . . We dress as men do, in uniform. . . .'. (6) Power dressing in its mimicry of male business style indicated the desire of some women at least to get a share of the status and power hitherto exercised by men.

However, styles associated with career or power dressing spread more widely than the woman executive or business woman. The style reflected an image to which many woman particularly those over twenty-five aspired as the success of shops like Next, Principles and the re-vamped Richard Shops with their 'working wardrobes' demonstrated.

In 1984 as fashion for women was being declared as 'mannish', Gaultier was promoting skirts for men and new sensuous and revealing styles. He declared 'Men too can be glamorous, they can be fragile and beautiful too. They have to be sexy and seductive today.' (7) On the fashion pages new looks appeared for men, longer hair, make-up, unstructured garments, flowered or paisley fabrics, 'peacock' and 'dandy' looks. We should not exaggerate the extent to which such developments have influenced the way most men looked. They did not wear skirts or make-up but their dress became more varied in colour, fabric, and style. It became more casual.

However by the mid-eighties more flamboyant styles were on the wane. The fears aroused by Aids seemed to be producing more conservative attitudes. Nostalgic themes were beginning to dominate, bringing with them traditional images of masculinity. This trend is perhaps best exemplified by the success of the Levi 501 advertisements which combined fifties images with sixties music. In parallel to the display of status and wealth in women's dress, suits had once again become popular. Greatest status was attached to 'designer suits' like those of the Italian Giorgio Armani.

The late-seventies to the mid-eighties was a period in which there were a variety of often contrasting looks for both men and women. Definitions of masculinity and femininity seemed less clear cut and dress styles seem to reflect a diversity in lifestyles and aspirations amongst both men and women.

References

1. Ferguson, M. (1983) *Forever Feminine*. (Heinemann).
2. Simmonds, D. (1984) *Princess Di: The National Dish*. (Pluto Press) 107.
3. Polan, B. 'Champagne and ski' *The Guardian* 12 October 1982.
4. *ibid*.
5. Carter, A. 'The recession style' *New Society* 13 January 1983.
6. Brampton, S. 'City slickers' *The Observer* 9 December 1984.
7. Brampton, S. 'Paris nexus' *The Observer* 28 October 1984.

11 Fashion for All

It is only relatively recently that fashionable clothes became readily available and accessible to women from all social classes and sections of society. In the past fashion was a mark of rank and wealth. (1) Only the rich could afford the luxury of beautiful clothes and the extravagance of changing styles of dress. Fashion was dictated from the top; it reflected the lifestyle and values of the elite and never reached the whole of society. Today members of all classes, people of widely different income levels, social status and age can be consumers of fashionable clothes. Of course, even today, not everyone wears fashionable clothes but today it is perhaps more a matter of *individual choice* and personal circumstance than a mark of status and wealth. This, however, is relative; fashion still exhibits an indulgence in *conspicuous waste*, and the rich do not wear the same fashionable clothes as the less well off. Distinctions in quality and style do remain. However, what is certainly true is that 'being in fashion' is no longer the prerogative of the rich and high-ranking in our society, and fashionable styles no longer simply reflect their lifestyle and values. A working class teenager from Bootle can dress fashionably in clothes inspired by workman's overalls. How much things have changed! (Figs. 11.1, 11.2)

The way fashionable clothes are produced has also changed. In the past, yarn, cloth and clothes were produced by hand either in the home, or by craftsmen or women in small workrooms or shops. Tailors produced men's and women's outer clothing until the end of the seventeenth century when seamstresses began to take over the making of women's dresses or mantuas as they were known then. The clothes, and the cloth from which they were made, were the products of time-consuming labour, and as such were highly valued commodities. (2) Fashionable garments for the well-to-do demanded particular skill and effort but even the simplest garments were made individually, cut out and stitched by hand. Clothes were made *bespoke*, made to order and to fit individual customers.

These days we have the convenience of walking into one of many shops and buying a garment or range of garments 'off the

Fig. 11.1 Edwardian fashion.

peg' − *ready-to-wear*. Relatively few people now have their clothes
made bespoke. Even at the top end of the market, *haute couture*
has largely given way to expensive designer label *prêt-à-porter*.
Most ordinary people are content to buy a garment which may be
one of a hundred, or even one of a thousand similar garments

Fig. 11.2 Seventies workwear.

produced in bulk in a clothing factory. Some people still make their own clothes but nowadays it is usually with the aid of mass-produced paper patterns and electric sewing machines. When and how did these tremendous changes take place?

FROM SLOW BEGINNINGS

It is from the nineteenth century that we can trace the beginnings of three important strands in our account:

(1) the gradual spread of fashion in society;
(2) the trend towards ready-made clothes;
(3) the trend towards factory-made clothes.

However, the precondition necessary for these developments, the first step, was the *mass-production* of cloth.

The first step

The development of the textile industry in Britain was at the heart of the Industrial Revolution. It was the cotton industry which produced the first industrial towns based on the new form of production, the 'factory'. The cotton industry exemplifies clearly the link between Britain's role as a trading nation and colonial power and its early industrialisation. Britain's colonies provided both the raw material and an important market for products. Originally cotton products, calicoes, had been imported from India. These imports were bitterly resisted by the domestic silk, linen and wool manufacturers and the English woollen industry succeeded in banning them altogether in 1700. This left the market open for domestic manufacturers and eventually small manufacturers established themselves near the great colonial and slaving ports of Bristol, Glasgow and Liverpool. The industry was finally concentrated near the latter. The raw material came first from the slave plantations of the West Indies and then from the plantations of the southern USA. The industry produced a substitute for linen, and for wool and silk stockings for the home market and a substitute for Indian goods for the foreign market. Until 1770, ninety per cent of British exports went to the colonies, mainly to Africa, and from the end of the eighteenth century the industry exported the greater part of its output, with the colonies remaining very important markets. It was the expansion of trade that gave the industry its impetus in the second half of the eighteenth century.

The increase in trade and demand for cloth stimulated interest in machinery which could speed up and increase production. During the Industrial Revolution new spinning and weaving machinery was devised and the power of first water and then steam was harnessed to drive them. The nature of the machinery and source of power led to the removal of production from the home and workshop to large-scale factories.

The technical problem which determined the nature of mechanisation in the cotton industry was the imbalance between the efficiency of spinning and weaving, especially after the introduction of Kay's flying shuttle, invented in 1733 and introduced by 1760. The spinners could not supply the weavers fast enough.

The machinery developed to alleviate this problem, such as Hargreaves' spinning jenny and later Compton's mule could be used in the cottage. But Arkwright had already established mills using water and then steam power to drive his spinning machines, and the 'mule' was soon harnessed to water power for use in factories by 1790. Factories were slow to develop at first because of the shortage of skilled mechanics to construct the complicated machines and workers skilled enough to operate them. But the mule was 'improved' and in 1830 a mule was developed by Roberts which could be tended by women and children instead of the more highly paid skilled workers. The cheap and plentiful thread turned out by the new mills at first brought prosperity to the weavers and an increase in their number. The invention of the power loom, by Cartwright in 1785, depressed the wages of the hand loom weavers reducing them first to poverty, and finally replacing them. The period between 1815 and 1840 saw the spread of factory production throughout the industry.

As factories turned out more cloth there was a demand for more bleachfields to whiten the cloth, new and faster dyes, and new methods of printing it. The long, drawn-out process of bleaching fabric in leys and sulphuric acid was replaced at the end of the eighteenth century by a much shorter process using chlorine. In 1775, Bell invented a new method of printing using copper cylinders which replaced the laborious process of printing by hand using wooden blocks. In the past a customer would often choose her own pattern and colours but Bell's cylinders changed the scale of operations. Patterns were engraved on cylinders, several colours could be printed by using several rollers on the machine, and it could turn out 5000 yards a day. However, British dyes were generally poor and the work of the printer could disappear in a shower of rain. Fabric was frequently streaked in the dyeing, spotted in the rain and 'ran' when washed. A number of improvements were made during the nineteenth century but a real breakthrough was made by Perkin in 1856 when he made the first dyes from coal tar. Cheap, bright and *fast* dyes were available. Even these tended to fade in light and were spoilt by washing but in 1880, a chemist named Holliday found a method of fast dyeing the yarn.

So, the major developments in spinning had taken place by 1830; the combing and carding of wool was mechanised in the 1850s; the power loom dominated in the English worsted industry by 1850 and in the Lancashire cotton industry by 1870; the printing of fabrics had been mechanised and dyes had been much improved. From the beginning of the nineteenth century a new source of cheap *warm* fabric for the less well-off was being supplied by the shoddy industry. By grinding woollen cloth and rags to a dust, it was reprocessed with new wool to produce a warm cloth at a price competitive with that of cotton. Attractively coloured, printed fabrics and warm cloth could now be produced in large quantities at much greater speed than hitherto and *more cheaply*.

Mass-production of fabric had been achieved and the fashionable styles of the Victorian period seem to celebrate this abundance in their extravagant and ostentatious use of fabric. *But what of the garment-making side of the industry — was there a corresponding development in large-scale mechanised production?*

The evidence from the early nineteenth century suggests that clothes production remained a small-scale 'craft' industry. It was still normal to make your own clothes or have them made for you, and although 'people spoke of buying a gown or a dress...what they had purchased was the material for making it'. (3) Some ready-made garments were available and advertised in the previous century but these were mainly underwear and childrenswear and, of course, these were all handsewn. The style of clothes, and the number which an individual could afford depended on his or her social and economic position, but this also determined how he or she obtained them.

Well-to-do women generally obtained fabric from drapers and haberdashers. They would have their clothes made by a local dressmaker, or some families might have a dressmaker stay for several weeks to make clothes for the family. It was expected, however, that a young woman would be able to make some of her everyday clothes.

Many upper class and some middle class families employed a permanent sewing maid. She would spend her time repairing clothes and other household linen, making underwear, children's clothes and simple dresses for the women of the household. Sewing maids were still employed for these purposes at the beginning of this century; one sewing maid in a middle class household was paid £25 per annum for her services. (4)

The upper class would purchase their better clothes from a dressmaking establishment in a town, sometimes in London. At this level, dressmaking could be a lucrative business for its proprietor. The best dressmaking establishments had an impressive façade and the lady client would be led into an elegant showroom where she would be shown materials and could discuss possible styles. Fittings would often take place at the client's home, and be delivered there after it had been completed in the crowded workrooms above the showroom. In the eighteenth century, dressmakers had been able to make a silk gown for a ball or special occasion in a day but as the simplicity of early nineteenth century styles gave way to the complexities of Victorian fashions the demands placed on the dressmaker became greater. By 1830 sleeves were much more complicated and dresses decorated with piping required hours of fine stitching, but ladies still demanded that their clothes be made in a matter of days if not hours! For London dressmakers the problems were particularly acute in the 'Season' which lasted from April to July, when 'Society' came to London for the round of social events and activities. The vast majority of seamstresses worked fifteen hours a day during the season, although there is evidence that many worked for over eighteen hours a day for two or three months of the year. (5) The seamstresses were not well-paid, and some found themselves without work when the season came to a close. Some of these unfortunate women were forced into prostitution in order to survive.

The increasing complexity of styles, and the extension in time needed to complete them did not lead to an increase in dressmakers' charges. Prices and wages remained low because dressmakers feared a loss of trade if customers had to pay a more 'realistic' price. The low wages did not, however, deter women and girls from entering the trade in large numbers, mainly because there were so few occupations open to them apart from domestic service.

The existence of so many dressmakers and the low prices of, particularly, the less skilled meant that their services were not beyond the reach of the less well-off. Women did make many of their own clothes, sometimes recutting and remaking them from old ones, but for special occasions, they would have their fabric

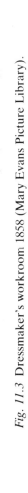

Fig. 11.3 Dressmaker's workroom 1858 (Mary Evans Picture Library).

made up by a dressmaker. The fabric and trimmings would have been bought from a draper, or perhaps the *talleyman*. He took his pack of assorted materials around remote and rural areas, as well as industrial towns. Customers could pay for the goods they purchased by instalment. Those going into service were expected to take a stock of clothes made up at home, but later on drapers supplied gift parcels which contained materials out of which to make uniforms for employers to give to their servants at Christmas.

But what of those too poor to afford either material or the services of dressmakers? Decent clothes were a sign of respectability even among the poor, but the provision of such clothing was extremely difficult for many families. Ladies wishing to help the poor lamented the lack of skill shown in dressmaking. They were advised by publications such as the *Ladies' Economical Assistant* on simple dressmaking techniques and were given patterns for clothes suitable for charitable gifts. Some drapers offered Christmas parcels suitable for distribution to the poor by charitable ladies. Charity schools gave instructions to girls on how to make clothes so they could dress themselves decently, but also with the view to earning their own living.

Although women could sew for themselves and their children, few had the time to spare for needlework. For the poor the second-hand trade was an essential source of clothing. Second-hand clothes were sold at rural fairs and in towns in street markets like Manchester's 'Rag Fair'. In London the second-hand clothing trade was substantial and it was one of the chief sources of clothing in the capital. Mayhew records the importance of markets like Petticoat Lane and Cutler Street where garments were sold not only second, but third-, fourth- or even fifth-hand. The stock was supplied by travelling buyers, often Jewish or Irish in origin, but some of the goods would undoubtedly have been stolen, perhaps from washing lines or stripped from well-dressed children. (6) Some dealers had extensive businesses; for example, Mayhew mentions a Mr Isaacs whose Clothes Exchange had separate sections for the retail and wholesale trade. (7) The wholesale section alone measured 100 feet by 70 and contained about 90 stalls. Other traders displayed just a few garments in the street.

Goods retailed at about 15 per cent of the new price and were in great demand. For women, plain clothes in sturdy washable cloth were the most sought after. But there was a good trade in furs, and in fancy silk dresses of a 'fashionable' kind which after being cleaned with turpentine, were sold to the large number of prostitutes found in the capital. The most popular items for men were great coats and flannel shirts, but also jackets and trousers, which were of much better quality than the cheap ready-to-wear clothes now available to men.

In the nineteenth century, cheap ready-made clothes were being produced mainly for men through what was known as the *slop* trade. (8) In London, shops such as E. Moses and Son Ltd of Aldgate were selling ready-made clothes. *Their stock was not made in factories*, or in large workrooms as in the case of bespoke tailoring but were supplied by outside contractors or middlemen – 'sweaters'. The work was done by outworkers, often in their own homes where they drew on the help of their families to earn a mere pittance. In 1849, a woman making men's shirts was paid 3d (just over 1p) per shirt and even less by the dozen. Outworkers desperate for work were used to undercut the prices of tailors who worked on the premises of shops in regulated conditions. The slop trade did provide a cheap and 'convenient' source of clothing, mainly for men. However, the method of production was small-scale and based on handicraft methods and the exploitation of the producers. Although they were new, respectable people tended to look down on such clothes because their quality and fit were poor.

However, the population in the nineteenth century grew dramatically and with it the demand for clothing. The wealthy and expanding middle classes required fashionable clothes as befitted their status, but there was also a growing demand for cheap, ready-made clothes. The growth of an elite group of skilled workers within the working class whose regular earnings continued to grow throughout the century, and the growing number of lower middle class clerks and office workers who were not well-paid inspite of their higher social status, created new patterns of consumption. Clothing was the mark of those entering the realm of Victorian respectability. *How was the demand for clothing met?*

The sewing machine

A turning point in the production of clothes came with the invention of the sewing machine. An early version had been developed by the French in 1829, another by an English shoemaker, but it was not until Elias Howe invented his lockstitch machine in 184? and

Isaac Singer patented his machine in 1851 that really efficient machines became available in large numbers. Many other brands were soon on the market. However, the invention of the sewing machine did not lead to centralised and mass production of clothing in factories as the development of power looms had done in the textiles industry.

Clothing factories were established, particularly in the North. John Barran of Leeds is said to have been the first in this country to install sewing machines in his tailoring workrooms in 1856. The sewing machines increased the pace of production so much that in 1859 the company developed the band knife, a device for cutting through several layers of material, in order to meet the demands of the faster sewing speeds. In 1879 the oscillating shuttle made it possible for sewing machines to be power-operated. George Holloway and Company were said to be the first in the world to use steam-driven sewing machines and it was claimed that each machine turned out 150 pairs of trousers a week. Although John Barran pioneered the factory production of high grade men's tailoring, and companies like Selincourt and Coleman were to supply good quality womenswear to stores like Barkers of Kensington, factory produced ready-to-wear clothing was generally confined to cheap menswear such as workmen's clothing, cheap maids' outfits, childrenswear, and mantles and underwear for women.

But there was not an immediate and widespread change to large-scale production in factories. In his study of the London clothing trades, Schmeichen suggests: 'As late as 1915 there was probably no industry as untouched by factory production or in which the methods of production had been standardised so little as the manufacture of clothing'. (9) In fact, the large-scale mechanised production of good quality ready-to-wear fashion for women was not achieved until over seventy years after Singer patented his machine. What caused these delays?

The nature of the sewing machine itself must explain to some extent the delays in the change towards factory production of both ordinary clothing and fashionable styles for women. It was (and still is today) small, comparatively cheap, and just as suitable for use in the home or a small workshop as in the factory. Singer lost no time in mass-producing his machine and in making his hand- and treadle-operated machines available to amateur and professional alike. He opened what is said to be the first chain of retail shops, beginning with a branch in Glasgow in 1856. For those who could not afford to buy a machine outright, Singer introduced a hire-purchase scheme.

Schmeichen suggests that the sewing machine encouraged the use of sweated, unskilled labour working in small workshops or at home, and as a result most ready-made clothes were not made in factories. Other technology did not counter this tendency; machines like Reece's buttonholing machine (1881) were also suitable for domestic use, and the band knife, although not suitable itself for domestic use, provided the cut out pieces of material at a rate which could keep many outworkers occupied.

The ready availability of machines under hire and leasing schemes meant that the trade now attracted many unskilled workers. Sweaters encouraged this tendency with the practices of subdivision and subcontracting. Subdivision meant that instead of a skilled craftsman or woman making a whole garment, the making-up process was broken down into a series of tasks. As an outworker had only to learn how to do one task, unskilled labour could be used. Subcontracting became an extensively used form of production in the ready-to-wear trade. A sweater might agree to supply a quantity of garments to a manufacturer, wholesaler or shopkeeper. After paying a deposit for the cut out pieces he would distribute the work to a number of workshops or homeworkers, who in turn might contract out to a smaller sweater or to outworkers, and indeed it could be subcontracted out again. Each time, of course, the recipient of the work would receive a lower rate of pay.

An abundant source of labour prepared to work for very small rewards made the sweating system possible. Sweaters made use of cheap labour — mainly women who worked in their own homes using sewing machines which were often on hire from their employers. From 1880 onwards the pool of cheap labour was swollen by an influx of Jewish refugees fleeing persecution in Russia and Poland. Large numbers of Jews settled in Britain, particularly in those areas associated with the clothing industry — Leeds, Manchester and the East End of London. Many were skilled tailors and entered the men's tailoring industry, but in London many entered the women's tailoring industry and provided the basis for much of the early development of ready-made tailored clothes. They provided an important source of labour at all levels of the clothing trade, from high class tailors to sweatshops in the East End. Like women homeworkers, immigrants were, and still are, particularly vulnerable to exploitation.

The plight of such workers did not go completely unnoticed. A Lords' Committee in 1880 drew attention to 'the unduly low rates of wages, excessive hours and unsanitary conditions of the workplace'. However, legislation intended to protect employees in small workshops – such as the Factory Acts of 1891 and 1895 – by introducing registration and inspection of workplaces had the effect of causing a decline in the number of workshops and an increase in the number of outworkers, workers who could not be protected by the legislation. Public feelings were roused by an Anti-Sweating Exhibition sponsored by the *Daily News*, in which nineteen out of the thirty-two trades exhibited were clothing trades. As a result the National Anti-Sweating League was founded with the aim of establishing minimum wages. The report of a Parliamentary Committee resulted in the establishment of trade boards to improve conditions of employment in the sweated industries. These boards were to set minimum time and piece-rates for *all* workers whether in factories, workshops or their homes. However, the Trade Boards for Wholesale Mantles and Costumes, and Dressmaking and Women's Light Clothing were not established until 1919 and 1920. Women at home making slip bodices which would retail in shops like Harrods at 7s 11d (40p) were paid 11d (5p) a dozen. Most underwear makers would earn a maximum of 8s (40p) a week. The elaborate Edwardian blouse, with many small tucks and lace inserts, would retail for about 18s (90p) to 25s (£1.25) but the maker would probably have been paid 10d (4p) per blouse and earned less than 10s (50p) a week.

The use of the sewing machine had resulted in an increase in the production of clothing particularly cheap ready-made clothing. But those who benefited from these goods did so at the expense of the sweated labour which had produced it.

The slow development of the factory production of fashionable clothes for women has many causes but the sewing machine may have contributed to the delay by encouraging the trend towards ornate and elaborate styles. The sewing machine came on the market at a time when there was an increasing demand for fashionable clothes from the growing ranks of the middle classes eager to show off their new-found wealth in their dress. At the same time, and by no means unrelated to this, fashionable styles were becoming more ornate and the amount of clothing worn was increasing. As a labour-saving device the sewing machine must have been a godsend to dressmakers, sewing maids and home

Fig. 11.4 Skirtworkers' Daily News Sweated Industries Exhibition 1906 (Mary
Evans Picture Library).

dressmakers as the amount of required sewing to make fashionable
clothes was reaching a peak. It is estimated that a machinist could
do the work of five seamstresses.

However, the sewing machine, instead of speeding up the production of clothing, may have actually encouraged an increase
in the amount of sewing and the complexity of styles. As the
Englishwoman's Domestic Magazine suggested in 1867:

> 'Great as is the saving of labour by the introduction of sewing machines,
> what lady can say that her sewing is less a tax on her time and strength
> than it was before the sewing machine appeared?...As soon as a
> lovely woman discovers she can make ten stitches in the time one used
> to require, a desire seizes her to put in ten times as many stitches in
> every garment as she formerly did.' (10)

Fig. 11.5 Ornate styles of the 1870s.

It is true that from 1860 fashionable styles did become even more elaborate in cut, construction and decoration. The bustle of the 1870s, the mass of pleats and frills which accompanied it and the tight-fitting bodice were products of the dressmaker's craft and were totally unsuited to factory production.

Other devices to aid the dressmaker were developed — from kilting and pinking machines to dress stands and tracing wheels. Paper patterns had been available since 1830. But they were so complicated, with numerous pattern pieces for several garments all on one printed sheet, and so costly that it seems likely they were used mainly by professional dressmakers. In 1850, the magazine *World of Fashion* included a collection of paper patterns in each issue 'in order that Ladies of Distinction and their dressmakers may possess the utmost facilities for constructing their costumes with the most Approved Taste in the Highest and most Perfect Style of Fashion'. (11) Paper patterns were soon readily available. An American, Butterick, laid claim to the invention of the paper pattern in 1863. This claim was apparently unfounded, but he did produce less complicated patterns. By establishing a network of agencies in drapers' shops all over Britain and opening a shop in Regent Street in 1875, he made them readily available to the public.

New sources of knowledge about fashion trends encouraged the spread of fashion amongst the middle classes. In the second half of the nineteenth century, the number of magazines for women increased dramatically, and their circulation figures grew steadily. (12) Magazines such as *The Englishwoman's Domestic Magazine* catered for the needs and interests of middle class women. It was one of the first to provide engravings of the latest Paris fashions. Paris had taken the lead in fashion and magazines with their sketches and detailed descriptions could keep their readers in touch with not only the styles in vogue in London but also current Parisian modes. Armed with such knowledge, many middle class women were eager to reproduce the styles in their own wardrobe, and in order to assist them in this endeavour many magazines included advice columns on the problems of making clothes and provided a paper pattern service. However, the styles they wished to copy during the latter part of the century were so complex that many had to rely on the skills of the professional.

So even after the invention of the sewing machine, the dressmaking trade enjoyed considerable growth. In London the number of dressmakers increased from almost 55 000 in 1861 to 80 000 in 1911 in order to serve the needs of the rapidly expanding population. These dressmakers provided services for all sections of society; from the fine Court Dressmakers of Bond Street who supplied dresses at eighty guineas each to the richest women in society, to the humble dressmakers of the back alleys who charged as little as 5s 6d (27.5p) to their working class customers. Dressmakers continued to be a major source of clothing and fashion for middle class women.

However, the department store was developing as an alternative source of fashion for the middle classes. The growth of the department store runs parallel to the growth of the middle classes. Most of these stores started as small shops; some — Harrods and Fortnum and Mason, for example — started as grocer's shops; others, like Debenham and Freebody and Swan and Edgar as haberdashers or drapers. From selling fabric, trimmings and accessories it was a small step into producing garments, and by the late nineteenth century most leading stores had set up workrooms for making bespoke women's fashions. Clothes were made to order and made to measure. They were of high quality and stores were able to attract the upper end of the middle class market. Debenham and Freebody even described themselves as Court Dressmakers. The stores were popular with wealthy provincial women who wanted the prestige of London fashions but who did not know the best dressmakers in London. The stores kept their regular customers' patterns and measurements on file for reference.

The department store was part of a new structure which was developing within the fashion industry and which was to facilitate the spread of fashionable styles designed for the elite in society to other less wealthy and prestigious groups. Dressmakers of the highest quality had been concerned with producing splendid and *unique* garments made to the individual customer's specifications. This practice continued well into the twentieth century but the idea of selling a design rather than just one garment began to change the role of the top 'dressmakers' or 'couturiers' in Paris.

In the mid-nineteenth century, Paris had regained its image as the centre of the fashion world. Its fortunes had been revived by an Englishman, Worth, who became the dressmaker of the Empress Eugenie, and then of many of Europe's royal ladies. His business developed on a large scale, employing 1000 workers by 1864. Methods of production remained those of the craftsman, of course, as did for the other couturiers and Court Dressmakers in England. However, Worth set in motion a new business structure for the fashion industry when he produced model gowns not only for sale to private customers but also for copying by top dressmakers – and eventually manufacturers and big stores in France, Britain and America. English department stores frequently advertised Paris models, alongside their own designs, and both would be made in their own workrooms. They provided middle class women with the opportunity to wear 'Paris fashions' created by the names who dressed royalty. High fashion began to be associated with names of designers rather than the great ladies who wore it.

This spread of fashion, however, was limited to the well off. Department stores cultivated an air of luxury and exclusivity towards the end of the nineteenth century and it was not until the American Gordon Selfridge opened his store in Oxford Street in 1906 that there was an appeal to the wider public. He launched the first purpose-built store with a massive advertising campaign and as a result a million people visited the store in the first five days. The new store maintained the luxurious image with a winter garden, lounge, reading room and aerial garden but it had an open door policy. It provided the first bargain basement in a British store to appeal to the less well off.

Department stores had been making fashion accessible to a wider range of people by selling fashions through catalogues and mail-order. At first they produced loose-fitting garments like mantles but later on 'ready-to-wear' gowns and costumes were advertised. However because sizing was so rudimentary such garments were *partially made* rather than ready-to-wear. Generally, ready-made garments were produced in one size, 'stock size'. If larger or smaller sizes were attempted, it usually meant that an inch or so had been added or subtracted all round! Department stores had begun to offer ready-made clothes for sale at the store and customers could have them refitted and altered by the workroom staff. But this obviously was not possible for those buying by mail-order. This meant that advertisements for 'dresses' rarely referred to completely made-up garments. Sometimes the garment arrived completely unmade and had to be assembled and fitted by the purchaser; sometimes she would be provided with a made-up skirt and material for a bodice; or perhaps the back seam of the garment would be left open to allow the purchaser to fit the garment to her own measurements. In some cases the customer was required to

The Dedication of a Great House·

A DAY WELL SPENT
IS PASSED AT SELFRIDGE'S

THIS HOUSE
IS DEDICATED
TO WOMAN'S SERVICE
FIRST OF ALL

AND for this there are many excellent and satisfying reasons.
To begin with, everything at Selfridge's is obviously and charmingly
NEW—the great building itself and its equipment the vast stocks of
varied merchandise in their entirety the methods of displaying them to best
advantage and the unaccustomed and luxurious appointments instituted to provide every possible comfort for daily visitors.

We intend that the Selfridge reputation shall be for Enjoyment as well as for
Honest Value to be obtained, for Time as well as Money to be profitably spent.

This House is dedicated to Woman's Service first of all, and our purpose is to
make her Shopping more attractive than it has ever been before; so to satisfy her
with Value, Stocks, and Prices that she will discover a wider and more pleasurable
meaning in the word " Shopping " than she has hitherto read into it ; and learn
regard for Selfridge's as the best equipped place of Merchandise in London for every
Shopping purpose in which she takes an interest.

There is a home-like lounge for smoking, and gentlemen are invited to use it
as they would their club.

SELFRIDGE & CO.
OXFORD STREET, LONDON, W.

Fig. 11.6 Invitation to luxury.

supply details of her measurements, or a well-fitting bodice. It was
probably to keep the staff of bespoke workrooms occupied during
slack periods that the deparment stores started to produce ready-
to-wear fashion.

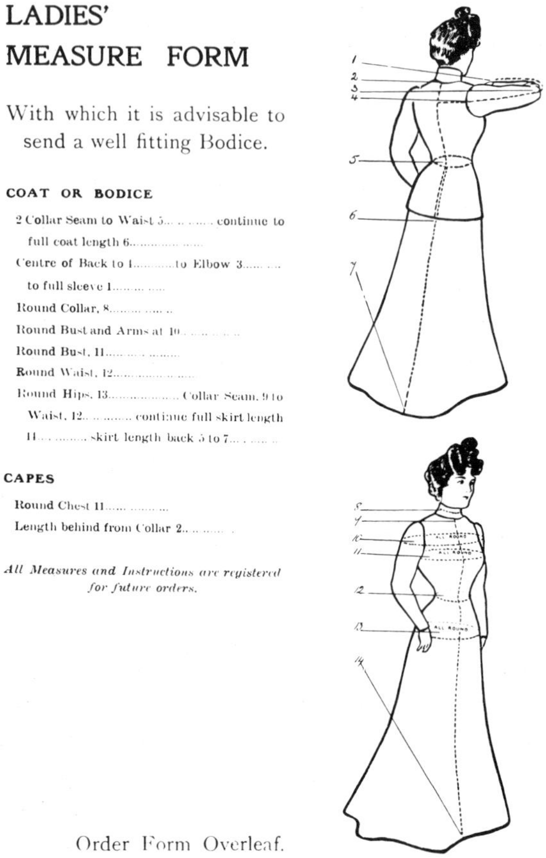

LADIES'
MEASURE FORM

With which it is advisable to
send a well fitting Bodice.

COAT OR BODICE

2 Collar Seam to Waist 5.............continue to

full coat length 6................

Centre of Back to 4............to Elbow 3..........

to full sleeve 1..........

Round Collar, 8..............

Round Bust and Arms at 10..........

Round Bust, 11..........

Round Waist, 12..............

Round Hips, 13................Collar Seam, 9 to

Waist, 12.........continue full skirt length

11..........skirt length back 5 to 7..........

CAPES

Round Chest 11..............

Length behind from Collar 2..........

*All Measures and Instructions are registered
for future orders.*

Order Form Overleaf.

Fig. 11.7 Ordering by mail 1904.

The lack of adequate methods for sizing certainly inhibited the
development of good quality ready-to-wear clothing but the very
nature of fashionable styles increased the problems of achieving a
good fit in fashionable ready-made womenswear. The styles of the
late Victorian and Edwardian fashion − the close-fitting bodices,
high collars, tight sleeves, bustles or bell-shaped skirts which had
to fit smoothly over the hips meant there was still no real alternative
to time-consuming fittings of bespoke clothing for fashionable
women.

The nature of fashionable styles and the social values implicit in
them also inhibited the spread of fashion in society. Despite the
invention of the sewing machine, the growth of a woman's press

informing the public about fashion, and department stores — which contributed to an increase in the number of women participating in fashion and the ease with which they could do so — fashion was restricted to a minority.

This was because fashion at the turn of the century was led by High Society, the aristocratic and the extremely wealthy, and reflected their lifestyle and values. In order to be fashionable a woman required considerable resources and a life of leisure. Both men and women had to follow a strict code of dress which necessitated an extensive and expensive wardrobe. A lady had different outfits for morning, afternoon and evening; for teas, garden parties and balls; for staying at home or going shopping; for cycling, motoring or walking. A lady may be required to change her dress five or six times a day. Edwardian fashions were characterised by a mature S-shaped figure created by a corseted waist, a large overhanging bosom and ample hips thrust back; a profusion of lace fur and ribbons, enormous padded out hairstyles and even larger hats decorated with feathers and artificial flowers. Apart from sportswear and tailor-mades, women's fashions were made of light translucent fabrics such as silk chiffons and cotton lawns in delicate 'sweet pea' colours. Long rustling skirts and later, the tight hobble skirt, restricted a lady's movement. These styles were not only evidence of wealth and the ability to buy luxury goods, but their delicacy and restrictiveness showed that the wearer did no work of any kind. The most wealthy could not even dress themselves and required the services of a maid to achieve the elaborate and spectacular results. Servants were required not only to launder, iron and thread underwear with ribbons but generally take care of all domestic tasks.

The social position of members of Edwardian society was clearly visible from the style and quality of their clothes. Fashionable clothing distinguished the minority, the social elite, from the majority, who had neither the time nor money to indulge in such finery. Out of a population of 33 million people in England and Wales, only 400 000 people declared their incomes at more than £400 a year and less than one million people were liable to pay income tax which was set at 1s (5p) in the pound on incomes of £160. In 1913–14 the average wage was £80 per annum but many women received less, not only working class women but also those working in the lower professional grades.

For example, the budget of an invoice typist living in London shows her total income for 1910 to be £66 18s (£66.90). A representative of the new breed of lower middle and middle class working woman, she probably adopted the style of dress associated with the 'New Woman' — tweed suits or high-collared shirts and skirts made popular by the Gibson girl. But in no way was she 'fashionably' dressed given her annual expenditure on dress of £5 9s 2d (£5.46) and the limited nature of her purchases.

> 'The material for a blouse was bought and made up, and a dress was dyed. No new dresses or skirts were bought. A new coat was bought and two hats. All the underclothing was bought ready-made. One pair of walking boots, one pair of shoes and a pair of sandshoes were bought, and boots were repaired three times...shampoo powders, hairdressing, toilet soap, dentifrice...'. (13)

Her purchase of ready-made underwear but bespoke blouse is typical of the period. Although not fashionable her dress was no doubt neat and highly respectable.

Many women found it a struggle to keep themselves adequately clothed. In her account of working class life in Lambeth in 1913, 'round about a pound a week,' Mrs Pember Reeves described the overcrowded conditions in which most families lived — often without proper facilities for cooking or washing. These were not the poorest families but those of respectable regular wage-earners. Even so, they had little if anything out of their weekly budget for clothes.

> 'Clothing is, frankly, a mystery. In the budgets of some women 6d (2½p) a week is set down opposite "clothing club". This seems meant to provide for underclothing — chiefly flannelette. One shilling (5p) is down perhaps, against "boot club". In the poorer budgets items for clothing appear at extraordinarily distant intervals, when, it is supposed, they can no longer be done without. "Boots mended" in the weekly budget means less food for that week, while any clothes which are bought seem to be not only second-hand, but in many cases fourth- or fifth-hand.
>
> 'The women seldom get new clothes; boots they are often entirely without. The men go to work and must be supplied, the children must be decent at school, but the mother has no need to appear in the light of day. If very badly equipped, she can shop in the evening in the Walk, and no one will notice under her jacket and rather long skirt what she is wearing on her feet. Most of them have a jacket, a hat, and a "best" skirt to wear in the street. In the house a blouse and a patched skirt under a sacking apron is the universal wear.' (14)

Even if the typist or one of these women had been able to afford fashionable clothes, what use would a Merry Widow hat or silk tea-gown have been to them?

In summary, then, the following factors had delayed the development of mass-produced ready-made fashionable clothes. First, technological developments were limited and as yet had not encouraged widespread factory production. Furthermore, sizing and grading, key elements in successful ready-to-wear were not well-developed in this country. Secondly, the styles of fashionable dress for women were unsuited to both ready-to-wear and factory production, and to the lives led by the majority of women. Thirdly and most significant the majority of women did not have the time or resources to indulge in the conspicuous waste implicit in the act of following fashion; there was as yet no mass market for fashion to stimulate production. As a consequence the retailers of fashion remained elitist and exclusive; there were then no retailers providing fashion for the masses.

THE GROWTH OF READY-TO-WEAR FASHION BETWEEN THE WARS

The combination of stylistic, technical and social changes which occurred in the period between the wars promoted the growth of factory-produced fashionable clothes for women which could be bought 'off the peg'.

Changes in style

After the First World War there was a radical change in the appearance of women. A number of factors had led to the decline of cumbersome and ornate styles for women, and lighter, more comfortable and plainer styles were fashionable. Although on the whole fashion was still led by and created for the rich, there was a new mood of simplicity and practicality amongst some of the designers. Poiret may have initiated the trend but designers like Chanel followed it through. For example, she was inspired by the Deauville fishermen's clothes to design casual and practical clothes for women, adapting their sweaters and creating 'matelot' dresses with wide sailor collars. She also made popular what was known as

Fig. 11.8 Simple lines – Chanel's jersey suit.

'the dressmaker's suit', a cardigan jacket with or without collar worn with a straight skirt and made out of jersey. This kind of simple design inspired Jaeger to update its image of specialising in 'health' clothes and enter the field of fashionable ready-to-wear for a wider public by launching a range of Chanel-type easy-fitting suits.

Styles such as the dressmaker's suit, the chemise dress and simplified daywear with boat or V-necklines, or Peter Pan collars, were much easier and cheaper to manufacture than the tailor-mades – the very fitted and elaborate styles with high-boned necklines of the Edwardian period. They presented fewer technical problems for the manufacturer and because they required less fabric, less trimmings and involved less sewing, they cost less to make. The tubular shape which became popular in the twenties reduced the problems of sizing and fit. Because these clothes were looser fitting, a wider range of women could wear the same garment (Fig. 11.8). In the late thirties, the square padded shoulders which were so fashionable also allowed more flexibility of fit for the buyer of ready-to-wear.

The styles of the twenties and thirties were suitable for the use of a new and cheaper fabric rayon. Rayon had been developed towards the end of the nineteenth century. It provided an excellent fabric for the production of cheaper fashion, and was used as a substitute for silk. Once again, Chanel provided a lead when she used it in her collection in 1915. Rayon was better adapted to the making of fashionable ready-to-wear than the cheap cotton fabrics available at the time; it was light and draped and printed well. What is more, rayon became a very cheap fabric. Protection was given to the rayon industry in 1925 when import duties were imposed on silk, and all imported rayon and rayon goods. Rayon production and weaving expanded and many manufacturers turned from cotton to rayon production. The price of rayon fell from 18s 6d (92½p) a lb in 1920 to 2s 2d (11p) in 1937.

The popularity of simple styles which could be produced in a cheap and easy to handle fabric encouraged factory production. Increasingly, dress factories were able to produce attractive fashionable clothes at reasonable prices and this encouraged women to buy ready-to-wear clothes.

Technical change and factory production

Although Margaret Wray suggests that women's outerwear production could be largely described as a factory-based industry by 1939, producers of womenswear in Britain had been very slow to adopt existing technology. (15) The American ready-to-wear industry was well in advance of the British in terms of its size, the quality of its products and the degree of its mechanisation. It provided a lead for Britain not only in the manufacture of fashion, but also in methods of retailing. Until the Second World War there were large-scale imports of American ready-to-wear into Britain because the goods were superior to those made in this country.

Most of the technical innovations introduced into Britain were from the United States. The use of the sewing machine, in the nineteenth century, had established bulk cutting and high speed sewing but in 1900 the making of buttonholes, sewing on buttons, felling of hems, padding of collars and lapels in factories were still done by hand in Britain. In the United States, Reece Machinery were pioneering buttonholing machinery in the 1880s, as were Singer. In 1900 Dearborn developed a blindstitch machine for felling hems and in 1902 an improved machine was introduced for padding collars and lapels. The Eastman cutter was developed in 1888 and was used in this country by companies with cutting rooms too small for the band knife. The Hoffman Press was introduced in 1907 into this country to speed up pressing operations. Margaret Wray writes: 'The main innovations in clothing machinery on which factory production has been based was in general use in the larger men's tailoring factories by the time of the 1914—18 war. But apart from the basic sewing machines, these innovations were little used in the women's tailoring industry until the late 1920s and in the dress industry until the 1930s'. (16) As we have seen, women relied largely on dressmakers, the products of sweated labour, or second-hand clothes, rather than factory-produced clothes.

Gradually, things began to change. The First World War was a decisive factor in changing the character of the clothing industry. It affected the use of labour and production techniques. One of the factors which had inhibited the development of factory production was the use of the homeworker and sweated labour. The demand for labour during the war reduced the number of people, and women in particular who were available for and willing to take such work. Many women continued to work long hours but now it was outside the home in factories such as munitions where conditions were regulated and the pay was relatively good. The sweating system depended upon plentiful supply of cheap labour. Alternative forms of employment after the war reduced the number of women willing to work in this way and post-war immigration restrictions limited the supply of new workers. In theory, cheap labour came to an end when the Trade Board for Dressmaking and Women's Light Clothing set minimum time and piece rates for all workers whether employed in factories, workshops or in their own homes. Conditions did improve but the evils of the sweating system have not been completely eradicated even today. (The Low Pay Unit is still campaigning against sweated labour and there are still cases of women working for derisory sums making garments in their own homes.)

The First World War also affected production techniques, initially in menswear but the benefits eventually spread throughout the industry. The demand from the Government for millions of uniforms of standard quality and style in a range of standard sizes brought about improvements in manufacturing standards and more efficient methods of production. Manufacturers learned important lessons from the need for long steady production runs a steady stock supply and the need to make best use of scarce labour. There was a growth in larger production units and labour-saving machinery such as mechanical cutters and power machines were introduced.

In womenswear, the economies of factory production began to outweigh the previous advantages of home workers. Factory production was encouraged by the simplification of styles, machinery from the United States and Germany was becoming more efficient and less expensive to buy, and some machinery like the overlocking machine were too specialised for home use. Firms like John Barran of Leeds, a pioneer of factory production of menswear, began to produce women's coats and costumes in the twenties. During the thirties factory production of women's ready-to-wear became firmly established.

Such developments were encouraged by the protection given to the British industry from foreign competition and in particular from American dress imports. In 1931 the British Government imposed a 10 per cent duty on all cloth and clothes entering the country, and increased the duty to 20 per cent the following year.

The industry was not, however, deprived of the advantages of advice or technical innovation from abroad. During the thirties an influx of German and Austrian refugees from Fascism were to make a contribution to the technical skills required for organising factory production, particularly in the London area. The clothing workers among them brought a knowledge of continental styling and bulk cutting which improved the attractiveness of British ready-to-wear.

American advice was sought on sizing, a key element in the

development of ready-to-wear production. British sizing was extremely rudimentary, until the thirties when a number of British fashion producers invited American experts to this country to introduce systematic sizing and grading on lines which had given them a lead in ready-made clothing. (17) The Americans set new standards of manufacture and planned production.

The improvements in machinery, in techniques of cutting and grading, and methods of production meant that dresses of reasonable quality could be produced on a large scale in a range of sizes (though still far from perfect) for a price that many women could afford.

The growth in demand for ready-to-wear fashion

Important changes occurred in British society between the wars that were to lead to the growth of a mass market for fashion: radical changes in industry and the economy, changes in the position of women, in the lifestyles and living standards of the social classes, and the development of the modern mass media.

During the twenties and thirties there were periods of industrial decline, industrial unrest, economic catastrophe, and prolonged periods of large-scale unemployment. In the period immediately after the First World War, there was a slump in world demand for the products of those British industries, such as coal, shipbuilding and textiles, on which Britain had built its prosperity over the past hundred years. Massive unemployment followed; in 1921 there were over two million registered unemployed and this figure did not fall below one million throughout the decade. There was considerable hardship despite extensions of the 'dole' system. There were a large number of strikes, primarily against the general drive against wage reductions, and strikers included groups like the police as well as shipbuilders and engineers. The culmination of this action was the General Strike of 1926 which was called when the coal-mine owners threatened a lock-out of miners who refused wage reductions. After nine days, despite the support of all the major unions, the Trade Union Council backed away from revolt and called off the strike in what amounted to an unconditional surrender. The miners went back to work eventually on terms involving less pay and longer hours.

Three years later in 1929, the world was taken by surprise by the

Wall Street Crash. The 'Depression' followed. Within the next four years world trade had dropped by half and unemployment rose to over two million by 1930 and over two and a half million by 1933. The 'National Government', an alliance of all major parties, had no real policy to solve the problems facing the country, but in order to save the country's finances introduced cuts in government spending. It reduced the pay of the armed services, of civil servants and school teachers and cut unemployment benefit by 10 per cent.

It was the North, North West and Wales which were particularly hard hit by unemployment, areas which depended on the old and now stagnating heavy industries. For many the thirties was a period of great misery and hardship, squeezed by the Means Test and with little prospect of finding work. Despite attempts to draw public attention to their position, the plight of groups such as the Jarrow marchers seemed to go largely unheeded by the more fortunate. For, indeed, the situation was not the same all over the country. Despite the Depression and to some extent the policies of the National Government, the nature of British industry and the economy were changing. New industries were emerging and expanding, bringing prosperity and a rising standard of living to those in work.

New sources of power, electricity and the petrol engine were replacing coal and steam power. The chemical industry was expanding and producing new materials, such as bakelite which were used instead of metals, and synthetic fibres like rayon which replaced natural fibres. The nature of the goods produced was also changing. Britain was in a period of transition from an economy dominated by heavy industry and the manufacture of capital goods to one increasingly involved in the supply of consumer goods.

In the inter-war period, electricity became an important source of power for both industrial and domestic use, and the petrol engine an important part of transport, both commercial and private. All kinds of mass-produced consumer goods were available − motor cars, radios, gramophone players and records, electrical goods for the home, razor blades, rayon stockings, canned and packaged foods, cosmetics and toiletries, all promoted by new forms of advertising. Entertainment, reading matter, house-building − all aimed at the private consumer − boomed during the thirties.

These industries provided new and increased employment opportunities but not for everyone. The prosperity brought by such expansion tended to be concentrated in the South-East and the West-Midlands. In the period 1932 to 1937, out of a net increase of 644 in the number of factories in Britain, 532 were in Greater London. Almost two-thirds of the employment provided by new factories in Britain was in Greater London although it had only one-fifth of the population. (18) Those living in such favoured areas and those in employment enjoyed a rising standard of living during the thirties, and for the first time those people who produced the goods were seen also as large-scale *consumers*. The mass-produced consumer goods were aimed at the working class market.

The market for fashion was part of this change in the buying habits of working class people. Working class women, particularly single ones, in employment had disposable income to spend on relatively cheap consumer goods. They were becoming more knowledgeable about fashion through mass-produced reading matter and they would no longer be satisfied with cast-offs. They wanted attractive fashionable clothes to wear and, as they worked, the convenience of buying them off the peg.

The lifestyle and standard of living of many people from the middle classes also underwent change during the inter-war period. The ranks of the middle classes were swollen by the new salaried workers, the rising number of civil servants and the increasing number of clerical and management staff in business. The increased burden of taxation both during and after the First World War meant that few middle class families could now sustain the lifestyle of their Victorian counterparts.

The decline in the number of girls and women in service meant that the middle class housewife had to take on a new role. The new industries and technology brought important changes in the middle class home. The slogan 'Let electricity be your servant' reflects the shift to all kinds of labour-saving device for the middle class housewife – cookers, refrigerators, vacuum cleaners, electric irons and fires.

Ready-to-wear clothing for the middle class was part of the same trend towards economy and convenience. Women still wanted stylish clothes but now they were without servants to perform domestic tasks or to make clothes. Many women lacked both the skills and time required for making all their own clothes. Neither the married woman burdened by domestic work, nor the single working woman had as much time to devote to choosing fabric and to visiting the dressmaker for fittings. Both were lured away from their dress-makers by the convenience of off-the-peg fashion when good quality goods were produced.

The expansion of the mass media during the inter-war period contributed to the growth in demand for fashionable clothes in a number of ways. By 1931 one in three homes had a radio, and there had been a general expansion in the popular press and in all forms of advertising. These developments contributed to a growing uniformity and standardisation of taste among the population as a whole, and disseminated knowledge about the kind of consumer goods available on a much wider scale than ever before. The demand for fashion was perhaps influenced most by the growth in magazines aimed at the working and lower middle class woman. The first *mass* circulation magazines for women − *Woman's Own* and *Woman* were launched in the thirties. Like the women's pages in newspapers, they included features on fashion amongst other 'womanly' topics. Women all over the country became knowledge-able about the latest styles and it was no longer possible for manufacturers to sell London's fashions years afterwards in the North or rural areas.

The cinema was another important influence on the way women wanted to look. It was a mass form of entertainment enjoyed by all classes and by 1937 twenty million tickets were being sold a week. Some people went several times a week to enjoy the spectacle and excitement − the glamour and romance on the screen and the atmosphere of some of the picture palaces built in the thirties. Millions of women (and men) were subjected to the same images of feminine beauty, beautiful clothes and make-up. Inevitably tastes became more uniform.

The cinema system created types − 'the blonde', 'the brunette', exemplified by stars from rival studios. The stars were seen to be admired and loved on and off the screen by the audiences. Women sought to emulate their looks and their clothes, to conform to the 'type' and thus to be considered as desirable as a Jean Harlow or Joan Crawford.

Cinema had also created the notion of 'glamour'. Quite ordinary girls were transformed into 'stars', 'goddesses' and 'queens' by the use of certain cosmetics, certain hairstyles, certain styles of clothing and jewellery, indulging in certain activities in certain kinds of surrounding defined as 'glamorous'. You, too, could be glamorous given the right equipment — you could look glamorous in the right style of evening dress, in the right kind of expensive restaurant or nightclub!

Styles of dress from films did influence fashion. Although top designers like Schiaparelli and Chanel did design for Hollywood, costume design was distinct from the design of couturiers and high fashion. It was important that cinema costumes did not date too quickly, and thus make the film look dated. However, people did admire the clothes of the stars on and off screen, and the taste for clothes worn by stars in films or in 'glamour shots' published in magazines could be exploited by fashion manufacturers. A London manufacturer, Julian Lee of Marley Gowns, was able to produce and sell *thousands* of what were known as Joan Crawford dresses (a dress with a long white roll collar caught up at one side above the waist) and Ginger Rogers coats (a coat with caracul collar and three caracul buttons). (19)

The growth in the mass media during the twenties and thirties meant that information about fashion was brought to a wider public, that increasingly a wider range of people shared similar tastes, and the desire to be attractively and fashionably dressed was fostered. In combination with the changes in lifestyle and standard of living for many women during this period, it meant there was now a mass market for fashion to be exploited.

The mass marketing of fashion

The growth of a mass demand for fashion and the mass-production of clothes had important consequences for the relationship between the producer and the retailer, and forms of retail outlet appropriate to selling such clothes.

Manufacturers of menswear had found the method of selling through a large number of small independent shops inadequate and had started to develop their own outlets for direct selling. Hepworths had been among the first in the late nineteenth century, and these were followed by Burtons at the beginning of this century. After the First World War, when millions of men required demob-ilisation suits, there was a boom in all sections of the tailoring trade but the multiple tailors like Burtons, with their integrated system of factories and retail outlets, did particularly well. Before long there were few towns in Britain where a man could not walk into a shop of one of these chains and be measured for a factory-made suit.

The methods for making and selling women's clothes developed on rather different lines. There was, for example, little direct selling to customers by manufacturing companies. Notable exceptions were companies like Burberry, Aquascutum and Jaeger, all of which had started as suppliers of menswear or, in the case of Jaeger, specialist clothes for both sexes. All, of course, supplied goods for the middle class market.

During the inter-war period, as we have seen, there was a growing demand for good quality ready-made clothing which could compete with bespoke clothing in its standards of fit and finish. A number of manufacturers developed goods to meet this demand and this section of the trade became known as 'wholesale couture'. This term obviously embodies both the notion of high quality and innovative design but also the notion of large-scale production. Elizabeth Ewing suggests that it was this kind of manufacturer who was among the first to adopt American sizing, grading and manufacturing techniques. (20) She cites, as examples, Lou Ritter who founded Dereta and who worked closely with buyers from stores such as Harrods to adapt Paris lines to the requirements of ready-to-wear production and markets; Olive O'Neill who set up her own company to manufacture her designs and who worked with fabric manufacturers to create fabrics for her designs; and Frederick Starke who was to be the first manufacturer to show a wholesale collection in the style of couture in 1945, and thus create a whole new image for ready to wear.

In addition to these innovatory producers of high quality clothes, the number of manufacturers of moderately priced, but good quality, fashion grew during the thirties. Some of these companies began to market their goods under *brand* names, many of which are well-known today – for example, Windsmoor, Berketex and Alexon. A brand name could enhance a manufacturer's reputation, encourage customer loyalty to his products and thus stimulate a demand for *that* company's products. Manufacturers began increasingly to sell direct to department stores, and other shops, instead of relying on a wholesaler.

The role of the department store had changed since the turn of the century. After 1914, although some stores had opened up their own factories to supply them with ready-made clothing, most department stores had ceased to be *producers* of fashionable clothes as they had been in the past. Their main concern was now *distribution*, and as the demand and production of fashionable clothes grew, their trade expanded. Margaret Wray suggests that they took the initiative in marketing fashion 'by placing considerable orders with manufacturers at the beginning of the production season and timing their advertisement to the consumer, in the local and national press, to coincide with the deliveries of the completed garments to the stores'. (21)

Department stores provided an ideal outlet for good quality ready-to-wear. In addition to their efficient use of advertising, they provided a pleasant and comfortable setting in which to display the goods, and they were able to offer the customer extensive alteration facilities. In these ways department stores were able to make ready-to-wear fashion an attractive alternative for the large middle class market to which they catered. (Although they could also appeal to quite a different type of customer with the cheaper goods for sale in their 'bargain basement'.)

This expansion in the trade of the department store was accompanied by growth in another sector of the market, that of the multiple stores which catered predominantly for the working classes. These stores were important in the spread of fashion, not only because they provided outlets for factory-made clothes but also because some of them were to give an impetus to the *development of products* which brought fashionable ready-to-wear within the reach of those who in the past had to be content with badly made, ill-fitting or even second-hand clothes.

The term 'multiple store' refers to a shop which is part of a chain with a central organisation and buying policy. There are two types — speciality and variety chain. The speciality chain deals in one type of product. For example, Burtons specialised in menswear and Etam in lingerie. Variety chains — such as Woolworth's and Marks and Spencer — on the other hand, sell a variety of goods. The fore-runners of multiple stores were the co-operative stores which provided a variety of products for the working class market. By the late nineteenth century there were a number of chains which had grown from one or two shops, and they and the co-ops were expanding rapidly. In the period between the wars there was a substantial growth in the number of chains, the number of shops and their share of retail trade (see Table 1). Their share of trade grew from 3–5 per cent in 1900 to 7–10 per cent in 1920 and 18–20 per cent in 1939, whereas the department store increased its share of trade from 3.5 per cent in 1920 to 5 per cent in 1939.

Their development was encouraged by the increase in mass

Table 1. Estimates of the number of multiple shop branches, 1905–1939

	1905	1910	1915	1920	1925	1930	1935	1939
Variety chains	55	130	247	300	3 400	667	981	1 202
All multiple shop branches	15 242	19 852	22 755	24 713	29 628	35 894	40 087	44 487

manufactured consumer goods, the rising standard of living of some sections of the working classes, and the growing uniformity of taste promoted by the mass media. The increasing use of motor transport, lorries, motor cars and buses, was affecting both the distribution of goods and changing the shopping habits of the public. People were able to travel more easily to towns and cities and this made it possible for retailers to serve much larger areas. Improvements in transport and roads encouraged the trend towards large-scale retailing.

However, the success of the multiples lay in their ability to supply goods at a price which appealed to the working class consumer. They, in particular, were able to do this for two reasons. First, they were able to reduce costs through the style of shopping they offered which contrasted with that of the personal service of the small retailer and the luxury of the department store. They adopted a different approach to customer service. The shops were plain with long counters where goods were displayed. Prices were clearly marked so that each customer did not need the aid of an assistant to make a choice.

Secondly, during the periods of economic slump and mass unemployment between the wars, manufacturers found it difficult to sell their goods and price reductions were offered to retailers who bought stock in large quantities. This obviously gave the multiples an advantage over the independent retailer and all kinds of multiple expanded during this period − Boots (The Chemist), W.H. Smith, Sainsbury's, Dorothy Perkins, etc. By the late thirties a number of department stores were amalgamating to form a 'multiple' group with central control over buying. The John Lewis Partnership, and Great Northern and Southern Stores are examples of this trend.

We should perhaps mention here the development in the thirties of companies dealing exclusively in mail-order. They, too, could take advantage of price reductions for bulk orders and were able to keep their overheads to a minimum. They were part of the same trend in retailing of appealing to the working class consumer with competitively priced goods. Littlewoods issued their first catalogue in 1932, and 'catalogues' became an increasingly important outlet for all kinds of mass-produced goods including clothes.

During the thirties, chains specialising in women's *outerwear* developed, but they were not on the scale of, say, men's tailoring multiples. C & A Modes were one of the most important. They, in fact, established a factory to supply part of their stock and thus combined mass-production with multiple distribution.

Marks and Spencer were the first variety chain to sell women's outerwear. The company was soon to become a leader in the field, bringing not only innovations to retailing but also encouraging mass-production. Marks and Spencer started off as a Penny Bazaar in the 1880s, selling a variety of goods for 1d (about ½p) in market halls, mainly in the North. By 1914, the business had expanded considerably into a chain of fixed shops, a third of which were in the South. The shops still preserved the features of a market stall with the open display of goods and prices, and self-selection by the customer.

One of Marks and Spencer's main competitors was Woolworth which had opened in Britain in 1909. As an American company, it was backed by American finance but also had the advantages of American expertise and methods of large-scale retailing. Simon Marks, the son of the founder of Marks and Spencer, went to the United States to study American retailing. He came back with the idea of developing large premises, 'superstores', introducing modern methods of administration and statistical stock control, and a five shilling (25p) price limit. These policies were to be the key to success:

'Despite the variations of boom and slump (in the inter-war years) popular needs and tastes, and particularly those of the working classes, were changing at a speed which we now recognise to be one of the characteristic features of the twentieth century. Any retail organisation which could interpret the public's changing needs, adapt itself rapidly to them, and satisfy them at a price which was within the income of the working class household was certain to receive a rich reward. The creation of the superstore, combined with the reintroduction of the fixed price limit, placed Marks and Spencer in an exceptionally favourable position to take advantage of this opportunity. The superstore, with its very large turnover, served as a kind of laboratory in which the demands of the public were tested day by day and minute by minute and the results quickly and accurately reported to the central administration. The fixed price limit ensured that nothing sold in the stores should be beyond the reach of the working class household; that is, of the overwhelming mass of the population.' (22)

Throughout the inter-war period the company continued to expand and by 1939 had opened a total of 234 stores.

The decision to adopt a five shilling price limit also had important consequences in terms of the kind of goods which were sold in the shops, and the relationship the company developed with its suppliers. Marks and Spencer had previously obtained most of its goods from wholesalers, although from the very early days it had some close links with suppliers. However this new policy meant it could no longer be a passive recipient of what the wholesaler or manufacturer had to offer. Marks and Spencer had to discover or create a range of merchandise which could be sold within the price limit, and they had to assure sources of supply.

One consequence of this policy was that Marks and Spencer had to reduce its range of goods to those which could be most efficiently produced within the five shilling price limit. The range of goods became much narrower and there was an increasing concentration on 'textiles' − which included women's outerwear. By 1936, two-thirds of sales were 'textiles' and by 1950 the company was classified as a clothing multiple.

In order to obtain a regular supply of goods at the right price, Marks and Spencer decided on a policy which excluded the wholesaler and which promoted instead a special relationship between the retailer and manufacturer, one which would *generate* goods of the required quality within the price restrictions. This policy met with resistance from both wholesalers and manufacturers but Marks and Spencer had the powerful inducement of large orders. Marks and Spencer began to reserve part of a plant exclusively for their own orders on a guarantee to accept the whole of its production. This policy obviously gave great security to a manufacturer, but it also helped him reduce costs. It enabled him to plan ahead, reap the advantages of long runs and continuous production, and also relieved him of the costs of marketing and advertising.

Marks and Spencer got drawn into closer relationships with both primary producers of goods and the manufacturers of finished products. In their attempt to reduce costs or improve the quality of

Fig. 11.9 A Marks and Spencer's 'superstore'.

existing goods, they began to take on an educative role in relation to their suppliers. In the case of the women's light clothing industry this involved encouraging manufacturers to use the best available technology and most efficient methods of factory production.

As part of their endeavour to improve the quality of the goods they sold, Marks and Spencer began to exercise increasing control over the quality and uniformity of products. They began to draw up specifications to which the manufacturer must conform in terms of the materials and processes used. As many manufacturers lacked the knowledge and expertise to make improvements themselves, Marks and Spencer took on the role by providing a pool of experts who could advise on the latest technical advances in materials and processes, layout of equipment or labour problems.

As part of this policy the company established its own textile laboratory in 1931, originally to test quality, but later it began to draw up specifications for suppliers on quantity, quality and types of material, and methods of manufacture. In 1936 the Merchandise

Development Department took these concerns even further and were particularly interested in introducing manufacturers to the benefits of scientific and technical discoveries. In the thirties, this included those discoveries which were making possible the large-scale production of synthetic materials with qualities equal or even superior to natural substances.

The Design Department was also established in 1936. Its purpose was to keep the company abreast of the latest fashion trends and to provide a team of experts to advise suppliers. Eventually the Department created styles and supplied the manufacturer with fully graded patterns, and explicit and detailed making up instructions down to the number of stitches per sewing operation.

Marks and Spencer were able to expand whilst the country as a whole suffered the terrible effects of economic depression. We have outlined above the reasons for the growth in demand for women's ready-made clothing. Because of their policies of trying to supply goods at the lowest prices compatible with high standards, Marks and Spencer were able to take advantage of that demand. But their role as we have seen went far beyond that of the traditional retailer and they became actively involved in *encouraging the manufacturers of clothing to adopt the most efficient methods of mass-production whilst improving the quality of their products.*

Other chains developed in the thirties which were similar to Marks and Spencer but smaller in scale. British Home Stores (founded in 1928) and Littlewoods sold a wider range of goods than Marks and Spencer but both sold dresses, blouses and skirts in the lower price range.

Multiple stores became well-established and successful retailers of women's fashion. Even in 1930 and 1931, Marks and Spencer were selling over a million dresses. However, we must put their growth into perspective. A very substantial part of the trade in women's outerwear was still carried on through single small shops, such as draper's shops, and what were known as 'madam' shops (specialist dress shops which were probably the 'descendants' of the old local dressmaking establishments). (23)

By the end of the thirties all the conditions we outlined above as necessary to the development and successful growth of the mass manufacture and mass retailing of fashion were in existence. The industry had *not* been completely transformed; many of the old problems of small-scale production remained. But fashion was now available to the majority of people at a price they could afford.

FASHION FOR ALL AFTER THE WAR

The trend towards mass manufacture and mass retailing was to continue and ready-to-wear clothing came to dominate the fashion industry after the Second World War.

In some senses, developments in the fashion industry were interrupted by the war and by government restrictions on production, styling and sales. However, the stability those restrictions brought, in particular the almost total elimination of fashion changes, resulted in substantial improvements in manufacture. The austerity restrictions made women's clothing more suitable in many ways for mass-production. Simple line became more important in garment styling when the fussy types of trimming typical of pre-war styles were no longer permitted. Manufacturers were encouraged to adopt the methods of mass-production widely used in men's tailoring and shirt production when styles were simplified, the number of styles in production was reduced and guaranteed sales made longer runs possible. The experience of a number of firms in making uniforms and other products for the Government also led to a wider adoption of mass-production methods.

Manufacturers saw the advantages of simplified styling and long runs when productivity and therefore profit increased. The constant demand for clothes and the stability in styling permitted manufacturers to turn their attention to solving technical problems and improving production methods, rather than worrying about a market for their goods. There were important lessons to be carried forward into the post-war period, for those who wished to learn them.

These wartime developments and the establishment of Development Areas after the war led to an increase in large-scale factories with advanced sectional production methods. It is this kind of factory which was most innovative in terms of introducing new technology and production techniques. However, it must be pointed out that even today the vast majority of clothing manufacturers are relatively small-scale businesses employing less than fifty people. The nature of fashion with its rapid changes of style and tendency to produce short runs has continued to discourage large-scale production.

Large-scale manufacturers found it difficult to survive on a vast number of small orders for individual independent traders and in the post-war period they turned increasingly to the multiple stores in order to stabilise production. The multiple stores had experienced setbacks during the war but with the end of rationing their sales of womenswear and childrenswear increased dramatically and they were able to provide the manufacturers with large orders. The major trends in shopping since the war have been the increase in self-selection and a decline in the total number of shops. Multiples have gained an increasing share of the retail trade, currently running at over 50 per cent.

In the sphere of clothing, Marks and Spencer built on their pre-war policies and established overall dominance. Between 1950 and 1968 they doubled their share of the clothing market, and by 1970 their sales represented one-tenth of all consumer spending on clothes. As they concentrated at that time on womenswear and childrenswear, their dominance was even greater than this figure implies. In the seventies, they sold one-third of all bras and slips, one-quarter of all knitwear and nightdresses, one-fifth of all skirts and one-tenth of all ladies' dresses.

This expansion obviously depended on a continuing growth in the demand for mass-produced clothes. During the fifties and sixties, standards of living for the majority of people continued to rise. Lifestyles changed with the new patterns of affluence, and although spending on clothes did not rise at the same rate as spending on other consumer goods, taste and requirements in dress became more uniform. Both working and middle class consumers were now content to shop at the multiples, and the greatest growth in demand was for the lower- to medium-priced garments of good quality. Surely it was the final accolade for mass-produced ready-to-wear when it was rumored that Royalty had been seen shopping in Marks and Spencer. It really was fashion for all!

Finally, we should consider the decline of *haute couture* as the leaders and definers of what the fashion is in any particular season.

Immediately after the war, Parisian Couture reasserted its dominance in the world of fashion through Dior and his notorious 'New Look'. Dior went on to produce a whole series of new looks which the world felt obliged to follow. During the fifties, the structure of *haute couture* was like that of pre-war days. The exclusivity was maintained: the rich customers attended evening presentations which were great social events; photographers and sketchers were rigorously excluded. Manufacturers paid very large sums just to see the collections and, of course, to buy toiles or patterns for copying.

But the war had separated Paris from the rest of the world, and

Britain and the United States had developed some independence of design. In Britain the pre-war couturiers had become well-established and they were determined in the fifties to attract the world's press and buyers to their collections. Indeed they had some success but were soon challenged by another group for the lead in British fashion, namely the London Model House Group. It had been formed by fourteen leading ready-to-wear manufacturers under the leadership of Frederick Starke in 1947. It was created to provide a means of coordinating the dates for showing their whole-sale collections to overseas buyers. Autumn collections were shown in May and spring collections in November. While couture shows, as in Paris, were staged in January for spring and July for autumn. Gradually the ready-to-wear openings replaced the couture shows as London Fashion Week, attracting the press and buyers, and when the group reformed into a larger and more influential association of twenty-eight manufacturers under the new name of Fashion House Group of London in 1960, they became the leading force in British fashion. Couture designers like Hartnell had been working in both areas since the early forties when he designed ready-to-wear dresses for Berkertex, and combined such activities with couture until 1970 when he closed his couture house.

In Paris, too, couture came under threat from ready-to-wear. As early as 1948 Fath designed a special collection for mass manufacture in the United States but he died before he could bring his plans for mass-producing fashion in Paris using American methods. But changes were inevitable. In 1955 the French couturiers sent a committee to study American fashion and methods of production, and gradually *prêt à porter* began to develop. Some couture houses developed direct selling to stores, instead of selling models or toiles for manufacture. For example, Harrods bought Courrèges; others, like Yves St. Laurent, set up their own retail outlets. The fashion calendar began to change and the ready-to-wear collections in France and Italy, as in England, attracted more attention from the press and buyers. The turning point came in 1971 when St. Laurent announced his final couture collection for the press. In future he would show only to private customers and his new lines would be introduced in his *Rive Gauche prêt à porter* collections. As in England there was a conflict of interest in showing new lines at both the couture and ready-to-wear collections. The ready-to-wear collections were shown in May to allow orders for retailers to be made and delivered. If a couturier introduced a new line into his or her couture collection in July, the ready-to-wear collection would immediately seem out of date. It did not make business sense. As most couturiers had ready-to-wear interests they followed St. Laurent's lead and ended couture collections for the press.

Couture houses are still patronised by rich private clients wanting unique clothes, but it is to *prêt à porter* that journalists look for the innovations which might change fashion overnight and affect the clothing styles of millions of people all over the world.

References

1. See the discussion in Chapter 4.
2. Wellington's officers fighting at Bayonne two years before Waterloo are said to have protected their precious clothes from the rain by putting up their umbrellas during the battle!!
3. Adburgham, A. (1964) *Shops and Shopping 1810–1914.* (George Allen and Unwin) 3.
4. Bishop, J. (1977) *Social History of Edwardian Britain.* (Angus and Robertson) 40.
5. Children's Employment: 'Reports of the Commission for Trades and Manufacture,' 1st Report 1842.
6. Dickens gives a fictional account of child stripping in *Dombey and Son.*
7. Mayhew, H. (1969) *Mayhew's London*, ed. P. Quennell (Spring Books) 208.
8. Tailors selling easy fitting ready-made suits for the lower end of the trade and were common in market towns and in seaports. In the latter, they were called 'slop shops' because they provided the clothes for the 'slop' chests carried on every ship and which contained clothing and bedding for sailors.
9. Schmeichen, J.A. (1984) *Sweated Industries and Sweated Labour: The London Clothing Trades 1860–1914.* (Croom Helm) 26.
10. Arnold, J. 'The dressmaker's craft'. In: *Strata of Society.* Costume Society 34.
11. Adburgham, A. (1964) *Shops and Shopping 1810–1914.* (George Allen and Unwin) 115.
12. White, C. (1970) *Women's Magazines 1693–1968* (Michael Joseph) 58.
13. 'Accounts of expenditure of wage-earning women and girls' (1911) Board of Trade: Labour Department In: *Human Documents of the Lloyd George Era*, ed. E. Royston Pike. (George Allen and Unwin).
14. Reeve, Mrs 'Round about a pound a week'. In: *Human Documents of the Lloyd George Era*, ed. E. Royston Pike. (George Allen and Unwin) 51.
15. Wray, M. (1957) *The Women's Outerwear Industry.* (Duckworth) 26.
16. *ibid.*
17. Ewing, E. (1974) *History of Twentieth Century Fashion.* (London: B.T. Batsford) 127.
18. Branson, N. and Heinman, M. (1975) *Britain in the Nineteen-Thirties.* (Weidenfeld & Nicolson).
19. Ewing, E. (1974) *History of Twentieth Century Fashion.* (London: B.T. Batsford) 126.
20. *ibid* 129.
21. Wray, M. (1957) *The Women's Outerwear Industry.* (Duckworth) 36.
22. Rees, G. (1973) *St. Michael: A History of Marks and Spencer* (Pan).
23. Margaret Wray suggests that the proportion may be over half, but as the figures include childrenswear it is difficult to obtain an accurate figure.

12 Youth

A study of the clothes worn by children and young people in the past reveals that for much of history they have been dressed like mini-adults. At other times such as at the end of the eighteenth century, and at various times this century, special clothes thought to be suitable for the needs and activities of children, as distinct from those of adults, have been worn. However, whatever was worn, it has been determined by *adult* views of what was appropriate for children and frequently has been influenced by contemporary adult fashions. Children's dress has reflected changing attitudes to childhood but children and young people remained at the mercy of adults' definitions and taste.

Since the war, a new development seems to have taken place in relation to young people and dress. (In this Chapter we are concerned with those young people who are no longer considered 'children' but who are not yet regarded as mature adults. We therefore include not only teenagers but also some people in their early twenties.) Young people not only began to assert their own tastes, they also became a dominant force in fashion and one of the largest markets for fashion.

In the twenties, youth also exerted an influence in terms of the silhouette and mood of some of the fashions, but since the Second World War the affect of youth has been of quite a different order. Groups of young people have generated quite distinct styles of dress and appearance, some of which have had a strong influence on mainstream fashions. It has become widely accepted that young people in general have different tastes in music, clothes and forms of entertainment from adults. In addition, young people have become a very important but separate market for *fashion* goods.

It is of course true that gangs and groups of young people developed their own distinct styles of dress and behaviour before the post-war period. R. Roberts, describing youth in an Edwardian slum, writes:

'The groups of young men and youths who gathered at the end of most slum streets on fine evenings earned the condemnation of all respectable citizens.... In the late ninteeth century the Northern Scuttler and his "moll" had achieved a notoriety as widespread as that of any gang in modern times. He had his own style of dress — the union shirt, bell-bottomed trousers, the heavy leather belt, pricked out in fancy designs with large steel buckle and the thick, iron-shod clogs. His girlfriend commonly wore clogs and shawl and a skirt with vertical stripes.' (1)

However, since the war, styles have been created by groups of young people which have been adopted not only by small local groups but hundreds and even thousands of young people. Their influence has been widespread among young people but, as we shall see, styles like those of the Hippies profoundly influenced dress styles in general.

Before the war there no shops selling fashion specifically to young people; fashion was sold to the 'fashionable', old and young alike. During the sixties and seventies, many people began to think of fashion in terms of the clothes that young people were wearing. Shops catering specifically for the young had opened everywhere; they had a different atmosphere and introduced a new approach to selling fashion. In major shopping centres, soon most of the shops selling fashion were aimed at the young and those who wished to appear young — both men and women. In recent years this has begun to change with more and more shops aimed at the over-25s, but this development belongs to the eighties. For nearly twenty years the young seemed to dominate mass market fashion.

In this Chapter we are going to look at the background to the development of a separate identity for youth and, in particular, at the development of youth culture. We shall examine the ways in which the fashion industry was both influenced by youth and also sought to exploit it as a market. Lastly we will consider the importance of youth as an inspiration and market for fashion today.

The development of youth culture in post-war Britain

Why did a sense of 'youth culture', a generationally specific 'way of life', and a series of distinct youth styles develop in the post-war period?

In what ways did social conditions encourage different attitudes to and among young people, and in what ways had their position in society changed?

How were things different in the fifties? In the fifties, the economic boom and the social and political atmosphere encouraged feelings of optimism and security which were to last into the sixties. The construction of the welfare state, the emphasis on 'consensus' politics and the promise of affluence for all, encouraged people to think that the days of poverty and deprivation were at an end, and that everyone could look forward to full employment and a continuing rise in the standard of living. In this atmosphere people began to look to the future with a sense of confidence; their children were to live in a better world.

Indeed, without the rising standard of living that the economic boom brought it is unlikely that there would have been the development of youth cultures at all. Young people, and particularly working class youth, shared in the affluence and prosperity of the post-war period. The demand for labour pushed up wage levels and those of young people at a faster rate than those of adults. In his pamphlet, *The Teenage Consumer*, Abrams suggested that 'as compared with 1938, their real earnings...have increased by 50 per cent, and their real 'discretionary' spending has probably risen by 100 per cent'. (2) Teenagers could now enjoy the period between school and marriage; they had disposable income to spend on themselves.

Before the war many young people had been paid relatively little and much of their wages had been handed over to their parents to contribute to the family income. Abrams suggested that, by 1959, the average wage for boys was about £8 a week and the average wage for girls was £6. Perhaps because many families were now better off, children were not required to contribute such a high proportion of their wages to the family budget. On average, Abrams estimated that boys contributed 35 shillings (£1.75) a week and girls 25 shillings (£1.25). After allowing for such payments, tax, National Insurance deductions and savings, Abrams estimated that the amount spent each week by the average teenager (including those not employed) was 71s 6d (£3.58) for boys and 54s (£2.20) for girls.

> 'By and large...one can generalise by saying that the quite large amount of money at the disposal of Britain's average teenager is spent mainly on dress and on goods which form the nexus of teenage gregariousness outside the home. In other words, this is distinctive teenage spending for distinctive teenage ends in a distinctive teenage world.' (3)

Without this free spending money it would have been difficult to sustain the development of distinctive youth sytles.

During this period, people *felt* themselves to be living in a rapidly changing world. Indeed, people's lifestyles were changing, as we have said elsewhere – living standards rose, new patterns of consumerism were developing, and people's outlook and aspirations were changing. Some commentators thought that the political emphasis on 'consensus' politics and growing affluence would lead to a withering away of class differences. Everyone would become 'middle class'. People did seem to think that a new order based on education, employment and patterns of consumption was around the corner – educational opportunity would lead to job success and affluence.

Of course, things did not change as dramatically as people thought and time has shown that poverty and hardship did not disappear with the setting up of the welfare state, that class differences did not disappear, and the dream of full employment and growing affluence did not last.

These views, however, contributed to the sense of a 'generation gap'. People felt that the war represented a watershed between two worlds, and both older and young people felt that youth were living in a different world, in different social conditions. Young people, who had not known pre-war Britain, were identified with this changing world. Youth did experience post-war social change in very specific ways: they were the beneficiaries of the welfare state, the generation brought up on free school milk and orange juice. They all went to new kinds of school after the 1944 Education Act, they all had the carrot of educational opportunity and social mobility dangled before them. To be young was an enviable situation.

The sense of 'generations' was given further substance by the way certain industries directed themselves to the youthful audience and, of course, their spending power. The record industry, the cosmetic industry, the fashion industry, all produced products specifically directed to youthful consumers. Television programmes were created for a young audience, starting off with the *6.5 Special.* *Thank your Lucky Stars* and later *Ready, Steady, Go!* Radio was slower to cater for the young and it was left to illegal pirate stations to lead the field before Radio 1 was established and commercial stations tolerated.

The fact that young people did generate their own clearly identifiable styles of dress, tastes in music, ways of behaving, ways of speaking and favourite forms of entertainment gave further credence to the notion of 'youth culture', a generational way of life. Many adults looking at Teds, mods, hippies or punks felt they were not only looking at people of a different age but people from a different world.

By the sixties the idea of a 'generation gap' had been transformed into the 'Youth Revolution'. The children of the post-war baby boom were now reaching their teens, and society seemed to be mesmerised by youth and their culture. So strong was this sense of a 'generation gap', the notion of 'Youth' as a homogeneous group in conflict, or in rebellion against age that the author Colin MacInnes could write:

> 'The "two nations" of our society may perhaps no longer be those of the rich and the poor (or, to use old-fashioned terms, the "upper" and working classes), but those of the teenagers on the one hand and, on the other, all those who have assumed the burdens of adult responsibility.' (4)

Although such views may express the way many people *felt* in relation to young people, they do exaggerate the degree of generational identification, and the extent to which all young people participated in 'youth culture'. For example, although Abrams in his study of spending patterns identified 'a teenage world' he also pointed to clear, class-based differences in those patterns amongst teenagers. All young people did not share the same culture. It is also important to make a distinction between youth subcultures which contain stylistic innovation and genuine oppositional and rebellious elements, and the wider youth culture which consists largely of the products marketed by the teenage leisure industries.

We have tried to set out the conditions in which the development of youth styles and a youth market took place. Now let's look more closely at what the distinctive youth cultures which appeared in the fifties, sixties, and seventies were about, to what extent they constituted genuine innovatory and oppositional styles.

What are youth styles about?

It has been argued that the 'youth culture' of the post-war period was the product of manipulation of impressionable young people by commercial interests, that youth culture is really no more than the range of products available specifically for the young. This argument was developed in relation to what people feared would be the effects of the development of mass communications and, in particular, the effect of television which was still a relatively new medium.

In 1964, Paul Johnson wrote in the *New Statesman*:

'Both TV channels now run weekly programmes in which the popular records are played to teenagers and judged. While the music is performed, the cameras linger savagely over the faces of the audience. What a bottomless chasm of vacuity they reveal. Huge faces, bloated with cheap confectionery and smeared with chain store make-up, the open sagging mouths and glazed eyes, the hands mindlessly drumming in time to the music, and the broken stiletto heels, the shoddy, stereotyped, "with it" clothes: here, apparently, is a collective portrait of a generation enslaved by a commercial machine.' (28 February 1964)

Although it is undoubtedly true that many adult entrepreneurs were eager to exploit the youth market, to accept this extreme view would be to deny the quite unprompted emergence of groups with their own distinctive styles like those of Teddy boys, and punks.

Others have tried to explain youth subcultures, not in terms of mindless consumption but in terms of genuine style innovation, and the generation of styles which 'say' something about the social and economic conditions in which those young people live, their experiences and their aspirations. (5) Style innovation, it is argued, takes place when groups of young people take already existing commodities, ordinary consumer objects, put them into a new context and endow them with a new meaning. They rearrange them in a pattern which reflects their values and aspirations – not that of their makers. Youth cultures in general are about leisure, having a good time, looking good and getting high. They are about friendships and group activity, not about work or how to change the conditions in which you live. To a large extent youth cultures pretend the 'real' world of routine jobs, failure at school, etc., do not exist. But it is also argued that in youth cultures such real life experiences and aspirations of social groups are symbolised and put into the language of style.

Tony Jefferson's study of Teddy boys exemplifies this approach. (6) He argues that Teds style can be seen as an attempt to defend symbolically a constantly threatened space and a declining status. Teddy boys appeared in South London in the early fifties and the style spread quickly throughout London and then the rest of the country. Most of them were early leavers from secondary modern schools where they had been in the lowest streams, leaving without any qualifications.

They were easily identified by their distinctive form of dress but their behaviour also became infamous in fifties' Britain. They displayed a great sense of territory, a strong sense of group identity and were extremely touchy in relation to actual or imaginary insults. They fought with other Teds, people who insulted them, Cypriot café owners, blacks, and bus conductors. *Why did they behave in this way?*

The Education Act of 1944 had introduced the system of selecting children at the age of eleven for particular types of schools. The system was thought to be fair. So, if you found yourself in the bottom stream of a secondary modern, you found yourself at the bottom of the educational hierarchy and this was felt to be a fair assessment of your worth. In terms of the system you were a failure. The pervasive belief in educational opportunity, social mobility and affluence contrasted strongly with the position of unqualified early leavers. Many Teddy boys, having failed at school, could not look forward to successful careers; unskilled work and phases of unemployment were taken as yet another *personal failure*. In short, Teddy boys enjoyed none of the conventional forms of prestige.

Their toughness and flamboyant clothes were one way of trying to get a kind of respect. The importance of their appearance and being tough is reflected in the number of fights caused by insults to Teds. Their group-mindedness and sense of territory was probably a response to the post-war upheaval and destruction of working class local communities and the need to feel in control of at least part of their environment. The fights with immigrants were obviously a kind of scapegoating, blaming them for the Teds, frustration in realising their ambitions.

Appearance was a key element in being a Ted, despite periodic unemployment and involvment in unskilled work. Teds, like other teenagers, had disposable income, they had money to spend, and as that was *all* they had in terms of socially accepted forms of status, it was of great importance to them. Much of their money went on clothes.

In 1950 the tailors of Savile Row produced a neo-Edwardian suit for young aristocrats with long lapelled and waisted jackets, narrow trousers and fancy waistcoats. This style was taken up by working class youths who as a result were known as Teddy boys. Since the

Fig. 12.1 Teddy Boy.

clothes were originally worn by the upper class, this can be seen as a simple attempt to buy status. But this did not last for long because the style was rapidly dropped by the upper class and second-hand suits became available in markets in 1954.

The style was modified by the Teds and made their own. They added the bootlace tie, thick crêpe-soled suede shoes, skin-tight drainpipe trousers and straighter, less waisted jackets with moleskin or satin collars. They introduced vivid colours such as pink, red and bright green − and, of course, fluorescent socks. The hair was worn greasy and long, combed into a D.A. with long side whiskers, or swept up into an 'elephants trunk', or shaved at the sides in an 'apache'.

They made the style working class, but it also communicated something of their aspirations. Jefferson suggests that, for instance, the adoption of the bootlace tie might have revealed both the way they experienced their social position and their aspirations:

> '(The bootlace tie was) probably picked up from the many American Western films viewed during this period, where it was worn, most prevalently as I remember them by the slick city gambler whose social status was, grudgingly, high because of his ability to live *by his wits* and *outside* the traditional working class *mores* of society (which were basically rural and hardworking as opposed to urban and hedonistic)... I believe its symbolic cultural meaning for the Teds becomes explicable as both an expression of their *social reality* (basically outsiders forced to live by their wits) and their *social "aspirations"* (basically an attempt to gain high, albeit grudging, status for an ability to live smartly, hedonistically and by their wits in an urban setting).' (7)

The same approach can be used to 'explain' the styles of other youth cultures. For example, the appearance and behaviour of skinheads can be seen as an attempt to recreate and affirm the core values of a 'traditional' working class culture. They rejected the narcissistic tendencies of the mods and the studied 'un-dress' of the hippies with their flamboyance combined with ethnic and working clothes. Their activities centred on establishing territories through 'mobs', on football, and drink. They were critical of those with 'airs', who tried to better themselves, and of any deviation from traditional working class views about sexuality. As such they also put a high value on toughness and aggression. Their dislike of anything which deviated from the white working class norm manifested itself in 'paki-bashing', 'hippy-bashing' and 'queer-bashing'.

Fig. 12.2 Skins.

The use of Dr Marten boots, short working men's jeans and braces clearly indicates a desire for an authentic 'working class-ness' with no pretence of social mobility. Their extremely short hair and tattooes contribute to their aggressive and 'masculine' appearance, even when worn by girls.

Of course, it is important to remember that only a small proportion of youth at any time was fully identified, and actively involved with any of the youth styles. Even for those who really did become one of the 'faces', a real mod, a Teddy boy or punk, it was usually an interlude, a part of growing up. Furthermore, many young people do not have the time, the money, or the opportunity ever to get fully involved in a style. Girls, in particular, may be forbidden by their parents to participate fully in the required activities, or an extreme form of appearance. They may be obliged by such circumstances to accept a watered down version of the style or wait until it is made more acceptable by becoming fashion. Nevertheless, such young people are identifying with those styles and the small group who could participate fully in it – and the values implicit in them.

Hebdige points to another aspect of identifying with subcultures – it helps youth deal with problems of identity:

> 'Amongst kids, this desire for coherence is particularly acute. Subculture provides a way of handling the experience of ambiguity and the contra-dictions, the painful questions of identity. Each subculture provides its members with a style, an imaginary coherence, a clear-cut *ready-made identity* which coalesces around certain chosen objects (a safety pin, a pair of winkle-pickers, a two-tone mohair suit). Together, these chosen objects form a whole – a recognisable aesthetic which in turn stands for a whole set of values and attitudes.' (8)

The styles, as symbols of subcultural identity, are precarious. Almost as soon as objects have been used to 'say' something on behalf of the members of the cult there is the drive of the market to catch up, to harness it for their own financial gain. The styles no longer 'speak' about the values or aspirations of the cult and its followers but of 'the latest', 'the fashion'.

Not all youth cultures have generated styles which have been taken up in this way but let's look at some of the styles which have had a considerable impact on fashion in general.

Mods

Mods like Teds devoted a great deal of attention to their appearance, but with them it became an obsession. They appeared about 1960 and were mainly working and lower middle class in origin. Their name was coined from their interest in 'modern jazz'. They developed a sharp style, wearing impeccably cut Italian suits which suggested an up and coming European type, worn with hand-made shoes, shirts with pointed collars and knitted ties. They had short neat hair which was often lacquered into place. This smart appearance was obviously acceptable to the outside world, although of course the mods' behaviour was not. But the mods' appearance was subversive in the way it inverted the hierarchical equation of status and dress. They were so smart they put their middle-aged bosses to shame, and they expressed the prevailing myths of the sixties — upward mobility and classlessnes — in their dress if not in their working lives. If male mods expressed a kind of defiance in their fastidious appearance, girl mods did so by wearing styles which hitherto had not been regarded as feminine. They often wore men's shirts and trousers with round-toed shoes. They used quite a lot of eye make-up but no lipstick.

The dull routine of work had to provide the cash for the expensive clothes, the Lambretta, the imported soul and ska records, and money for evening activities. A mod, interviewed for *The Sunday Times* in 1964, described an average week in life of a London mod as: Monday night dancing at somewhere like the Mecca or Hammersmith Palais; Tuesday at the Scene Club in Soho; Wednesday at the Marquee; Thursday washing his hair; Friday back to the Scene Club; Saturday afternoon shopping for clothes and records; dancing on Saturday night and into Sunday morning, and finally Sunday evening at the Flamingo Club. (9) The probably very small number of youth who actually maintained this lifestyle did so with the aid of 'speed'.

The mods projected an image of the good life and a taste for impeccable clothing. However all those around the country who wished to identify with mod ideals and culture could not necessarily achieve such extremes of activity or dress. For the majority being a mod meant wearing casual clothes, Fred Perry shirts and Levis, and a parka when riding on your scooter, and saving up for a leather or suede coat, and suits to wear at dances.

The mod style was to become in many ways *the* fashion of the mid-sixties for the young and those wishing to look young. Mod tastes for the simple pared down look and unisex tendencies were all to be manifested in fashion and, as we shall see, their influence was a key factor in the development of fashion retailing for the young. It is perhaps a measure of their influence that Lord Snowdon was called a mod when he appeared in a polo neck sweater.

Hippies

Hippies are different from members of the other youth cultures we have discussed in that they were middle class, and they did not form identifiable groups. The hippy movement developed in Britain

Fig. 12.3 Mods in Clacton 1964 (BBC Hulton Picture Library).

Fig. 12.4 Hippies on their way to a love-in 1969 (BBC Hulton Picture Library).

mainly among the student population. It really came to the fore in 1967 – a hippy summer in Britain when people put flowers in their hair and bells round their necks. Hippy culture was a strange mixture of drug-taking, exotic religion, radical politics, pacifism and a desire to get back to nature.

In a reaction against the affluence of the sixties and the emphasis on social mobility and materialist values, people were attracted to the mystical religions of the East, and some also sought alternatives to the consumerist lifestyle. By 1967 more and more young people were experimenting with marijuana and hallucinogenic drugs like LSD. They used drugs like LSD as a means of self-exploration and to 'extend their consciousness'.

The search for cheap drugs and alternative philosophies took many hippies on pilgrimages to Marrakesh or Katmandu − the hippy trails. Because this was a time of affluence, expansion in higher education and graduate unemployment was as yet unknown, students could experiment with drugs, alternative living, politics, travel the world and still return to education or a job.

Two strands developed in hippy culture, particularly in America. One focused on drugs, mysticism and a revolution in lifestyle which led to alternative lifestyles and the commune movement, while the other grew out of the anti-establishment, anti-capitalist, anti-war feelings which led to the student revolts of the late sixties and the anti-Vietnam protest, and culminated in activist politics.

The preoccupations of hippies are clearly manifest in their dress. The long hair of the men was perhaps the most obvious expression of their rejection of straight society's norms of appearance. It was extremely offensive to the older generation. But eventually, of course, longer hair, beards and moustaches became fashionable, as did the long hairstyles of the women.

Their interest in drugs and drug-induced experience led to a fascination with intricate patterns and 'psychedelic' colours. Their travels in the East, and those of American hippies in South America in search of drugs, introduced dress and jewellery from these cultures. Afghan coats at first brought back as trophies from their actual trips abroad were soon imported directly into Britain. In Britain, dress from North Africa and the Indian subcontinent − kaftans, beads and silk scarves all became widely worn. The ornate and intricate patterns and styles were soon adopted by mass producers of fashion. From the hippy culture of the United States came the influence of traditional Red Indian dress with beads and fringed leather clothes; and from the South American Indians, the poncho and embroidered blouses and smocks.

The search for a simple life, and in the United States a return to the rural life, was reflected in the adoption of old-fashioned rural work clothes − dungarees, boiler-suits and, for women, pioneer-type long flowered dresses (in this country represented by Laura

Ashley's milkmaid look). Rejection of straight society and their commodities, led to a vogue amongst hippies and for second-hand and antique clothes partly because they were unique, and had to be 'found'. The most highly valued of hippies' clothes were the well-worn, intricately decorated jeans; they could not be bought — they had to be created.

A concern with the 'natural' as opposed to the artifice of modern consumer capitalism led hippies to prefer natural rather than man-made fabrics, to experiment with 'natural' cosmetics made from fruits and vegetables or from old recipes, and to seek alternative medicines and healthier foods. It was hippies who promoted the return of wholewheat bread, and had considerable influence in creating the current health food boom.

Lastly, their involvement in politics and particularly the anti-Vietnam movement and the Civil Rights campaign meant that some hippies developed a style of dress modelled to some extent on guerrilla leaders like Che Guevara, and on army surplus. Army greatcoats and camouflage jackets which had been bought cheaply became standard student wear.

The four main features of hippy dress had a tremendous influence on mainstream fashion. Ethnic and nostalgic styles were soon to be found in the couture collections and have been recurring themes, and workwear and uniforms became major influences on casual clothes for *all* ages.

Punk

Punk seemed to develop as a reaction against the massive commercialisation of both music and fashion for the young in the mid-seventies. The products available for the young were incredibly dull and bland. Punk culture seems to have developed in 1976 around a shop called 'Sex' on the Kings Road and a rock club called 'Roxy' in Covent Garden. The style of dress and the behaviour of punks involved everything that was unpleasant, even revolting, by conventional standards. The name itself implied something rotten and worthless.

Punk is often seen as a reaction to unemployment and the general pessimism of youth, as its slogan 'No careers' implies. However, it was also a reaction to imposed youth culture and the rejection of 'idols', as implied by their 'No heroes' slogan. At first punk was a do-it-yourself culture; anyone could play in a band, produce a photocopied magazine, create an outfit. It seems that they attempted to build up an authentic youth culture which was independent of the industries serving and profiting from youth.

Their style was constructed out of the most remarkable and often offensive (to conventional eyes) items possible:

'Objects borrowed from the most sordid of contexts found a place in punks' ensembles. Lavatory chains were draped in graceful arcs across chests encased in plastic bin-liners. Safety pins were taken out of their domestic 'utility' context and worn as gruesome ornaments through the cheek, ear or lip. Cheap trashy fabrics (PVC, plastic, etc.), vulgar designs (e.g. mock leopard skin) and "nasty" colours...were salvaged by the punks and turned into garments (flyboy drainpipes, "common" miniskirts) which offered self-conscious commentaries on the notions of modernity and taste.' (10)

Previous youth cultures seemed to have been dominated by boys, their style and activities seemed to be the most crucial, but in punk girls seemed equally involved. A key element of punk seems to have been its rejection of conventional femininity. Punk girls turned the 'nice girl' image on its head. They certainly did not look how nice girls should look or do what nice girls should do. They shaved their heads, mutilated themselves, wore dirty and torn clothes, explicitly tarty styles, or bondage gear. They de-naturalised the use of make-up and hair products to produce 'outrageous' styles.

Despite the distaste of the media for these spitting, pogoing, swearing young people in their even stranger clothes, perhaps no style was taken up more quickly by the fashion business. Punk has had an incalculable effect on late seventies and early eighties fashion. Particularly in the fields of cosmetics and hairstyles, where the 'unnatural' colours and a played down version of the totally unruly hairstyles persisted into the mid-eighties. Initially it was zips and rips which appeared in high fashion garments and the 'nasty' colours of lime green and shocking pink, but the influence continued in the loose and baggy styles of the eighties and parodies of the tarty look. In the early eighties, *Vogue* ran fashion features playing around with the tarty and bondage images created by punk. The use of unlikely motifs, in real punk razor blades or tampons, in fashion icecream cones or parrots continued in jewellery and, particularly, earring design. Lastly, the way models looked, the way they scowled at the camera, their stance, all reflected the influence of punk.

Fig. 12.5 Punks.

Let's now look at how the fashion industry harnessed the innovations of youth style.

Selling to the young

Youth were a significant force, demographically, economically, socially and stylistically. By the sixties, the post-war baby boom was reaching its teens. As we have seen, these teenagers had free disposable spending money, they were regarded as a vanguard of the future, and they were generating new styles of behaviour, new tastes in music and new styles of appearance. They were to become a key market for fashion. How did the fashion industry respond?

Before distinctive youth styles had begun to influence fashion, changes were taking place in the training of designers which were to contribute to the youth revolution in fashion. In 1947, the Royal College of Art opened its School of Fashion. The aim was to equip young designers with an understanding of the demands of modern methods of production as well as develop a flair for fashion. Other art colleges were to follow suit and art colleges became a major source of recruitment of new talent for designers and manufacturers.

However, an important consequence of these changes was the production of a generation of designers with a new approach to fashion. They were not inhibited by what was happening or what had happened in mainstream fashion. They related their concept of fashion to the world of popular culture which they inhabited and to the preoccupations of their friends and associates. The education policies of the post-war governments which made provision for local authority grants to support students meant that there was a greater social mix in the art schools. Talented young people who would have been excluded in the past because of lack of funds now could enjoy further and higher education. The sense of 'generation gap' or youth rebellion was not confined to members of youth subcultures, but was shared by many young people. By the sixties, young people seemed to rule in the sphere of 'popular arts' – music, photography, fashion. 'Swinging London' became the youth capital.

Many of the designers who were involved in creating the new fashions for the young which appeared in the fifties and sixties were the product of the art school – such as Ossie Clarke, Zandra Rhodes, Sally Tuffin and Marion Foale, Thea Porter and, of course, Mary Quant. Like Thea Porter, Quant did not train in fashion. She emerged from the 'art school' scene when she took a course to become an art teacher at Goldsmiths College.

Although we have stressed the affluence of young people and their potential as a market for consumer goods, established companies were slow to respond and seemed hesitant about breaking into this new field. Nowhere was this clearer than in the field of fashion. It was left to the young designers and entrepreneurs to lead the way and open up the market. Mary Quant and her husband Alexander Plunket-Green were perhaps *the* fashion entrepreneurs of the fifties and sixties. They started in 1955 by opening a shop called 'Bazaar' in the then unfashionable Kings Road and sold clothes to the sophisticated Chelsea set.

'Mary Quant's genius was to stylise the clothes of poor but imaginative art students, to throw a custard pie in the face of every rule of what up until then had constituted British fashion, to spell "chic" as "cheek".' (11) In her autobiography she says that 'I had always wanted young people to have a fashion of their own, absolutely twentieth century fashion'. (12) She believed that young women 'were tired of wearing clothes essentially the same as their mothers'. (13)

The boutique was a great success; few garments stayed on the rails for more than a day. By 1961 they had opened another shop in Knightsbridge and boutiques and coffee bars were opening all along the Kings Road. In 1961 Quant started to supply her designs wholesale for other retailers. The market for youth fashions was growing. Quant suggests 'It was the mods who gave the dress trade the impetus to break through the fast-moving, breathtaking, uprooting revolution'. (14) As we have seen, dress was essential to mods' sense of identity, and Quant turned her attention to this market and the teenagers this style influenced. It was a market which was growing in size and influence.

Around the same time Carnaby street was becoming a new focus for fashion for the young. Sally Tuffin and Marion Foale left the Royal College of Art in 1961 and took a house and shop in a dismal back street — Carnaby Street. They turned their backs on establishment fashions: 'We suddenly didn't want to be chic; we just wanted to be ridiculous'. (15) They wanted to produce fun clothes. Their first success was with lace dresses and by 1963 they had a successful business.

Changes were occurring in menswear, too. The Teds had opened up the way for more flamboyant and distinctively youthful styles of menswear. American rock and roll artists like Jerry Lee Lewis, Little Richard, Wee Willie Harris set a precedent for wearing extravagant and eccentric clothing and hair styles. Although in comparison British stars like Cliff Richard, Billy Fury and Adam Faith seemed much more subdued, a new era of fashions for young men was beginning. John Stephen, a Glaswegian, came to London in 1956 and worked for Moss Bros. Soon he had saved enough money to open a shop in Carnaby street in 1957. Although he was selling the traditional formula of shirt, jacket, trousers and tie, he tried to introduce more colour and a certain flamboyancy of style. To counteract any impression of homosexuality, he had 'macho' types like boxers model his clothes.

Stephen's ideas were to have a strong appeal. He had four shops in 1961 and eighteen by 1963, six of them in Carnaby Street. Carnaby Street and John Stephen had been discovered by mods. It became the mecca of serious mods who would go there every Saturday to inspect the new styles on offer.

Figures like Stephen and Quant not only influenced styles but the way fashion was sold. Boutiques selling fashion to the young were springing up all over the country. They were different from the department stores where assistants waited ready to pounce on any customer to show them the goods, and let them try them on under their watchful eye. They were different from the large chain stores with mass-produced, middle of the road styles.

Boutiques were small shops, with young sales assistants, where customers could rifle through the rails at whim or just chat without any great pressure to buy. Some even served coffee. John Stephen initiated the vogue for special lighting and the playing of loud pop music and these became essential parts of the boutique atmosphere.

Their clothes were different; many boutiques clothes sold for both sexes and some sold 'unisex' garments. In general there was close contact between the customers and the owners or managers of the boutiques, and so the owners could respond very quickly to changes in taste and demand. John Stephen described watching young men pull up their shirt collars to get a higher looking collar, and pulling the waistband of their trousers down onto their hips. By watching the way people tried on clothes he got ideas for high-collared shirts and hipster trousers and put these into his shops. (16)

Styles changed rapidly and no attention was paid to seasons. The essence of boutique fashion was rapid change and there was often only a few weeks between the conception of a design and the garment actually being on the rail. Because big manufacturers were geared to seasonal collections and programmed delivery dates, they could not supply the demands of the boutique market. So, at first the boutiques brought new scope to outworkers who were used to the high speed production of small quantities of endless designs.

The original mods became disillusioned as they saw Carnaby Street turn into a major tourist attraction in 'Swinging London', visited by TV crews and tourists. At the same time their style was being copied all over the country by teenagers wishing to identify with mods. They, like tourists, made pilgrimages to Carnaby Street to obtain 'mod' styles. Mod style was being diluted and turned into fashion.

Barbara Hulanicki launched Biba in 1964 as a mail-order business in an attempt to cater for the mass teenage market. Hulanicki and her husband felt that despite boutique fashions, and the relative cheapness of some clothes they were still too expensive for the average teenager, particularly those still at school. When she opened a shop in Kensington High Street it was a great success and customers would queue outside, waiting for the van loads of clothes to arrive. Cathy McGowan who introduced the hugely successful *Ready, Steady, Go!* wore a different Biba dress each week.

The success of these entrepreneurs and the evidence of the spending power of young people attracted big manufacturers and retailers into this undoubtedly profitable market. Big manufacturers started to employ young art school-trained designers and to launch 'young ranges'. For example, Polly Peck launched Miss Polly, and Sambo launched their Dollyrocker range. Big retailers opened boutique sections within their shops — Harrod's Way In, Peter Robinson's Top Shop and Miss Selfridge at Selfridges. Chains like Etam and Dorothy Perkins started to switch to youth fashions. Whereas retailers could imitate the 'boutique atmosphere', manufacturers could not produce the variety or rapid change of style that characterised boutique fashion. But, by the mid-sixties, Quant had gone into mass-production with the Ginger Group, and John Stephen acquired his own factory and established a chain of shops in the suburbs and provinces.

Eventually, the fashions sold by the big retailers for the young

Fig. 12.6 Biba dress.

Fig. 12.7 Biba boutique 'where dresses are so cheap girls collect them like postage stamps' 1965 (BBC Hulton Picture Library).

From tomorrow. *Miss Selfridge* **at Selfridges.**

Fig. 12.8 From tomorrow Miss Selfridge at Selfridges.

became the bland and uniform, the intimate atmosphere of the boutique was reduced to impersonal self-service with large communal changing rooms and absolutely no sense of contact between the customer and the designer or producer of the styles.

The publishing industry was also to cash in on the youth market. *Honey* was launched in 1960, after surveys by Mark Abrams had demonstrated the potential spending power of teenagers. Its target audience were young women with education − several 'O' levels and possibly some 'A' levels − who were earning £10−15 per week. Although it included features of general interest to the educated girl, *Honey*'s main aim was to stimulate interest in fashion. To help readers get the clothes they wanted, '*Honey* has sponsored its own boutiques in department stores all over the country, and encourages girls to badger shops for anything they cannot get so that their requirements are brought to the notice of manufacturers'. (17)

A sister publication for younger girls, *Petticoat*, appeared in 1966. It was geared to the fast growing teenage market. The prelaunch folder distributed to prospective advertisers summed up the potential of the market.

> '*Petticoat* will be a brand new opportunity in a brand-free market. *Petticoat* offers you a potential two million young women in the 15−19 age group. *Petticoat* will be telling them about the clothes they ought to buy, the beauty products they ought to try, and fashion accessories, holidays, books, careers and pastimes that are big news for Miss 1966. Girls in the *Petticoat* age group command more than £250 million a year of uncommitted spending money...Statistics show that over 70 per cent of girls aged 15−19 have left school and are earning themselves − the highest incidence of earners in any age group. The potential *Petticoat* readers spend far more heavily on footwear and stockings than any other age group − an average of six pairs of shoes and forty pairs of stockings a year for each girl − and the largest amounts of nail varnish, eye shadow, mascara, eye-liner and deodorant!' (18)

Youth was big business indeed! Other magazines were to follow, like *19* in 1968, and magazines for an even younger market of teenyboppers like *Jackie*, all promoting youth fashions and also providing a shop window for advertisers.

In the late sixties and seventies, big retailers began to reassert their dominance but hippies made some innovations in retailing. The hippy movement brought with it its own entrepreneurs, and a market for 'ethnic' and 'nostalgic' goods. Shops selling kaftans, silk scarves, beads, joss sticks and bits of orientalia became commonplace as did shops and market stalls selling antique or second-hand clothes. The second-hand 'nostalgic' market is still important. But both these themes had a profound influence on mainstream fashion as we have seen.

By the mid-seventies, fashion had become bland and — as we pointed out earlier — the selling of fashion had become large-scale and impersonal. With the arrival of punk there was once more a flurry of activity on the Kings Road where entrepreneurs opened small shops selling clothes and accessories to the 'punk rockers'. Reviled and celebrated at the same time in the media, punk was more rapidly diffused and defused than previous youth styles.

Although youth styles may start out as subversive, challenging accepted customs of behaviour and accepted modes of dress, they have fed into and have been absorbed by mainstream fashion. They may establish new looks, new sounds, etc., but they are soon taken up by entrepreneurs and then big business and turned into profitable commodities which are sold as 'fashion' or the latest thing to the majority of young people. The styles lose their power as signs of subcultural identity and become fashion. This tendency is clear in both punk music and styles of dress.

At first the major record companies refused to take on punk bands, and small independent record companies were set up to produce the records. When the records began to appear in the charts, it was not long before major companies were hurriedly trying to sign punk bands. Punk styles first appeared on the streets in 1976. They were self consciously anti-fashion, anti-elitist, and thoroughly shocking. By 1977 the clothes were available by mail-order, and in September Zandra Rhodes' collection inspired by punk was reviewed in *Cosmopolitan*. The 'outrageous' make-up, hair styles and colours were soon part of fashionable looks. Bright, artificial-looking colours and eccentric make-up styles became fashionable as did tousled hair, and gels were mass-produced so that everyone could get their hair to stand on end.

Just as Quant and Stephen became members of the fashion establishment, Viviene Westwood one of the leading figures of punk fashion is now part of the elite fashion establishment.

Youth in the eighties

Since punk, there have been a number of short-lived styles — New Romantics, followed by gender benders, various revivals of fifties looks, a mod revival, rockabilly and so on.

The Kings Road has become a tourist attraction, where visitors can go to see the weird and eccentric street styles for which Britain has become famous in recent years. In most towns in Britain these days the whole array of youth styles for the last thirty years are paraded before one: Teds, mods, soul boys, skinheads, punks, casuals, heavy metal kids, etc. The most recent styles have a strongly revivalist and nostalgic feel, harking back to the 'Golden Age' of youth cultures. But, unlike in that 'Golden Age' it is no longer possible to identify *a style* which the majority or even a large proportion of youth wear which is in opposition to the mainstream styles of today.

In an article entitled 'Golden Oldies of 85' Jon Savage argued that this extravagant diversity is a sign that the fashion dictatorship of the under twenty-fives is over:

'The apparent flourishing of youth fashion that you see if you walk down the Kings Road or through the new youth superstore Hyper Hyper is, in fact, indicative of a severe identity crisis. The sharp end of the youth market is busy reviving every past youth style − mod, ted, punk, hippie − in every possible permutation, as the past whirls before the eyes of a drowning man.' (19)

Is the fashion dictatorship of the young over?

Although young people remain an important market for fashion and street style, and young designers are closely watched for 'new ideas', attention does seem to be turning away from youth.

In the media, spaces once reserved exclusively for the description of youth styles now report 'nouveaus', 'yuppies', 'yappies', 'fogeys' and so on. Writers like Peter York, who 'discovered' the Sloane Rangers, seem obsessed with social categorisation, and a whole industry seems to have grown up describing new types and publishing their handbook. Groups like 'yuppies' are not defined so much by their age − although they do tend to be in the mid-twenties or thirties − but by their lifestyle and social position. The yuppies, 'young upwardly mobile professionals', are obviously defined by their jobs, but there also key yuppy activities, and key products which mark them out.

The biggest growth area in fashion over recent years has been in retail outlets catering for 'customers in their twenties and over in relatively well paid jobs'. (20) These are people who are least likely to be affected by unemployment and down-turns in the economy. Shops like Next, Next for Men, Principles, and the revamped Richard Shops, are all aiming at this market, providing fashionable clothes but less extreme than some of the current youth styles, at a reasonable price. They have all placed an emphasis on private changing rooms and better facilities for the customer. Assuming their customer to be leading a busy life, not able to spend time seeking out different parts to an outfit, accessories, etc., these shops provide the total outfit — the clothes, the shoes, the accessories and jewellery and all of them colour co-ordinated.

The marketing policies seem to be based on demographics. 'We're aiming Richards at the 25 to 45 age group, which by the end of the 1990s will be the largest in the country.' (21) By the turn of the century the 25—45 age group will constitute 28 per cent of the population, whereas the 16—24 age group will have dropped from the present 15 per cent to 13 per cent. However, it is not simply a matter of the demographics of particular age groups. It is also to do with occupation, lifestyle and disposable income.

The shift in marketing focus must reflect the high level of un-employment amongst the young. It is no longer the fifties when young women who spent their lunch times in dance halls did not worry if they got the sack when they returned late to work, for they knew they could find another job that afternoon. (22) The young are no longer the most affluent group; many are unemployed and others on lowlypaid government training schemes.

The situation for young people is so different from that which sustained the boom in the youth market. They are becoming less significant demographically and perhaps what is more important, youth no longer seem 'special'. In the eighties there is no longer a sense of optimism, a looking forward to the future; youth as a whole is no longer in the vanguard of change. The change in the status of youth is perhaps seen most clearly by those who are now middle-aged or in their thirties who were part of that 'special' generation. (This sense of their own stylish youth may account for the continuing interest of some of them in fashion.) Youth are certainly no longer envied; people are more likely to say 'I feel sorry for young people today!' The sense of common identity and shared beliefs sustained by disposable income and goods directed at the young, the sense of generational identity, has been un-dermined.

Unless social and economic circumstances change it does seem that the dictatorship of the young is over, or at least will be held in abeyance for the foreseable future.

References

1. Roberts, R. (1971) *The Classic Slum.* (Manchester University Press) 123.
2. Abrams, M. (1959) *The Teenage Consumer.* (London Press Exchange Ltd) 9.
3. *ibid* 10.
4. MacInnes, C. (1961) *England, Half England.* (McGibbon and Kee) 56.
5. This approach is known as 'Sub-cultural Theory'.
6. Jefferson, T. (1975) 'Cultural responses of the Teds.' In: *Resistance Through Rituals* (Working Papers in Cultural Studies 7 & 8) (Centre for Contemporary Cultural Studies, University of Birmingham).
7. *ibid* 86.
8. Hebdige, D. 'Putting on the style' *Time Out* (17 August 1979).
9. Interview with Denzil *Sunday Times Magazine* (April 1964).
10. Hebdige D. (1979) *Subculture-The Meaning of Style.* (Menthuen) 170.
11. Melly, G. (1970) *Revolt into Style.* (Allen Lane) 145.
12. Quant, M. (1966) *Quant on Quant.* (Cassell).
13. *ibid.*
14. *ibid.*
15. Bernard, B. (1978) *Fashion in the Sixties.* (Academy Editions) 16.
16. Speaking on Channel 4 series *The Sixties.*
17. White, C. (1970) *Women's Magazines 1693−1968.* (Michael Joseph) 173.
18. *ibid* 188.
19. Savage, J. 'Golden Oldies of '85' *Observer* (February 1985).
20. Vliet, A.Van de 'Hepworth's Next Trick' *Management Today* (December 1984).
21. Stephenson, J. marketing director of Habitat, Mothercare. In: 'Golden Oldies of '85', J. Savage. *Observer* (February 1985).
22. You'll never be sixteen again' Radio 4 programme November 1985.

Index